FRANZ BOAS

Franz Boas

In Praise of Open Minds

NOGA ARIKHA

Yale

UNIVERSITY

PRESS

New Haven and London

Yale University Press books may be purchased in quantity for educational, business, or promotional use. For information, please e-mail sales.press@yale.edu (U.S. office) or sales@yaleup.co.uk (U.K. office).

Set in Janson Oldstyle type by Integrated Publishing Solutions.
Printed in the United States of America.

Library of Congress Control Number: 2024948358
ISBN 978-0-300-24123-5 (hardcover : alk. paper)

A catalogue record for this book is available from the British Library.

This paper meets the requirements of ANSI/NISO Z39.48-1992 (Permanence of Paper).

10 9 8 7 6 5 4 3 2 1

Frontispiece: Franz Boas with his wife Marie Krackowizer in their study, circa 1900. (Courtesy of the American Philosophical Society.)

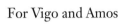

For Vigo and Amos

CONTENTS

FRANZ BOAS

Introduction: The Self as Other

By the time of his death in the midst of World War II, in December 1942, Franz Boas had become known as the highly influential father of cultural anthropology. He had famously argued for cultural relativism, against the pseudoscientific biological racialism that was prevalent in his day and brandished to justify racism. A German in New York, well ensconced within the circle of German émigrés there, and a secular Jew brought up in a comfortable German middle-class family, a well-educated product of Germanic *Bildung*, he had been one of the 250,000 from his country to settle in the New World during the 1880s. Professional opportunities and wider horizons had brought Franz to America, but he was also disturbed by the increasing nationalism and antisemitism of Bismarck's Germany—and by its new colonial forays.

Today, as the third decade of the twenty-first century opens with growing echoes of the obscurantist forces Franz Boas fought against, the man who made a vivid case for cultural humility when observing peoples different from one's own—in particular the First Nation tribes of the Pacific Northwest—is returning to the forefront. Within the world of anthropology, he was never forgotten: his research, methods, ideas, and convictions were immensely influential, resonating in the work of his students and followers who became prominent figures of anthropology— such as Margaret Mead, Ruth Benedict, Zora Neale Hurston, Alfred Louis Kroeber, Edward Sapir, and many others, including, notably, Claude Lévi-Strauss. But among the general public, he has remained a vague name at best. It is often noted that he did not produce a magnum opus, which may explain why he isn't as celebrated today as Lévi-Strauss, who learned a lot from him. The apocryphal legend still circulates that Boas died in the arms of Lévi-Strauss, though all we know for sure is that the latter was one of the guests at a jovial dinner Boas was hosting at the Columbia University Faculty Club in honor of ethnologist Paul Rivet—who had founded the Musée de l'homme in Paris in 1937—and where, in the middle of a sentence, Boas dropped dead.

His many students are also perhaps better known today than their teacher. Boas focused on methods of data collecting via emissaries, multilingual tribe members, and artifact collectors, and it is generally thought that he tended to disappear behind this data. It has been argued, however, that in doing so he was actually adopting a precise theoretical stance: he stood against the focus on systems from which to deduce facts, instead inducing from a potentially infinite multiplicity of facts a historical picture that was nevertheless never totalizing. My telling of Boas's life will emphasize the clarity of this theoretical stance, which is precisely the one that can help us today, when totalizing notions of identity abound again. I will engage with the abundant scholarship on him but also return his voice to him, showing how much he in fact does appear, loud and clear, rather than disappearing behind the scenes, in his numerous writings: articles, letters, and diaries.

In 2019, a wide-ranging narrative biography by Charles King, *Gods of the Upper Air*, set Boas back on the stage, taking on his ideas and followers in America and presenting him to a general audience.[1] In an academic volume published posthumously two decades ago, historian Douglas Cole told the story of his early life in Germany and during his first decade in the United States.[2] Most recently, his life has been retold by Rosemary Lévy Zumwalt in two volumes.[3] All three biographies rely on rich archival sources to recount Boas's life, using some of his vast correspondence. In turn they have been rich sources for my own account, which looks closely at the intellectual traditions that enabled him to develop his views, methods, and teachings. Engaging with the debates and questions about the relations between nature and culture that drove him throughout his life, and to which he contributed so much, this is a journey into his life that will reveal his significance, in his lifetime and in ours. It will illuminate what he can bring today to the concerns of anthropology in its relations with psychology, philosophy, and, not least, politics, in a world where we need to redefine humanity's relation to nature, and where we can no longer consider our culture without also considering our psychology and its embeddness in our biology. The main question underlying his investigations remains open and has acquired a new urgency in our age of increasing nationalism and identitarianism: how do cultural environment and sociopolitical conditions shape the human mind?

Born in 1858 into a secular, middle-class Jewish family in Germany, Boas had been living in the United States since the 1880s. He brought to America a rich German education and culture that he would hold on to throughout his life. There is much within the anthropological literature that examines Boas's thinking within the broader context of German intellectual history (most notably *Before Boas* and numerous publications in academic journals), but it is the histories of psychology and philosophy that constitute the background to the development of the anthropological approach as we have come to understand it today, in large part thanks to Boas himself.[4] He was especially interested in how human psychology was inflected and expressed within the diversity of cultures, eventually establishing anthropology as the discipline at the nexus of what had long been viewed as a dichotomy between nature and nurture. His aim was to record and collect all there was to preserve of the cultures, myths, history, and languages of the First Nations before these peoples were entirely wiped out by modernity. It was an urgent job that stemmed in part from the 1871 Indian Appropriation Act, which facilitated the expropriation of land from Native individuals. His task of preservation was necessary for the sake of posterity, of collective memory, and perhaps even of collective wisdom.

Boas accepted his Jewish identity but did not identify with his Jewishness any further than that. And yet it bears consideration that although the people he studied were very *different* from a middle-class product of German *Bildung* such as he, there were similarities. Not unlike Jews, the First Nations were very ancient peoples alienated by modernity and displaced by it, disenfranchised, and dispossessed of their lands: they were familiar with the kind of frustration, pain, and loss that Jews too had long experienced. They were at once of the land and expelled from it, severed from the connections that had bound their tribal identity to the land. There may be an extent to which Boas, as a Jew in Germany who, like many of his conationals, had left his country at a time of growing anti-Jewish discrimination there, and then as a German Jewish émigré in the United States, identified with these people who were autochthonous to the continent he had come to: non-Europeans who tended to be defined by both European and American moderns as *primitives*.

Boas would spend the rest of his life showing that nothing was "primitive" about them. But one may ask how far Boas's interest in them was also a product of a gnawing awareness at the time of how *tricky* origins are—and of the need to ask what, where, and how cultures develop from them. For these peoples were quite unlike the alienated *moderns* analyzed by another product of Germanic *Bildung*, an exact contemporary of Boas, Sigmund Freud—who was equally, though differently, interested in our origins. Boas's Jewish heritage may perhaps have accentuated his sensitivity to the dangers of establishing a hierarchy of peoples and cultures and claiming that one was superior to the other. He was politically engaged as a socialist, and he would actively help colleagues—Jewish and not—flee Nazi Germany. And yet his empathic method of study of different peoples, and his own empathy for all peoples, developed from specific intellectual traditions that had taken root in Germany long before his birth.

The anthropological impulse begins as an epistemological quest into the nature of the human mind itself. In the words of Boas's student Margaret Mead, cultures are "experiments in what could be done with human nature."[5] This observation already presumes concepts about what human nature may be and acknowledges that these assumptions are, in turn, culturally determined. When we look at another culture, we are observing a variation upon human nature, but tend to do so on the basis of assumptions about what counts as natural and what as cultural. And we may not always be aware of those assumptions: distancing from our own culture is necessary to perceive them. The anthropological gaze is characterized by such distancing—by a particularly acute awareness of how our understanding of another culture or language is conditioned by our own starting point. In turn, this very conditioning is modulated by psychological mechanisms whereby each individual is shaped by environmental, historical, and cultural factors. The biological and the cultural are tightly enmeshed. Ethnology operates by observing the practices and artifacts of another society on the assumption that neutrality is possible, and that the onlooker's starting perspective is not significant, but anthropology shows the naivety of such an assumption.

Boas knew firsthand what was involved in turning a scientific gaze from the natural world to the world of humans. An admirer from his childhood of the explorer and polymath Alexander von Humboldt, he started his career as a geographer, completing a thesis on the refractions of light in water. His first field trip, to Baffin Island in 1883–84, had as its goal the study of the physical conditions in which the Inuit—a people very unlike his own—lived, and it was the starting point for his interest in studying the peoples themselves: their languages, customs, beliefs, and modes of living. His Baffin sojourn certainly yielded reams of data and many ideas, but it was arguably the most significant nonintellectual adventure of his life: he called it one of *Herzensbildung*, translated literally as education of the heart or nobleness of the heart, or, ultimately, as emotional awareness. He lived with the Inuits—"my Eskimos," he called them—in ice huts, eating and learning to appreciate frozen seal meat and learning how to drive dog sleds, which apparently is quite complicated. The close quarters made him realize that one could not understand without empathy—and that realization in itself was a first in the history of what we currently call fieldwork.

Since he had migrated from his native German culture to the United States and had to acquire fluency in English, Boas also knew firsthand what it took to gain perspective on one's native culture and mother tongue—a perspective that is constitutive of anthropology. This is one way in which the biography of Boas overlaps with the history of the field he pioneered: one may surmise that a secular European Jew feels somehow "other," however much at home he or she may feel within the culture at large. Religious difference aside, cultural Jewishness is itself a marker of difference from the dominant society, characterized by the persistent continuity of a landless people whose identity was defined from the start by a rich textual tradition of societal laws and ethical deliberation. German Jews like Boas who were integrated within the wider society were, precisely, *integrated:* they were German citizens active within society, belonging and at home within it, but in relation to the Christian majority, they were others nonetheless. All Jews are aware of the historically recurrent perception of them as a social group whose unity seems to pertain to some sort of underlying essence, and of the anti-semitic narrative that characterizes this essence as menacing, bi-ologically determined, and featuring underlying negative moral qualities.

Essentialism itself is a construct poised on that shifting border between what counts as biological and what as cultural.[6] Whether it emphasizes—or imagines—biological or cultural sameness, it is a flattening of plurality into a single entity, the reduction of complexity to a generic name. It is a way not to engage, and not to empathize with individuals or societies per-ceived as different from one's own. Not only was Boas keen on specific facts about peoples and cultures—the latter a term he indeed promoted as plural, as we shall see—he was against es-sentialism, to which he opposed the cultural relativism he con-tributed strongly to shaping: that is, the notion that peoples differ solely in virtue of their respective culture, each of which is set within its own physical environment and has its own his-torical genesis and particular, albeit always changing, social char-acteristics, norms, and practices. It is important to emphasize this at an epoch, late in our crumbling modernity, when what we now call "identity politics" are fracturing societies in both the West and East, in a way that echoes the fractured world Boas lived in, but whose specific characteristics he perhaps might not have foreseen.

It is notable that Boas's life needs telling by virtue of his at-tention to the lives of *others*—of how he told, and taught how to tell, the stories of these First Nations, and because he revealed the richness of their cultures and, crucially, their many languages. (His work in linguistics, along with his attention to the centrality of philology, was remarkable for its richness and sophistication, and taken forward by his student Edward Sapir.) And herein may lie the paradox inherent in telling the story of his life. Yet his own life—his intellectual life, more specifically—offers many lessons. He was interested in the particular, the "individual phenomenon," not the general, because, as he put it in a lecture in 1909 entitled "Psychological Problems in Anthropology," "The science of anthropology deals with the biological and mental manifestations of human life as they appear in different races and in different societies," and these phenomena were both "historical" and "the objects of biological and psychological investigations."[7]

Historical phenomena because the anthropologist's mission was "to elucidate the events which have led to the formation of human types, past and present, and which have determined the course of cultural development of any group"—in other words, the historical approach would overcome the limitations he saw inhering in the "diffusionist" interpretation he otherwise took on board, which proposed a common origin to all cultures. The aim of the anthropologist, as he put it in an earlier *Science* article published in 1896, "The Limitations of the Comparative Method of Anthropology," was to find "the *processes* by which certain stages of culture have developed. The customs and beliefs themselves are not the ultimate object of research. We desire to learn the reasons why such customs and beliefs exist . . . , the history of their development."[8] Later, he proposed that imitation accounted for the transmission of culture within all societies, and that one could retrace what happened when and how by cataloguing languages, myths, artworks, and the like.

And *biological and psychological* phenomena because the anthropologist's purpose was also to "ascertain what are the laws of hereditary stability and of environmental variability of the human body," and so was akin to the psychologist's: "We are also trying to determine the psychological laws which control the mind of man everywhere, and that may differ in various racial and social groups. In so far as our inquiries relate to the last-named subject, their problems are problems of psychology, though based upon anthropological material."[9]

History itself is not law-like, as Boas well knew, but insofar as it is accepted, at least since Darwin, that all human individuals belong to the same species regardless of cultural variability— and Boas was convinced this was the case—the question arose of where to place the bounds of generalizability. Anthropology was grappling at this time with relatively new notions of heredity and biological universals. Using ethnographic fieldwork, it would eventually come to investigate how linguistically manifest concepts were embedded within cultural and artistic practices and within belief systems governing spiritual and social life. And it would ask questions regarding how these interrelated notions were informed by sociopolitical, religious, and ethical concerns, which themselves became objects of anthropological study once these were made explicit. The background of this questioning is the stuff of the anthropology we know today, whose demarcations Boas was instrumental in shaping—archaeological, cultural, linguistic, physical. And the complementarity of humanities and science was the central point around which all anthropological questions began to turn in the second half of the nineteenth century. Boas matters now in part because he stood on that fine line between the particular and the general, showing how the one nourished the other.

And it was by determining cross-cultural psychological laws that Boas developed what he remains most well known for today— powerful and influential arguments against biological racialism, and against the social evolutionism that was its entrenched bedrock. The story of social evolutionism is not so simple, though, since some of these ideas emerged, as ever, out of seemingly decent intentions. Lewis Henry Morgan was a businessman who explored America's "true roots," so to speak, in its Indigenous communities, eventually advocating for their reclamation into American society (in *The League of the Ho-de'-no-sau-nee or Iroquois*, 1851). But later, in his *Ancient Society*, he formulated a hypothesis that was attractive in its simplicity: that humanity advanced in hierarchical stages, that each society was at a particular stage of development—from savagery to barbarism to civilization—and that its evolution was inevitably from simplicity to complexity.[10] The idea was favored by John Wesley Powell, at the time the powerful head of the Bureau of Ethnology—a part of the then new Smithsonian in Washington—renamed the Bureau of American Ethnology in 1897. It was a view also shared by Frederic Ward Putnam, curator of Harvard's Peabody Museum of Archaeology and Ethnology and permanent secretary of the American Association for the Advancement of Science (AAAS), who hired Boas to set up the Anthropology Building at the World's Columbian Exposition of 1893 in Chicago, and who believed that, as Charles King writes, the purpose of "psychology, ethnology, and anthropometry" was to use "systematic observation of the outward traits of individuals to arrive at conclusions about the apparent differences across social groups." Anthropometry "was a way of looking back through time" in search of "nature's ur-types."[11]

Boas practiced anthropometry as well, in depth and at length—we will return to this. But he had also seen firsthand that there was no cultural hierarchy pointing toward the white man's idea of civilization: social evolutionists saw a progression in degrees of human civilization and devised a hierarchy all too useful for racist theories perpetuating the superiority of European culture. In a lecture he gave at Columbia in late 1907 simply entitled "Anthropology," Boas argued against the notion that "the manifestations of ethnic life represent a series, which from simple beginnings has progressed to the complex type of modern civilization."[12] He was a convinced Darwinian who accepted biological evolution, but he had no truck with the way in which the notion of evolution was being twisted and applied to groups of human beings. It was clear to him that social evolutionism was imposed on, rather than derived from, ethnographic data. He understood groups as shaped within and by historical contingency—which alone could explain similarities in myths, legends, and languages. He was committed to fighting any intellectual justification for racism and, indeed, antisemitism. As the Nazis came to power, and until his sudden death at that jovial dinner, he became extremely active in helping Jewish and other scientists escape Nazi Germany.

So, this story alone is a good reason to tell his life—and it is perhaps the most well-known aspect of it. Yet, again, to focus on him is precisely not to focus on those he studied, whose stories he made sure would be told and retold. To write about him is rather to engage in the dialectic between modernity, as embodied in the German intellectual he was, and the so-called "primitive"—or, in other terms, between what is given culturally and what biologically, between the culturally particular and the biologically universal. For in fact this tension is what is most interesting about his life, which is mostly adventurous in intellectual terms—as well as in academic and institutional ones, given how embattled his career was well into his forties, and how much of an activist he became later on. In his life are concentrated concerns and conundrums that suffuse Western intellectual history, the formation of the disciplines that constitute that tradition and, by extension, inform the principles of our very polity—which today has reached a state of crisis. Through Boas, we may be able to take stock of this crisis.

During Boas's formative years in Germany, there was an intense debate regarding the disciplinary divisions used to study and analyze the world. Boas took on board the distinction between the *idiographic* and *monothetic* sciences that neo-Kantian philosopher Wilhelm Windelband first developed, publishing in 1894 a volume on the history of philosophy in which he proposed this distinction to contrast the methodologies at work in the historical and in the natural sciences respectively, and which he viewed as complementary.[13] Windelband took his cue in part from another early influence on Boas, philosopher Wilhelm Dilthey, and from his definition of the separate realms of the *Geisteswissenschaften* and *Naturwissenschaften*—the complementary human and social sciences and the natural sciences. To each corresponded a method of study, and here too, a debate ran as to which method was best for which field of inquiry.[14]

Today, we have come to understand culture as an aspect of human nature, and, in turn, biological evolution as handmaiden to cultural adaptations. Increasingly, science is helping us understand the extent to which we are embodied, in the sense that "the body plays a key role in constituting and structuring our most basic sense of self."[15] The notion is thus becoming established in general, and within the humanities and social sciences, that we are *naturally* cultural: our cultural accretions are aspects of our animal nature, an evolved capacity on a continuum with the capacities of other creatures. We are embedded within the environment and adapt to it to such an extent that it shapes our very biology. The living body stands in a dynamic relation to the world. Yet this view is culturally situated too: *there is a history to the very idea of human nature.* Just as one may view history itself as a diachronic anthropology, one may say that as long as we are studying ourselves, we are conducting an anthropological investigation—taking leave of our own here and now, taking a step beyond our belief system, in order to look at this system's structure, or at the conditions of the here and now of others. As a proper discipline, the ambit of anthropology has its own history since the mode of relation between its areas of concern has shifted and changed over time. These areas of anthropology as we know it today—archaeological, cultural, linguistic, biological—

precisely encompass those that are modernity's tectonically shifting territory between what we understand as nature and what as culture, what as individual and what as social, what as evolved and what as acquired. Boas was, arguably, the one who most centrally set up these areas. And to look, via Boas, at the history of the inherently multidisciplinary field that is anthropology, navigating as it does between empirical investigation and theoretical speculation, is also to throw light on the roots of current concerns about the embodied, socially situated self in psychology. It is also, thereby, to redefine anthropology as the comparative psychology we need to expand our capacities for empathy. As anthropologist Clifford Geertz put it: "To see ourselves as others see us can be eye-opening. To see others as sharing a nature with ourselves is the merest decency. But it is from the far more difficult achievement of seeing ourselves amongst others, as a local example of the forms human life has locally taken, a case among cases, a world among worlds, that the largeness of mind, without which objectivity is self-congratulation and tolerance a sham, comes. If interpretive anthropology has any general office in the world it is to keep reteaching this fugitive truth."[16]

The primary site of investigation of anthropology is culture: as anthropologist Philippe Descola wrote in *Par-delà nature et culture*, anthropology understands culture as a "system of mediation with Nature" invented by *Homo sapiens*.[17] It records variations in technical ability, language, symbolic activity, and social and political organization, in their relation to a shared biological reality that in turn is the stuff of what biologists and psychologists investigate. Yet no investigation is free of bias. In a 2003 book, *The Hedgehog, the Fox, and the Magister's Pox*, whose subtitle is *Mending the Gap between Science and Humanities*, the late Stephen Jay Gould quotes Darwin wondering in an 1861 letter to economist Henry Fawcett, a convinced Darwinian, "How odd it is that anyone should not see that all observation must be for or against some view if it is to be of any service."[18] But how we get to our starting stance, for or against, is a story that is culturally, historically, and also psychologically laden.

Anthropology is inherently comparative—it is the study of one set of cultural assumptions by another, and of the ways in which individuals within that group negotiate them. One could say that ethnography first started in Greek antiquity, as most everything in the Western intellectual tradition does. Sociologist and anthropologist Florence Weber begins her *Brève histoire de l'anthropologie* with Herodotus's fifth-century BC *Histories* and his accounts of the mores of the Scythians, Carthaginians, and Libyans, many based on those of ethnographers who served as his correspondents—though one may also begin with the emergence of naturalistic accounts of the known universe first by the Hippocratics, then by Aristotle, the first great systematizer of nature into a causal taxonomy.[19]

But, as Weber tells it, this story was put on hold with the emergence of the Christian Church, which undermined naturalism, folding Aristotelian teleology into Platonist idealism. Weber observes that the openness onto the world of Herodotus, who wrote in the wake of the Athenian victory against Persia, stands in stark contrast to the later condemnation of the *libido sciendi* of Augustine, who wrote his early fifth-century AD and hugely influential *City of God* in the shadow of a once great Carthage and in the wake of the fall of Rome. As a result, according to Weber, anthropology became enclosed within the biblical narrative, where all of humanity descended from Adam and Eve and was then saved within Noah's Ark, while all its languages emerged out of the construction of the Tower of Babel. The Christian narrative, Descola writes, also conferred on us, self-conscious creatures, the right to dominate all of Creation, itself "a temporary scene for a play that will go on after the sets are gone, when nature no longer exists and only the main characters remain—God and souls, that is, humans as another avatar."[20] The Aristotelian chain of being remained, mind and body on a continuum. But the biblical narrative restricted for centuries empirical investigations into the origins of humanity, its genealogy, and its linguistic diversity. The known world was all there was to know in the West, and anything beyond its borders was the stuff of fantasy. Savages and monsters roamed the earth.

Yet there are substantial medieval narratives of travels to far-off lands, from missionaries' accounts to the diplomatic and commercial exchanges that never stopped, the ambassadors and interpreters who compiled and messaged information for use back home, east to west as well as west to east. There was the Venetian merchant Marco Polo, the explorer Ibn Battuta. Later there was Ibn Khaldun, the Berber dispatched to negotiate with Tamerlane in Baghdad, who constructed a sophisticated sociological theory. The ethnographic impulse has always existed as a search for windows into other worlds. At times, these windows turn into mirrors onto our own world, as was the case with Montaigne in the sixteenth century and his essay *On Cannibals:* his description of the Tupinamba tribe in Brazil shows up the barbarism of Europeans at a time of bloody conflict between Catholics and Protestants. We define ourselves in relation to others—and this is also the basis for psychic and social cohesion.

Montaigne was writing in the wake of the Europeans' discovery of the American continent, which expanded the borders of the known world, and gave birth to controversies in Europe as well as in the Americas on the rights and wrongs of conquest. During the famed Valladolid Controversy set up by Emperor Charles V in 1550–51, at which the rights of Indigenous peoples were debated, Dominican friar Bartolomé de Las Casas denounced the brutality of conquest and defended the Indigenous peoples, contra Juan Ginés de Sepúlveda, who saw them as "natural slaves," a long-lived argument used to legitimize colonialism, with all the horror we know about it and its aftermath. The colonial enterprise was also connected to the speciesism that had been the forte of Christianized Aristotelian teleology: humans had a special status in the created world, and "primitive man" was "merely" natural, not cultural, not illuminated by the One Creator. The respective realms of wild nature and human culture were clearly defined. Yet the encounters between peoples, mores, and languages mutually new and strange happened while Renaissance Europeans were confronting each other over religious dogma and reviving their own classical inheritance.

Then, over the seventeenth century came the mechanization of nature and the separation of its study from the throttle of theological constraint, the dismantlement of the old chain of being and the displacement of humanity from its place at the center of the universe, the establishment of the modern scientific method to explore the material world as well as some aspects of the human mind. The fossil record put in doubt the biblical age of the earth of six thousand years. Early modern natural philosophers collected their cabinets of curiosities, museums sprang up that collected and divided objects into kinds and provenance, while scientific explorers replaced missionaries. The demarcation of culture and nature became more problematic, and this very border zone eventually turned into the complex land of anthropology, or what the eighteenth-century naturalist Buffon called the "history of man, as an aspect of natural history and zoology."[21] The infinite regress that seems the hallmark of self-mirroring anthropological reflection starts with the joint assumptions of naturalism and cultural relativism. Descola opens his account of the genealogy of anthropology out of a "Great Divide," using art historian Erwin Panofsky's 1975 essay "Perspective as Symbolic Form" and, as an illustration for the self-mirroring that marks the entrance into modernity, a drawing by Flemish artist Roelandt Savery from the early seventeenth century, where he inserts himself into the landscape he depicts, in effect representing the particular point of view that is necessary to create perspective.[22] We may find the mathematical rules necessary to render a world that is separate from us, but we are the ones to find them. We draw the frame that creates the landscape. Without the frame, and without a point of view, there is no legible landscape in the first place, just a mess of elements. For a psychologist, of course, the point of view is the mind itself, which creates the frame. And always it is the mind that is studying itself.

Just as a method defines its object of study, so a stance can restrict the visible scope of the reality we want to describe. Ethnography is as neutrally static as any collection of uninterpreted data, yet even then, what we choose to collect as data for study can vary according to our cultural presuppositions, which can elude the viewer's grasp unless the viewer is included in the picture, as in Savery's drawing. Ethnography, as social anthropologist Tim Ingold puts it, "aims to describe life as it is lived and experienced," whereas anthropology "is an inquiry into the conditions and possibilities of human life in the world."[23] The collection of data about the customs, mores, myths, languages, and arts of a people becomes anthropology when a dialogue happens between cultures, when the observer becomes a participant. Participation *is* observation. Ingold is opposed to the notion that anthropological analysis *makes use* of the ethnographic stance, where ethnography is an idiographic enterprise, "dedicated to the collection of empirical particulars," and anthropology a monothetic one, "dedicated to comparative generalization and the search for law-like regularities in the conduct of human affairs."[24] And in fact, for Boas the two enterprises had to be conjoined.

For Boas was intent on exploring law-like regularities. In this he was a participant in the development of the scientific psychology of his time, which emerged out of and beyond metaphysics, in particular with Wilhelm Wundt, the first to define its ambit. For Wundt, individual psychology, based on but not reducible to physiology, was tied into general, comparative psychology, and his *Völkerpsychologie*, published in the early years of the twentieth century, would become a massive, ten-volume affair, translated as *Social Psychology: An Investigation of the Laws of Evolution of Language, Myth, and Custom.*[25] Wundt partly took his cue from Johann Gottfried Herder, who in the eighteenth century had mooted the notion of a *Kultur* specific to each *Volk*, or local people, expressed through language and customs. As anthropologist Adam Kuper has pointed out, this was an argument that weaved its way into a rejection by German ethnologists of "the Enlightenment view that there was a single evolutionary history of human culture, that culture progressed through a series of set stages to the pinnacle of civilisation," according to a hierarchy, as if only one criterion existed for the concept of civilization.[26] Instead, each *Volk* had an equally valid inalienable *Kultur.*

Herder's theory had a liberal intent, viewing all peoples as equal, despite its being later used to serve the cause of German nationalism. What matters here is his influence on the anti-evolutionist school that would make its way to America with Franz Boas when he moved there in the late 1880s, via ethnologist Adolf Bastian who, along with physician, anatomist, and polymath Rudolf Virchow, had created the Berlin Society for Anthropology, Ethnology, and Prehistory in 1869. Bastian had earlier founded the Royal Ethnological Museum. His arguments against the social evolutionism of the likes of Herbert Spencer and Edward Tylor in England, as well as Lewis Henry Morgan in the United States, helped Boas develop his own. Bastian posited what he called *Elementargedanken*, "elementary ideas" common to the whole of humanity, out of which grew the world's variegated *Völkergedanken.*[27] Everyone was inherently a social being, a *Gesellschaftswesen* and a *zoon politikon*, a political animal, for whom a specific language was the key to social exchange, just as Herder had seen. All societies developed in a similar fashion, albeit with multiple variations, because all of humanity constituted one species, endowed with the same physiology. The mono-genetic view of human history had earlier been justified on the basis of the story of Adam and Eve—the Christian Church could not have accepted a polygenetic view of a multiplicity of human species—but it was the discovery of prehistory in the nineteenth century, bolstered by Darwin's theory of evolution, that gave monogenism its scientific credentials. For the social evolution-ists, this also meant that "primitive" peoples were identical to prehistoric ones—that is, stuck in time. Boas, following Bastian, spent much of his career showing how deeply misguided and dangerous this latter supposition was.

And so, Boas wanted to look at the diversity of cultures, with the crucial assumption that they all were expressions of civiliza-tion. Like Wundt, Boas was explicitly interested in finding "the laws governing the activities of the human mind" necessarily inherent in the multiple cultural forms he studied.[28] Again, and crucially, he stood against the social evolutionists whose theo-ries served as a proto-scientific justification for racism, and whose consequences Boas fought against until his death. In his 1907 lecture, Boas stressed that "the genesis of the types of man, con-sidered from an anatomical, physiological, and psychological point of view, is the chief object of anthropological research," and thus "a separation of anthropological methods from the methods of biology and psychology is impossible."[29] In his ear-lier 1896 *Science* article, "The Limitations of the Comparative Method of Anthropology," Boas took on board the *Elementarge-danken* common to all of humanity—such as a belief in life after death, grammatical structure, and so on—and stated that sci-entific inquiry must ask what their origins were, and how they asserted themselves in various cultures. Or, as he restated it in 1907, "Why are the tribes and nations of the world different, and how have present differences developed?"[30] In response to these questions, Boas argued for a historical approach to the study of cultures that would overcome the limitations he saw inhering in the "diffusionist" interpretation he otherwise accepted, which envisioned a common origin to all cultures. He stood on that fine line between the particular and the general, showing how the one nourished the other—in the same way that sciences and humanities can.

In the following pages, I explore how Boas came to develop the cultural relativism he remains known and celebrated for, and how his fieldwork was informed by it even as he was shaping it. His life, by now well known, stands out by his engagement with others—with his family, his intellectual forebears and colleagues, his friends, and the individuals he encountered, befriended, or fell out with. In this short biography, I accompany Boas on his intellectual journey, focusing with more detail on his formative years, because the ideas for which he became and has remained known took shape then, as he confronted his own intellectual background and embarked on his first northbound travels. Starting with the embattled debates around Enlightenment universalism and the objects and methods of scientific and historical inquiry, we will cross the Atlantic with him, armed with the notions that had molded his mind as a young man in Germany. With him, we will ask the questions that led him to comprehend and seize some remains of the vanishing past of a continent that other Europeans, upon first encountering it, had mistakenly, and destructively, thought of as new. On that land, within the specificities of American culture, Boas, along with his colleagues, collaborators, and students, was able to deploy a set of methods and ideas to confront our human nature and to enrich the psychology of his time, as well as to create a whole field of study that still owes much to him today.

Boas didn't just create and launch a field further shaped by his many students. He also produced a body of thought. This has not always been recognized precisely because he never wrote that theoretical tome by which he could be remembered. He published massive amounts of raw data, hardly digestible for the nonspecialist. But he also produced many papers and lectures that allow one to follow his evolution. And his writings, from which I will quote at length, reveal a very precise methodology that serves a precise set of principles. He established these principles on the basis of a lifelong program of in-depth research in the field, while constantly gauging both his research methods and their outcomes, evaluating what anthropology was, what it was becoming, and what it told humanity about itself. He believed in the capacity of science to change minds, and in the importance of its proper communication. What he produced was aimed at fellow Westerners who sought guidance in understanding human nature as deployed in various cultures, but it also served those First Nations that he studied, and whose cultures colonialism had brutally suppressed.

Boas was ambitious from his youth on. But he was always pragmatic and grounded. There was no space or need in his life for pretention, ostentation, or intellectual narcissism. Boas's life was not flamboyant. He was excitable, passionate, resolute, and at times outraged, touchy, and choleric. But by and large, he was a man of virtuous measure. Lives of virtuous measure are notable for not making exciting biographies. But within this measure, and in the company of Franz, there is a lot to learn.

1

◆┼◆┼◆

From Physics to Geography

To UNDERSTAND what Boas did, how he did it, and why—
and why he remains an inspirational figure, especially today—we
must imagine the transformations wrought upon his German
background by the encounter with both American ethnology
and the Indigenous peoples he studied.[1] In 1938, a few years before his death, aged eighty, Boas wrote what he called "An Anthropologist's Credo"—published in the *Nation*—in whose opening paragraphs he summarizes his life, thought, and ideals with
lucidity and concision. "The background of my early thinking
was a German home in which the ideas of the revolution of
1848 were a living force," he begins. "My father, liberal, but not
active in public affairs; my mother, idealistic, with a lively interest in public matters, the founder about 1854 of the kindergarten of my hometown, devoted to science. My parents had broken
through the shackles of dogma. My father had retained an emotional affection for the ceremonial of his parental home, without

allowing it to influence his intellectual freedom. Thus, I was spared the struggle against religious dogma that besets the lives of so many young people."[2]

When he was born, on July 9, 1858, into this progressive, free-thinking, close-knit, and warm family in the small Prussian town of Minden, midway between Bielefeld and Hanover, Jews were mostly assimilated into the fold of the constitutional monarchy that was the kingdom of Prussia. The synagogue had stood proud since 1840, and a community building was inaugurated in 1865—which would be destroyed during Kristallnacht in 1938. The name "Boas" was fairly recent, chosen in 1808 by Franz's great-grandfather Bendix Levi during the short-lived reign in the "kingdom of Westphalia" of Jérôme Bonaparte, who gave the polity a written constitution, effectively the first of its kind in Germany. This constitution guaranteed, among other things, equal rights for the Jews. Franz's grandparents had been observant, but both his father, Meier Boas, and his mother, Sophie Meyer, had left the fold of their religious upbringing as they and their generation became emancipated and *verbürgerlicht*, joining the world of integrated Jews by partaking in the Enlightenment process of *Bildung*, a very German style of education and higher learning.

Sophie, as Franz alludes to in his brief account, had become politically engaged with the reformist movements that followed the 1848 uprisings. A strong believer in individual human rights and freedom of thought, she was close to members of the Communist Bund. Her future brother-in-law, a doctor named Abraham Jacobi, introduced her to a fellow doctor, Ludwig Kugelmann, who was a friend of Marx. In 1851, Jacobi sent to Sophie and her sister Fanny a copy of *The Communist Manifesto*. He even spent two years in jail because of his revolutionary politics, which were illegal in politically conservative Prussia.[3] Jacobi immigrated to New York soon after, in 1853—famously staying with both Marx and Engels in England before crossing the Atlantic.

In the United States he established himself as a renowned physician and pediatrician—eventually establishing the first hospital department of pediatrics in the country—and married Fanny, becoming the "Uncle Jacobi" who would play an important role in Franz's life.

Franz too was educated according to the principles of German *Bildung*, along with his elder sister Toni (Antonie), to whom he was very close. There were two other, much younger sisters, Hedwig (Hete) and Helene. As a young child, Franz attended a kindergarten that his mother had established, based on the progressive principles of German pedagogue Friedrich Froebel— the actual founder of what we know as the kindergarten. Franz often missed school as a child on account of recurrent headaches, but throughout his years in the Gymnasium, he studied the usual range of subjects: from mathematics to the Greco-Roman classics via history and German letters. Early on he also developed, independently, his interest in natural history and geology: "An early interest in nature and a burning desire to see everything that I heard or read about dominated my youth," he writes in his autobiographical sketch. While still in kindergarten, he grew flowers—he was four when he made his first herbarium.[4] And he loved imitating animals. Aged eleven, he wrote to his father that he had "been working out a little lecture in natural history whose theme is: What is the origin of the tides; life in the sea; the origin of the earth; fossils and the difference between land and water animals," which was "the hardest."[5] He was enchanted by *Robinson Crusoe*, and a little later, he was fascinated by the polymath, explorer, and geographer Alexander von Humboldt, who had died a year after Franz was born, and whose travels to the Americas impressed upon the young Boas the urge to see the world, especially the parts entirely different from his own land—he dreamed of Africa. Humboldt had written in the introduction to volume 1 of his influential five-volume *Cosmos: A Sketch of a Physical Description of the Universe* (published between

1845 and 1862): "It may seem a rash attempt to endeavor to separate, into its different elements, the magic power exercised upon our minds by the physical world, since the character of the landscape, and of every imposing scene in nature, depends so materially upon the mutual relation of the ideas and sentiments simultaneously excited in the mind of the observer."[6] Geographical observation could not be abstracted from the psychology of the observer.

Nor could geographical discoveries be divorced from the desire to discover the unknown. Boas described what can only be his own early dreams in "The Study of Geography," the first article he published in *Science*, in February 1887. He had already gone to America by then, and this was the article that clinched his permanent move there from Germany, since it led him to sign a two-year contract with the journal as an assistant editor in New York, in charge of overseeing the area of geography. Boas writes that "the mere thought of these vast territories which had never been sighted by a European could fill the mind of geographers with ardent longing for extended knowledge; with the desire of unveiling the secrets of regions enlivened by imagination with figures of unknown animals and peoples. But the more completely the outlines of continents and islands became known, the stronger grew the desire to understand the phenomena of the newly discovered regions by comparing them with those of one's own country."[7] Such desire, writes Boas, had yielded Humboldt's "admirable works" as well as the "comparative geography" of Humboldt's protégé Karl Ritter, a professor of geography in Berlin who, rather than set out on vast travels as Humboldt did, analyzed how nature and history related to each other. Ritter followed Gottfried von Herder in understanding historical processes as the outcome of geographical and environmental context rather than as the product of collective psychology, given how much geography can shape destinies.

Geography certainly determined Boas's intellectual destiny

to some extent, constraining the course of his studies. He began his undergraduate curriculum at the University of Heidelberg, considered at the time to be the Oxford of Germany. His parents, especially his father, had wished him to study medicine, but he had no desire to spend his life as a doctor: "I am not made for that, even though you don't want to believe it," he wrote to Toni in October 1876.[8] Sophie called upon Uncle Jacobi, who knew firsthand what it took to be a physician, to help sway Meier to let Franz make his own decision. And so Franz was able to study what he wished—mathematics and natural science. "I have dared!" he wrote to Toni in March 1877.[9] Full of wonder at the natural world, he managed to design a curriculum that reflected this, even though his "university studies were a compromise," as he would write in "An Anthropologist's Credo." "On account of my intense emotional interest in the phenomena of the world, I studied geography; on account of my intellectual interest, I studied mathematics and physics."[10] Music too became ever more important to him, and he played the piano regularly. Beethoven was his most beloved composer, as anthropologist Herbert S. Lewis observes in an essay that shows how central to Boas was the notion of the free-thinking, truth-seeking, post-Enlightenment individual.[11] (We will return to this, too.) He was entranced with the chemistry classes of Robert Wilhelm Bunsen (inventor of the eponymous Bunsen burner), "the first great scientist I had ever seen," as he put it in a letter to his mother in April 1877.[12] He tried to balance his fascination with science with his humanist bent, the two pulling him in very different directions—in this mirroring, as anthropologist Adam Kuper has noted, "the more general intellectual division in Germany between the positivists and subjectivists, the proponents of the natural sciences and the defenders of the humanities."[13] (Another theme that will recur in the following pages.)

He also engaged in the sort of revelry and heavy drinking familiar to undergraduate students everywhere. He confessed to his best friend in Minden, Reinhard Krüer—a friend who would, to his great sorrow, drown in the Weser River that summer, in 1877—what he avoided telling his parents in letters home informing them of his progress. "You have no idea what a loafer I have become and how much time I spend in cafés," he wrote in one letter, and in another: "We sacrifice to Bacchus more than enough here," though "Venus has turned away from me completely." No flirtations and few friends: Franz was quite lonely in Heidelberg. He avoided fellow Jews and Jewish societies where he may have been able to find some company, finding them "intolerable."[14]

He remained in Heidelberg for only one term: he had planned at the outset to move to Bonn to concentrate especially on physics under physicist Rudolf Clausius, famous for reformulating the second law of thermodynamics. Both physics and organic chemistry were better taught in Bonn than in Heidelberg. Boas stayed there for two years, from 1877 to 1879. Here he encountered one love interest, a Jewish woman who, he realized belatedly, had been present at the dedication gala of the city's Reform synagogue, which he had chosen not to attend. He had visited the synagogue before, with a Jewish acquaintance, and admired it—he was more accepting of his Jewishness here than he had been in Heidelberg. And he now regretted not attending the gala. The woman, a Fraülein Hirth, was the object of a youthful, undeclared infatuation, but nothing came of it—and in any case, as it turned out, she was bound for England.

And now Boas too was leaving Bonn. His hope was to go to Berlin to work with the great Hermann von Helmholtz and to continue his studies of physics. Helmholtz would remain influential in the development of his thinking. But he had to abandon the ambitious plan because his sister Toni had long been suffering from a joint ailment that caused debilitating pain, and, as a caring and concerned brother, he wanted to remain close to her. Her new doctor was based in Kiel, in northern Germany, and here, in 1879, she underwent a hip operation that helped her walk again, though she would have a lifelong limp. This is how Boas ended up doing his PhD in the small, provincial town of Kiel, which he once characterized in a letter to his parents, while still in Bonn, as "the abominable Kiel."[15]

He did manage to make the most of his time there, however. He was more mature now than he had been in Heidelberg and in Bonn, where he had participated in a few illegal duels, or *Mensuren*, typical of student life at the time, which left him with permanent scars on his face. Fresh wounds and scars would multiply, especially in Bonn once he became a member of the Alemannia, a fraternity—called a *Burschenschaft*—that was mainly a club of fencing and dueling, complete with rituals and featuring communal, extremely heavy drinking. No portrait of Boas fails to mention those scars, though he was serious, artistic, sensitive, and kind, hardly martial in temperament. Joining the Alemannia was a sure way for a secular, *verbürgerlicht* Jew to fit in, despite his opinion that mainstream German youth were "steeped in vulgarity."[16] It was, simply, the pragmatic thing to do. It ensured he would not again feel isolated as he had in Heidelberg: he was part of a warm community, a brotherhood, however much he ultimately remained on its outskirts. He was, in fact, already something of the observer that he would become.

At Kiel, he joined an equivalent group, here called the Teutonia. Student organizations of an antisemitic, nationalistic bent were increasingly active in various German cities, including Kiel, partly in reaction to the increasing number of Jewish students in those years. These organizations would coalesce into the Vereine Deutscher Studenten (Association of German Students), established in August 1881. Franz reported one incident in a letter to his parents: "A splendid anti-Semitic action happened to me," as he put it with verve. He was sitting in a tavern with friends when a student entered, "one of the 'Führer' who knew one of us very slightly," and sat at their table, having been granted permission by an undergraduate among them. "Of course, I immediately took my beer and sat at a nearby table saying that I could not sit at the same table with this man," Boas recounted, whereupon his comrades followed suit immediately, leaving the student embarrassedly alone in the crowded tavern. "I have never enjoyed myself so much."[17] He was well surrounded on that occasion, but antisemitism was widespread in Protestant Kiel. It was especially encouraged in the Germany of those years by the rhetoric of historian Heinrich von Treitschke and his contribution to what he and others called the *Judenfrage* (the Jewish question)—which would become prominent, for the Nazis, only a few decades later. But Franz's friends stood up against it. One of them had even gathered forty signatures for a petition against the *Judenhetzer* (Jew-baiter).

Still, Franz could not entirely avoid duels when his "honor" was at stake, as he confessed to his parents. His status as a Jew was inescapable in Bismarck's Germany, however much it had never been an important aspect of his identity. He was aware of this. He also wanted to fit in, to acquire competence, authority, and a social status worthy of the *Bildung* that had nurtured his intellectual development, his passions, and his self-perception. And as his studies progressed, he realized that the only way to stake out a place for himself was by fully engaging in science "as a way to reconcile the unfulfilled promises of his social existence and escape the limitations of the social world," according to Boas specialist and historian Julia E. Liss. "Science allowed him to transcend the boundaries which he could not surmount from within the exclusive community of the German university or through the ritualistic acts it encouraged."[18]

And so the dueling and student carousing became less frequent. Now he was studying hard. Most notably, he attended the geography classes of Theobald Fischer, a young specialist of the Mediterranean he had taken classes with and started befriending at Bonn, where Fischer had been a private docent before obtaining a professorship at Kiel—a promotion that gave Franz some hope about the possibility of having an academic career. Here in Kiel, Fischer, who had been influenced by Karl Ritter, became a real friend, and it was with him that Boas started concentrating on geography alongside physics, though his interests were still so broad that he had to force himself to focus. He was continuing mathematics and was tempted to write his PhD in the subject—he leaned toward Gaussian statistics—but his supervisor, the physicist Gustav Karsten, thought differently and directed him to study the optical properties of water, because of his, Karsten's, own involvement in a commission set up in Kiel to study the properties of water in fisheries along the Baltic and North Sea coasts.

The resulting thesis, on water's absorption of light, was not one that Boas would have thought of writing had it not been for Karsten. Its intellectual basis was solid enough, since it addressed a question central to post-Kantian thought—and Boas had read his Kant: what of the phenomenal world could we study to understand it, since sense perception could not yield direct apprehension? But the empirical work his thesis required was hard and unforgiving, especially as the equipment he had for the measurement of light was inadequate, and many of his experiments failed to produce any results. It was no labor of love. He did, however, get caught up in the processes of collecting data in the field (which was the Kiel harbor), analyzing it in Karsten's lab, and interpreting it, searching for equations that would enable him to calculate "the reflection of light against colored bodies," reporting on his progress in frequent letters to his parents and to his sister Toni.[19] And he managed to complete the dissertation in good time, by the summer of 1881. Nervous about the exams that followed its submission of his dissertation, insecure about his abilities and accomplishments, he nevertheless emerged brilliantly: summa cum laude for the dissertation, magna cum laude for the oral examinations.[20]

His research had proved more fertile than he may have imagined it would be at the outset because it led him to think about the nature of perception itself, and to question the rationale for his investigation of the physical world. He quickly became interested in the mind at work upon the world rather than in the physics constituting the world, or in exploring mathematical models for it. And from there, it was just a step to look into what exactly determined the differences between ways of seeing the world—that is, what went into the construction of cultures. In his 1938 "Credo," Franz looked back on this initial study, in which using "photometric methods to compare intensities of light" led him "to consider the quantitative values of sensations. In the course of my investigation, I learned to recognize that there are domains of our experience in which the concepts of quantity, of measures that can be added or subtracted like those with which I was accustomed to operate, are not applicable." As he formulated it as a twenty-four-year old in a letter to Uncle Jacobi dated January 2, 1882: "It is the mechanism of the life of organisms and especially of peoples that is before my eyes."[21] On April 10, Franz described to Jacobi with even more perspective the intellectual shift that he had undergone over the past few doctoral years and how, from his initial "objectives" of delving into mathematics and physics, he had "become aware of other questions which prompted me to take up geography," a subject that became his main focus of study, even though he remained "strongly influenced" by his scientific training, "especially physics." But it was precisely his deep engagement with problems of measurement that led him to realize how "untenable" was the "materialistic worldview" of physics. "This gave me a new point of view and I recognized the importance of studying the interaction between the organic and inorganic, above all the relation between the life of a people and their physical environment. Thus arose my plan to make as my life's work the following investigation: In how far may we consider the phenomena of organic life, especially those of the psychic life, from a mechanistic point of view?" And in order to "solve" this major question, Franz had by now realized that he needed to acquire "a general knowledge of physiology, psychology, and sociology."[22]

Over his lifetime, he would reconfigure the terms of this question. His dissertation research had first led him to realize that, in order to make sense of the complexities of perception, he needed to do so in the terms given by the scientific psychology that was burgeoning at that time, and in particular to engage in experiments in the psychophysics that was its bedrock. He was encouraged in this direction by neo-Kantian philosopher Benno Erdmann, on the basis that what had always been typically a philosophical inquiry regarding the nature of perceptual knowledge—that is, the relation between physical stimuli and the mind—could, and indeed should, be investigated empirically. Epistemological questions could yield answers if one turned away from metaphysics and followed the scientific method. This project was precisely at the heart of scientific psychology. Boas eventually wrote seven papers on psychophysics, a number of which would be published during his one-year military service, starting in October 1881. When he decided to travel to Baffin Island afterward, encouraged by Jacobi to make good on his old dream of traveling to far-off lands, he turned away from the theoretical approach inherent in psychophysics. But in fact its operative starting point would remain inscribed within his interrogations regarding the mode in which cultures shape people's perceptions of the physical world. Psychophysics was the theoretical base upon which his initially geographical project would give way to a keen interest in how *peoples* interacted with their environment, and in the phenomenon of cultural variation.

The psychophysics that Boas studied had begun earlier in the century with the medically trained philosopher and physicist Gustav Fechner who, afflicted in early middle age with serious eyesight problems, created an experimental methodology precisely to determine the physical laws that yielded perceptual experience. Boas was familiar with Fechner's major work *Elemente der Psychophysik*, published in 1860, whose intent was to unite scientific, quantitative investigations of the mechanisms involved in perception—the ability of the mind to perceive physical objects—with a metaphysical vision of the unity of all things that one could call panpsychist, and that Fechner inherited from Romantic *Naturphilosophie*. He wanted to find "a scientific rationale for linking the material and mental worlds. Material objects have mass and spatial extent, but mental experience has neither. Some have concluded that mental events belong to a spiritual world. Fechner, however, believed that mind and body are inseparable and that mental events are emergent properties of complex material systems, such as brains."[23] In Fechner's words, psychophysics examined the "functional relationships between the phenomena of body and soul as accurately as possible," and it asked: "What belongs quantitatively and qualitatively, far and near, in the physical world and the spiritual world together, according to which laws do their changes follow one another or do they go together?" In other words, "what belongs together in the inner and outer appearance of things, and what laws exist for their relative changes?"[24] His scientific response was "to make 'the proportionate increase in living energy . . . be the measure of the increase of pertinent mental intensity.'"[25] The human mind was not a mere receptor of phenomena: perception was inherently interactive.

Boas took up Fechner's challenge in a paper he published in 1881 as the newly matriculated young man he now was, the designation "Dr. phil." preceding his name as article author. The paper was on Fechner's law of thresholds, or *Schwellengesetz*, which governed what Fechner called the "apperceptions" that made up perceptual experience and that accounted for how "*dif-*

ferences in sensation correspond to differences in physical stimulation."[26] Boas concluded here that the smaller the difference between quantities, the more work was required for their detection. Within such a framework, quantitative analysis could in fact account for qualitative experience—in other words, epistemological puzzles could indeed yield a fertile program of empirical inquiry. Later, Wilhelm Wundt, the self-avowed founder of scientific psychology in Germany, would elaborate greatly on the notion of apperception, and we shall see how Wundt's work informed and enriched Boas's own investigations. (Wundt too had studied at Heidelberg and been fascinated by Bunsen.)[27] Although Boas was determined to "leave psychophysics in peace since it leads me too far afield," such empirical investigations into how the human mind interacted with the environment remained at the heart of his concerns throughout his life.[28] They also informed the ideological debates that fueled the core of developments in anthropology because they touched on the mechanisms whereby evolved, natural processes produced cultural variation.

Boas did not become a psychologist. Indeed, had he done so, anthropology would not be what it has become. But there was a continuity from his study of the physics of the refraction of light on water to his initial use of the massive project of psychophysics, and thence to his account of the phenomenon of alternating sounds, about which he published an article in 1889: this phenomenon was inherent in language, and it accounted for the perceptual differences between groups and between individuals.[29] These notions remained essential in Boas's quest—itself informed by his readings—to establish how cultural artifacts are the expression and outcome of specific modes of perception, themselves shaped by geographically determined historical incident and historically determined geographical circumstance. Such notions centrally inform one of his main legacies: the written record of the Indigenous languages he studied, for whose transcription he used a theory of phonetics based on the findings of psycholinguistics.[30]

But before he embarked on the epochal trip that would take him away from the experimental sciences and on to the study of his fellow humans, he had to enlist in the army. As a university graduate, he was entitled to reduce the usual three years' compulsory military service to one year, which he began in September 1881 as a lance corporal. It was an unpleasant year for him, as one can imagine. "Soldiering is really quite disagreeable," he wrote to Uncle Jacobi in early January 1882.[31] But since he was based in his hometown of Minden, he was able to spend time in the new house the family had moved into, getting reacquainted with his sisters Hete and Helene, now grown. Mostly, however, he studied very hard after his hours of duty.

And a momentous event had happened during the previous summer while on a family holiday initiated by Uncle Jacobi with Austrian friends of his, the Krackowizers, in the beautiful Harz Mountains in Saxony: he had met their American-born daughter, young Marie Krackowizer. (Marie and her sister Alice were to start attending a boarding school in Stuttgart after the summer.) The connection between the families was understandably strong. Her father, who had died in 1875, was a Viennese doctor named Ernst Krackowizer who had been a leader in the insurrection of 1848, had arrived in New York in 1850, and had become under President Lincoln inspector of Union army hospitals.[32] He had been close also to Jacobi's friend Carl Schurz—another former revolutionary and German émigré, who in the United States had been an abolitionist, a journalist who fought against political corruption, a senator, and the former secretary of the interior under President Hayes. The commonality of cultural, intellectual, and political backgrounds must have played a role in the development of Franz and Marie's relationship, but regardless, it was, if we are to believe Franz's own words, love at virtually first sight: "I do not think it took a whole day before you had won me entirely," he would write to her later.[33] The courtship, though, lasted a long while, from that July 1881 all the way to the spring of 1883. There were fluttering hearts, tortuous doubts on both sides, shyness, sighs, and worries—until, at last, mutual love would be declared.

Meanwhile, Boas was anxiously looking beyond his year of military service, preparing to find a position in order to become independent of his family. His parents suggested he take the state examination to become a teacher, but he wasn't at all keen to do so—not least because, as he wrote to Uncle Jacobi, "Jewish teachers have great difficulty in getting an appointment" in the secondary schools. He was impatient to kick-start a career that would enable him to fulfill his long-term, increasingly clear plan to investigate human geography, "what influence the configuration of the land has on the acquaintance of peoples with their near and far neighbors." For this, he acknowledged the need to study "physiology and sociology, for I believe that even a geographer cannot feel quite sure of himself until he has studied these."[34] He applied for a fellowship at Johns Hopkins University, encouraged to do so by Uncle Jacobi and supported by his mentor and friend in Kiel, Theobald Fischer. On April 12, 1882, he wrote to Jacobi: "The day before yesterday I sent you my certificates as well as a summary and my plans for the future. I do not know whether the last is well done, for I really have become so dull from my military duties that I can no longer think myself into my usual train of thought. . . . I do hope that something will come of the matter [Hopkins] for I regard it as very important for me to study a while longer. I am so overjoyed that the greatest part of my slavery is over—171 days more and I shall be free."[35] Eventually the disappointing news arrived that the application had not been successful—as still can happen to so many able young scholars today. His father had enough faith in his son that he decided to support him financially for an extra year after his military service, writing to him from Berlin that life was full of such disappointments, that he should use the extra year to prepare himself well for his future, and that Franz could count on his help. He also entreated him not to "let this disappointment depress you. Go with determination on your way."[36]

And so he did. As soon as his "slavery" was over, Franz went to Berlin. He immediately set to work on a paper about the geographical distribution of Eskimos, reporting to his parents that he was also studying Inuktitut, the Eskimo language, in view of the trip he was intent on undertaking to the American northern pole.[37] He took time to improve his English as well. His studies included "cartography, astronomical determination of places, and meteorological determinations," as he wrote to Jacobi in November 1882.[38] He held strong to his Humboldtian vision, which finally was defining itself, enriched by the university years he had so recently spent engaging with empirical research. His long-held fascination with the Inuits had matured into a concrete wish to understand how the region's geographical makeup determined their migrations. He was intent on "studying the wandering of the Eskimos, their knowledge of the country they live in and of adjacent lands, in the hope to prove a close connection between the number of persons in a tribe, the distribution of food supplies and the nature of the country." He was preparing an article on the topic for *Die Zeitschrift der Gesellschaft für Erdkunde zu Berlin*, and he would write his habilitation thesis on the basis of this research—a thesis he needed to be able to get a teaching job as a *Privatdozent* or university lecturer, on his way to achieving the rank of professor, as opposed to passing state examinations as his parents had first suggested he do.[39]

This fascination with the Arctic was common at the time: Fischer, his mentor at Heidelberg and Kiel, had studied polar geography as well, and over the previous decades there had been major expeditions to the North Pole, organized first by the British and then also by the Germans (who attempted two trips between 1868 and 1870). Many of the arguments about the interactions between culture, geography, and biology, and therefore around the nature of race, took these isolated populations as a case study. These debates were feeding into the development of ethnology—"a new knowledge of man as a being capable of culture," in the words of Carlotta Santini—in its relation to anthropology, which, in contrast to ethnology, encompassed biology, confronting the question of what in humans was culturally determined and what pertained to biological makeup.[40]

On the evening of October 21, 1882, Boas had met both Rudolf Virchow and Virchow's erstwhile pupil Adolf Bastian—a meeting that would prove to be historic, given its intellectual and practical impact on the course of Boas's life. The two, as mentioned earlier, had founded the Berlin Society for Anthropology, Ethnology, and Prehistory, and were respectively its president and vice president. The meeting, which took place at the society, was arranged by one of its members, geologist Wilhelm Reiss, who would prove invaluable in helping Boas set up his first journey. (Boas met Reiss via the Lehmanns, family friends. Rudolf Lehmann, with whom Franz often enjoyed Berlin's rich musical and theatrical scene, became a good friend who would eventually become his brother-in-law, marrying Franz's sister Hete in 1884.) Boas was eager to meet these colossal figures of German anthropology and ethnology, although he was intimidated at the prospect. Thus he was all the more agreeably surprised by how warmly he was received.[41] The meeting was primarily a meeting of minds, at this particularly effervescent moment in the history of thought about human culture and human nature. Boas had a lot in common with both Virchow and Bastian. He would also meet in Berlin, and become lifelong friends with, Karl von dem Steinen, another protégé of Bastian, who had first trained as a psychiatrist and then become an ethnographer, with notable fieldwork in Brazil.

Virchow was an impressive polymath who had also been studying the Inuits. He is remembered in particular as a physiologist and pathologist—inter alia, he first described and named leukemia in 1847—but he had long been involved in those debates, which raged not only in Europe but also in the United States, regarding Darwinian evolution, the role of the environment in shaping cultures and, inevitably, the question of race. (He was also a liberal politician.) His views on these matters, as Boas would describe it in the obituary of Virchow that he wrote for *Science* in 1902, were "determined by his fundamental researches on the functions of the cell in the animal organism," which he studied as a physiologist: "every new form is derived from a previous form," whether the cell is that of a healthy or sick organism, and indeed, for Virchow "there is no distinct line of demarcation between physiological and pathological processes," the latter of which are "physiological processes which take place under difficult conditions." Cells are mutable, and the origins of species can be understood in terms of "the relation between the mutability of the organism and the mutability of the cell." Virchow was not convinced by Darwin's theory of evolution. But Boas was careful to state in his obituary that, rather than being anti-Darwinian, as indeed he is remembered, and rather than doubting "the scientific value of the theory of evolution," Virchow declined "to speculate on the origins of species, until through researches on tissues a sound foundation has been laid." Underlying this was an awareness of the centrality of what today we would refer to as epigenetics: "Without a knowledge of the processes that take place in varying cells, it is impossible to determine whether a deviation from the normal form is due to secondary causes that affect during their period of development organs already formed, or if it is due to primary deviations which develop before the first formation of the varying organs."[42] There was no denying the antiquity of humankind, and Virchow, as a monogenist student of prehistoric archaeology, was convinced that bodily type and nation were separate, un-related entities. Geography and the history of migrations were crucial to the understanding of cultural difference.

The very notion of prehistory was fairly recent: the term itself was first coined in 1836, but only to refer to pre-Roman Britain.[43] It became more common currency and acquired its present meaning a few decades later, as multiplying excavations, in England and throughout Europe, revealed that life on earth had begun in a past far deeper than had ever been imagined even over the course of the "long" eighteenth century. Darwin's *Origin of Species* appeared in 1859. His mentor, the geologist Charles Lyell, published *The Antiquity of Man* in 1863, the very year in which Thomas Huxley published his *Evidence as to Man's Place in Nature*. Inevitably, attempts to tell the history of humanity as an animal species raised the question of how and when *culture* emerged in our biological evolution, and of whether we were one or many species: the monogenetic view was not a given everywhere, and polygenesis served well those who wanted to defend a hierarchy of "races" on what they considered, or felt they needed to consider, scientific grounds.

The responses to both these questions emerged out of the eighteenth-century Eurocentric view that social development was progressive and had led to white European civilization—itself based on the earlier mechanistic, post-Cartesian account of natural laws as uniform. "Human history," as George W. Stocking writes, "came to be viewed as a single evolutionary development through a series of stages which were often loosely referred to as savagery, barbarism, and civilization."[44] There were no historical records telling us how humanity and its various cultures had developed, and the conjecture of an actual evolution of the species seemed to make sense: it was an instance of a law of nature. British officer and ethnologist August Pitt Rivers (his collection became the core of the eponymous museum in Oxford), argued in the mid-nineteenth century that humanity *developed* from its infancy to adulthood: what he viewed as "savage races" represented our infantile stage. Darwin himself had called South American natives "our ancestors." In the United States, Samuel Morton, who died in 1851, divided humanity into a hierarchy of biologically determined "races" that could be identified from cranial measurements and facial characteristics—a notion that would persist and feed racism in America, in particular with his 1839 book *Crania Americana.* He famously attributed to biological rather than environmental causes the perceived differences in the crania earlier collected by German anatomist Johann Blumenbach. Also heir to the physiognomists and coiner of the term *Caucasian,* Blumenbach had used facial traits to infer mental characteristics, and established the practice of comparing skulls—including those of four Inuits from Labrador—whose differences could be understood as either environmentally or racially determined.[45] Just as races had evolved, so they could degenerate, or simply not develop, Blumenbach believed.

Racist theories were based on the claim that physical appearance translated essential characteristics and hierarchically determined qualities. This claim was rooted in the earlier tradition of physiognomics and in the complex, age-old, itself philosophically laudable attempt to pinpoint the material nature of mind. In the late eighteenth century, Viennese physician Franz Joseph Gall had developed the notion that cerebral functions were located in specific areas of the brain: this was an important contribution to the understanding of cerebral lesions, and helped advance neurology as well as psychiatry, since he believed that mental illnesses had an organic basis and were therefore curable, rather than being moral defects. He also believed that all humans had "the same brains," irrespective of origin.[46] But his locationism developed into the infamous pseudoscience of "phrenology," upheld especially by his close colleague Johann Gaspar Spurzheim, who coined the word: the belief that mental functions translate as visible bumps on the skull. Phrenology became highly popular but was discredited by the 1840s. Still, the wish to find an equivalence of shape with quality never disappeared, together with a morally inflected evaluation of such shape—and Morton would resort to phrenology to demonstrate what he thought of as the "barbarous" nature of Native Americans and Inuits. Phrenologists made use of the notion of degeneration as well, like all those who believed in a biologically determined evolution of races, and who upheld the famous notion mooted by the great zoologist and naturalist Ernst Haeckel, also a student of Bastian, that "ontogeny recapitulates phylogeny." Haeckel, though he was a liberal in social terms, was a social Darwinist who endorsed polygenism as well, a position that Virchow stood against.

Craniometry was a popular method of study from the 1860s on, and the renowned anatomist and anthropologist Paul Broca contributed to the tradition by inventing a "craniometer." Virchow also made use of craniometry, since, as a scientist, he was eager to base his investigations on as much empirical data as was possible to obtain. But he was deeply opposed to the notion of biologically determined races—ideologically, as a Humboldtian, progressive liberal, and also insofar as evidence trumped any a priori theory. In studying the Inuits from the 1870s on, he wanted to understand where this isolated people came from, what other peoples they might be connected to and, of course, their unique traditions and culture. In 1880, Johann Adrian Jacobsen, a former Norwegian fishing captain turned explorer and ethnologist, had brought to Hamburg two Inuit families from Christian missionary stations in the Labrador region, setting up a *Völkerschau* commissioned by a zoo director and animal trader, Carl Hagenbeck. Such *Völkerschauen*, human exhibits, were common in Europe from the 1870s on—peoples from far away were literally put on display for examination, not unlike zoo or circus animals. Not even the most liberal Europeans considered such a practice objectionable. This is an instance of historical distance operating much as geographical distance can, conferring a perspective on cultural forms that are nearly unimaginable to one's own, and on beliefs that may seem incomprehensible. Certainly, the existence of these *Völkerschauen*, and the widespread legitimized used of craniometry, for that matter, are aspects of the environment in which Boas was beginning his professional life. For Virchow, these existent methods were of use as entry points into gaining some scientific understanding of these peoples whose existence in their original form was menaced—aspects of the anthropological work required to record characteristics, cultures, and mores before they disappeared. He would become increasingly uneasy with this use of crania that he otherwise collected, and with these methods of physical anthropology. In the meantime, however, he taught Boas the basic techniques of craniometry, and of anthropometry more generally. There was a clear use for them. For instance, it so happened that the two families from Labrador were culturally very different from one another, and this difference raised questions. Much was still unknown about these "untouched" tribes. Virchow understood that environment shaped their biology, and that there were no biological races, but there was much more to understand about them, and measurements seemed a legitimate method of investigation. To us, of course, these methods do remain ethically questionable, not to say abhorrent. For one, craniometry and the measurement of bones generally required the practice of grave robbery—a practice that Boas did not shirk from. And more: all the visiting Inuit died of smallpox, since Jacobsen had overlooked having them inoculated in time.[47]

On that evening of October 21, Boas met Bastian before being introduced to Virchow. Bastian too was a larger-than-life figure, perhaps the best traveled European of his time, trained first in law, then in natural sciences, and finally in medicine, who systematically acquired an impressively vast quantity of objects from all parts of the world. His three-volume *Der Mensch in der Geschichte* appeared in 1860 after extensive travels, and more volumes followed over decades of further major travel. His was the mission of a highly educated European endowed with boundless curiosity about the rest of the world, a man who strove to create the theoretical superstructure that would allow us to make sense of the world's plural cultures—collecting artifacts for the sake of understanding the "folk spirit," or *Volksgeist*, of each culture, its *Weltanschauung*. His ambition was to map human thought, and indeed the human psyche, in all its cultural diversity, by cataloguing its manifold manifestations as so many expressions of humanity in the raw, so to speak. As he would put it in 1901, "We see (or meet) Man as such never and nowhere; rather he is each time presented to the view of anthropology only under his somatic coloring; and in ethnology, with the iridescent clothing of folk-thoughts [*Volkgedanken*], as historical-geographical transformations of social thought [*Gesellschaftsgedankens*]."[48] It was in asking how human diversity could be defined as essential to humanity itself that Bastian posited those *Elementargedanken*, which he had described as "the monotonously stereotypical elemental idea, naked, bald and bare," the basic particle common to all human matter, present beneath the variegated habits, customs, languages, and modes inherent in each culture, just as it defined each culture as such.[49]

This was the core of what would become cultural, as opposed to physical, anthropology. It was packaged into a psychological credo that would serve Boas—who became a student of Bastian—in grappling with the old problem of the "psychic unity of humankind" central to all anthropological thinking. Bastian, with his *Elementargedanken*, which he believed characterized all of humanity and which ramified into *Völkergedanken*, specific to each people, offered a solution to the puzzle Boas wanted to confront: how diverse cultures emerged, given this unity, which it was crucial to acknowledge. Bastian's liberal ideas too emerged out of Enlightenment notions about cultural belonging, those very notions that Herder had developed earlier, and that Kant had approached as well. His attempt to catalogue the diversity of thought was not uncontroversial. It was Karl Rosenkrantz, in fact, the holder of Kant's chair of philosophy at Königsberg, who said of it "a statistic of thoughts is a tremendous insanity," though Bastian countered that he did not conceive of thought in such terms.[50] It took conceptual work to understand how culture was at once universal and universally specific, and Bastian was hugely prolific—but he is little read today.

Upon meeting Boas, Bastian was pleased to learn that the young man was preparing a trip to the North Pole—to Baffin Island. He helped organize the logistics for the sailing, which would be aboard a schooner that had traveled in the Arctic before, a whaler, in fact, called the *Germania*, which belonged to the German Polar Commission and was heading to the Kinugawa Fjord in the Cumberland Inlet to pick up seven scientists and their staff. The boat was set to go through Kikkerton Island, where Boas would stop to connect with the Scots stationed there and hire some Eskimos as support before continuing on to Kinugawa. Both Bastian and Virchow assisted Boas in preparing him for the trip, academically and logistically. He learned about topography, since he was going to deliver surveys of the territory—charts from the British Admiralty existed, so he relied on those. He studied what was known about the physical geography of the Arctic region in order to understand the interactions between population and environment. Repeatedly trying to reassure his parents, who were clearly worried about their son embarking on such an adventure, Boas wrote to them in the autumn that he was preparing himself carefully and knew what he was doing, and that he would not be isolated in the north, since there were twenty Scottish seal hunters at the Kikkerton whaling station, which would be his base. For now, he was learning about cartography, hydrography, and meteorology, and was taught how to use a glass-plate camera. He was getting the best equipment. And he agreed to his parents' request that he be accompanied by their trusted longtime servant and gardener Wilhelm Weike at his father's expense.

Furthermore, he had "turned to the German Polar Commission, in order possibly to contact directly the German station which I could use as a good starting point and support."[51] He didn't obtain funding from the Humboldt or Ritter Foundations. But he managed to convince Rudolf Mosse, owner of the *Berliner Tageblatt* newspaper, to commission reports about his journey, which, Boas claimed in his presentation letter to him, "would cause a sensation in every way" because it "would determine the last of the unknown coastal regions of Arctic America and also that the method of travel would be unusual (such impudence)."[52] Franz was learning how to promote himself— calling such self-promotion "impudence" because it was clearly not in his nature, but he knew it was necessary if he were ever to fulfill his ambition. To convince Mosse, as he explained to his parents, he had shown him his plans and articles, dropping the names of people who mattered. He cleverly argued that he was "doing the *Tageblatt* a favor by letting them have my reports," rather than revealing that he desperately needed the funds to undertake the trip in the first place. Mosse requested a sample article, and upon reading it and finding it well written, agreed to commission the young man: he would pay him 3,000 marks for fifteen articles, to be published between August 1883 and April 1885. Franz was delighted with the outcome of this "impudent" attempt at earning money for his long-desired adventure, entirely on his own strength and merit, "through my own personal effort," as he put it in his letter. He was mapping his future, just as he planned to map the Arctic.

Over the next few months, Boas was busy preparing for his trip, traveling around Germany. He met with the men involved in the international effort to explore the Arctic's geography and climate—polar researchers not only in Germany but also from Denmark, Czechoslovakia, and the United States. Those in Germany included Georg von Neumayer, chairman of the German Polar Commission, with whom Bastian had put him in touch and of which Boas had written about to his parents. He gave Boas formal authorization to travel on the *Germania*. As it happened, 1882–83 was International Polar Year, which involved twelve countries, so the timing was perfect. Neumayer also offered to have the materials used by the current station's members loaned to Boas upon their outbound trip, to fund the purchase of materials—"instruments, guns, furs"—and to provide Boas with maps. He also invited Boas to give a talk at the Geographische Gesellschaft in Hamburg in early February. Franz accepted, performed nervously, but was heaped with praise. He then purchased his supplies in town, accompanied by a polar traveler, Captain Hegemann.[53] Mosse had expected Boas to write two articles before his departure, so Boas decided to report on the Third Assembly of Geographers taking place in Frankfurt at the end of March, which Neumayer was attending as well. This was another important occasion in the formation of Boas's thought, for he heard there a talk by Friedrich Ratzel, chair of geography at the University of Leipzig.

Over the course of the nineteenth century, and even starting before then, large amounts of ethnographic data had been gathered from colonial enterprises, fueled by the positivism that prevailed during that period—an application to all fields of knowledge of the methodologies and criteria of the scientific study of the natural world, which was growing increasingly intense and prolific. Anthropology, however, did not obviously lend itself to a positivist research model. While the scientific status of a field established its credentials within the positivist worldview, the application of positivism to the study of humanity risked yielding precisely the sort of evolutionism—and concomitant racialism—that Bastian, Virchow, and others, including Herder and Humboldt before them, stood against. But rather than classify humanity, perhaps one could map it. That is what Ratzel attempted to do, on a continuum with Bastian's mapping of thought and of culture—where culture was defined as the set of differentiations from universal characteristics, given the monogenetic nature of humankind. (Wundt, remember, had attempted something similar.) Culture was the output of geographical conditions and migrations, argued Bastian: "To study the groups of nations presented by history in the various periods, it is necessary, above all, to have a clear view of the map on which they move. To derive origins, one must study hydrography and orography (the science of mountains), even before philology."[54] Humanity, however, also influenced geography: that too was the nature of culture, after all. "*Elementargedanken* developed into distinct systems of thought," as Carlotta Santini puts it: "If, therefore, the cause of cultural difference was not to be found in geography, it was nevertheless through geography that the ethnologist would be able to outline the historical profiles of current configurations of peoples and nations and study the evolution of their thoughts and conceptions."[55]

Ratzel, believing exactly that, created a new discipline he called "anthropogeography" to account for the diversity of humanity *given* its psychic unity. (The eponymous work was published in two volumes, the first of which appeared in 1882—shortly before the talk Boas heard—the second in 1891.) All differences were cultural. To actually *classify* these differences bore the risk of falling into the trap of hierarchical comparisons. Instead, Ratzel created a dynamic map that considered together the movements of peoples, goods, and cultures, rather than sticking to a "static description of the *status quo* of a specific place and time" (again in Santini's words). Taking on board the Kantian notion of time and space as the preconditions for human experience and knowledge, Ratzel posited in his *Anthropogeographie*, "We are actually dealing with two humanities then. Their signs are *present* and *past*, they behave like *now* and *then*. One is the quantity of individuals existing today, those 1450 million human beings that you see, hear, feel, ask, measure, photograph, and finally dissect; and the other is the merely imaginary humanity of all times and countries, whose fictitious past, or its lower strata, rest in a deep shadow against which no ray of light of the mind has attempted to battle until today."[56] Human geography determined physical geography. But the map of human geography was a multiple palimpsest, comprising languages, ethnicities, religions, mores, artifacts, and arts, none of which— and this is crucial—were reducible to each other. The lecture on that day in late March 1882 was entitled "The Importance of Polar Research in Geography." Before the large audience gathered there on the occasion of the International Polar Year, Ratzel discussed how polar research, once "expeditionary," now consisted in "fixed stations where measurements and experiments agreed upon by an international scientific organization were conducted in a synchronized fashion" in order to obtain reliable data (fourteen stations, both in the Arctic and the Antarctic, had been established by the twelve nations involved in the Polar Year).[57] Ratzel, with his *Anthropogeographie,* "called upon scholars to examine common geographical areas, or clusters, inhabited by peoples of similar cultures, in order to better analyse how the natural environment shaped them," in the words of Rainer Baehre.[58]

Boas had gone to Frankfurt to report on the important conference for the paper. But his visit there was also a fine pretext: to pay a visit to the Krackowizers in nearby Stuttgart (less than two hundred kilometers away). Since meeting Marie the summer before, he had not been able to declare his feelings, nor did he know whether they were reciprocated. The doubts had been a tormenting backdrop since his year in the military, though he mentioned only to his sisters Toni and Hete the importance Marie had acquired in his life—never to his parents.

His sisters, in turn, had been in touch with Marie, and had figured out that both she and Franz were too shy to declare their feelings. Now that his departure for his yearlong trip was approaching, he had to see her again and declare himself. His visit to the household on April 1, which he announced to Marie's mother beforehand, was momentous. Soon after, he wrote to Marie: "Do you believe that the 1st of April was an easy day for me? I had to collect myself entirely in front of your door in order not to betray all my thoughts and feelings immediately and I did not know how you felt towards me." And Marie wrote to Toni: "Do I need to tell you how happy we were to have him with us yesterday? I had not let myself dream of such a beautiful surprise, to see him once more and to be allowed to speak with him before his long—trip. I would like to have put between *long* and *trip* the words terrible and horrible, but I may not do that anymore since he described it as not terrible at all."[59]

But still, nothing was made explicit on that occasion. Boas revealed his feelings in confidence to Jacobi, trying to put it casually. After telling him of his attendance as a correspondent for the *Tageblatt* at the Frankfurt conference, he revealed he had gone from there to Stuttgart "to again see the Krackowizers before my departure, or if I should be honest, to see Marie," for "I could not bring myself to undertake this trip without having spoken to her once more." The Krackowizers were about to head to America that October, and he hoped to be able to find there "a steady position so that I may tell her what I feel for her," since "I held it to be wrong at this time before the dangerous journey and considering my insecure future, to express myself even though my leaving becomes so very, very hard."[60] The letters between Franz and Marie remained restrained for a while, but Toni finally took things in hand and told Marie of Franz's love, sharing that letter in turn with Franz. Finally the torment— the "torture," in Marie's words—was over, and the two could freely exchange a series of intense, very touching love letters.

Franz was just twenty-five, Marie about to turn twenty-two. Emilie, Marie's mother, was at first concerned with this engagement, given that Franz was about to depart on a long journey into the northern wilderness, but she ended up accepting it, given the intensity and certainty of her daughter's feelings. Franz's parents were similarly concerned, but they had little choice in the matter. Marie wrote to Franz's mother: "I shall do everything in my power to make your Franz happy in order to be worthy of all the happiness that blesses me." Franz wrote to his parents: "Love her well, she belongs to us."[61] Marie was to stay with them for a few weeks before her departure for the United States in mid-October.

Meier Boas and Wilhelm Weike joined Franz in Hamburg on June 17. Franz and Wilhelm embarked on the *Germania* two days later. The ship sailed on the 20th. Boas wrote to Marie: "Behind the pain of departure lies an unmeasured and immeasurable blissfulness which makes a new man of me. My head goes to the Eskimos, my heart always and forever with you!"[62] As Zumwalt points out, Boas was still a physicist when he departed the port of Cuxhaven for Kikkerton Island in Baffin Island, noting his observations of the waves, for instance, but already "gently shifting to an expanded view, one that would embrace ethnology but would not abandon geography, though physics would slide ever so softly from his line of sight. He had all the ingredients for this gentle shift—language study, study of the people, and fieldwork, characterized at the time as travel."[63] Ten days prior to his departure, he wrote in his diary his plans: to make a name for himself, write for the *New York Herald*, to marry Marie within two years, and then go to Alaska. His goals were clear as he commenced his journey. Little did he realize, as he sailed northward, how they would change.

2

From Geography to Anthropology

Boas knew that without fieldwork experience, he would not be able to go far academically and obtain the professorship he was aiming for. Before departing, he had published two well-researched and well-received articles in reputable geographical journals, one in the *Zeitschrift der Gesellschaft für Erdkunde zu Berlin* and one in the *Deutsche Geographische Blätter.* But of course he was also fulfilling his Humboldtian dream of exploring distant shores. If he chose Baffin Island (as it is known today) and the Cumberland Sound, this was in part because of the ongoing expeditions and the whaling stations that had been in place there since the 1860s—and he departed at the tail end of the First International Polar Year—but also because, as he himself would put it later, the tribes there had hardly ever been observed by Europeans. These were "primitive" peoples, a term that Boas had no trouble using. "Primitive" has acquired a pejorative connotation, but for Boas the term was descriptive: it was not an evaluation. Comparison is inevitable in observation because there is no observation without a perspectival point. We saw early on with Philippe Descola how important it is to remember this. As he had repeatedly asserted, Boas was interested in the origins of these peoples and in their migratory patterns, within Baffin Island and also to Labrador, whence had come the two families for the *Völkerschau*.

On May 2, 1883, six weeks before he set sail on the *Germania*, he had written to Jacobi about the "genesis of this undertaking, and its purpose in my scientific plan." This was the letter in which, following the description of how difficult it had been to organize this trip and how he had found funding for it, he revealed to his uncle his visit to Marie. But it began with an intellectual credo that bears reporting here. He explained that all began with psychophysics, that he even had "the exact outline of a book on the subject which I hope I may write sometime later," and that Jacobi too should know about psychophysics. "But from the practical viewpoint I must willy nilly begin with geography, since that is the science that I have thoroughly learned." Hence his project on "the dependence of the knowledge of the land, and the range of wandering of peoples on the configuration of the land." He needed his "own investigation," he realized, and so he "selected a people living in the simplest circumstances," however "complicated" conditions were there. In his mind, he was "going primarily to collect material that will give me a point of view for more general studies": those would be "about the knowledge people have of the local geography, which will be followed by a psychological study of the causes for the limitation of the spreading of peoples. From here I wish to gain the starting point for the general questions which will be given possibly more rapidly and just as surely as psychophysics. Of course on my trip I must do many other things, make geographical observations, anthropological studies etc. but I shall keep my chief aim always in mind."[1] Psychophysics, in other words, remained at the forefront of his concerns, as a theoretical base of his empirical program. Virchow's interest in the Labrador Inuits, and in how different were the two families brought to the *Völkerschau*—who came from different parts of Labrador—played a role, no doubt, in Boas's wish to understand better how cultures were a product of geographical environment. So did Karl Ritter's studies on how geography determined societies, which had influenced him at Kiel. The Baffin Island Inuit were not "untouched" by the industrialized Western world (what one still called "civilization" in the nineteenth century). They had been in contact with whalers as well as with travelers exploring the possibility of a northwest passage. But much remained to be investigated scientifically.[2]

The voyage, however, was no theoretical undertaking. It was physical, concrete, sensorially rich. Boas would document his trip in detail—he would write a total of two hundred thousand words within a year. From June 23 he started keeping a letter diary for Marie—"And first of all I have to tell you how much I love you! I am always thinking of you, my Marie and wait longingly for the time I shall be with you again," he wrote her that day. (The diaries and letters, variously retranscribed by Boas during his sojourn for record-keeping as well as for correspondence, were carefully edited by Ludger Müller-Wille, and the following pages draw on this edition, in the translation of William Barr.)[3] He reported on how well one lived aboard the ship, describing breakfast and routines, the dour but trustworthy north German captain Mahlstede, Weike, the light, the birds, the colors of the sky, clouds, and water, the waves, and of course the all-important weather. He was an acute observer, attentive to details. And his clarity of purpose was just as precise. He felt strongly that it was also disinterested. On July 11 he wrote to Marie: "It is too funny to see how everyone believes that I have gone out to attain fame and honour. Not true; they don't know me at all, and I would stand very low in my own estimation if that was the *purpose* for which I was investing trouble and effort. You know that I am aiming for something higher than this and that this trip is only a means (in every sense) to that goal. And in so far it is perhaps correct that I am seeking *recognition* for my achievements from outside, because for my further purposes I must attain the situation that my word, which I can throw in the balance for the sake of my ideas, is accepted as that of a man of action. But that is all that comes to mind when I think of recognition. Empty fame is worth nothing to me."

As the ship sailed northward, the temperature fell. Boas recounted encounters with ice banks, days with no ice, fair winds and fine days, fog, ice floes, and icebergs. He put on his Eskimo boots for the first time on July 15, writing to Marie on deck when it was two degrees Celsius. Progress toward Kikkerton, the largest Inuit settlement, was slow and painstaking. On August 5 Boas wrote to Marie, "Over 6 weeks at sea is a rather long time!" Adapting to "shipboard life" was difficult. There was enough fresh water to wash just once a week, so "you can imagine how we all look by Saturday." But he made sure to "save the water in which I rinse my photographs and thus [I] can wash in fresh water at least every second day," unlike the seamen. The diet by now mostly consisted of bacon and salt meat, unlike the first days of plenty. Occasionally there were beans, dried cod, barley with plums. (Thankfully, there was plenty of coffee.) But Franz noted how he was adapting, getting used to the repetitive food—even appreciating it—the rhythm, the privations. For a while in August, the ship was surrounded by ice and made little or only intermittent progress: those were moments of great discouragement. Boas kept busy, hard at work making calculations and observations, and drawing maps. He had written about the voyage for the *Berliner Tageblatt*. But the lack of progress was draining. On August 24 he reported to Marie that he was "in a very depressed mood." By the next day, however, the ship made it to the sound at last, though there was "still a very great deal of ice at the entrance." All was quiet. There were seals. The water was "so transparent here that one can make out everything to a very great depth." On August 26, 1883, he reported to his parents that the *Germania* had arrived at Kikkerton Sound, and he asked them also to give his photographic plates, which he was sending to them, to a photographer in Minden with instructions: "He is to wash them all again properly, because we do not have enough pure water here; and where possible he is to expose the plates longer. He is to retouch them only where it is unavoidably necessary, e.g. those plates that have spots." On the 27th fog descended once again, and the prospect of the *Germania* making it to Kingawa was diminishing. It was a matter now of her making it past the Kikkerton Sound and into the harbor.

And she did, to the relief of everyone on board, on August 28—Franz's parents' wedding anniversary, as he noted. "A boat ahead! There appear to be 4 Eskimos and a white man in it; now we'll soon be going ashore and I can get to work. Can you imagine the joy of seeing the first land close by and the first new people, after 10 weeks?" The travelers encountered Scotsmen on a boat sailing alongside theirs. They included a whaler, Alexander Hall. After some maneuvering, they finally set foot on shore. Another Scots welcomed them, Captain James Mutch, keeper of the Kikkerton whaling station. A warm man and welcoming host, he would prove a great support to Boas, there on Cumberland Sound but also later in his career. As he wrote to Marie in late September, Mutch "is in every way obliging towards me and helps me with his better knowledge of the Eskimo language wherever he can, so I am greatly indebted to him for increasing my knowledge in this regard. Also he has been lending me his dogs for excursions; in short I must be grateful to him in every way. He is a very devout man, who allows no work in his house on Sundays."[4] The only other European there was Rasmussen, the Danish keeper of the American station. The compound was otherwise inhabited by a small population of local Inuits.

The adventure had barely begun. Boas's diaries afford us a detailed glimpse into daily life and into the process he underwent of acclimatizing to this new environment. He had prepared himself for it. And he was aware that his own reactions and observations would change with time: he had a strong metacognitive grip on his own experience, which was of course at once rich and new. He was there to study what he experienced in order then to be able to understand it better. All along, full, sensorial, embodied engagement in experience deepened his ability to analyze the nature of this experience. In his 1938 "Anthropologist's Credo," he wrote of how reading philosophy had ignited his "desire to understand the relation between the objective and subjective worlds," and of his early journey to the Arctic as a sort of "peculiar compromise," since he wasn't able to "continue this line of study by means of psychological investigations." Albeit "presumably largely dictated by the desire to see the world," he had therefore undertaken the trip "for the purpose of adding to our knowledge of unknown regions and of helping me to understand the reaction of the human mind to natural environment." That year "as an Eskimo among Eskimos," he wrote, "had a profound influence on the development of my views, not immediately, but because it led me away from my former interests and toward the desire to understand what determines the behaviour of human beings."[5]

But Boas was a resolute empiric, and the trip was no instance of armchair philosophy. As soon as he got to shore, he began measuring angles with a compass. He took care of his plant collection and photographic plates. Spending the first few days between land and boat, where initially he still slept, he also paid a visit to a *tupik* (an Inuit summer tent made out of animal skins) to begin collecting vocabulary. And then he sailed off in a whale boat with six Eskimos toward Kingawa and the German Polar Station via Tinixdjuarbing: the men there had to be alerted that the *Germania* would not make it in, and he also needed to pick up materials that were awaiting there. He watched as they tried shooting a seal (they missed). There were various stops, for coffee and breakfast. The landscape changed. Boas made observations on what he saw, the variations in ice, the magnificent light, the tidal shifts, the obstacles in the journey. He continued accumulating vocabulary. On September 7 the party arrived at the German Polar Station, whose members, he wrote, were "drinking terribly"—indeed, the station was in its last days, owing in large part to tensions and misbehavior among the crew, who had been there a whole year. Boas closed it down with the help of ten Inuit men. He then sailed back to the *Germania* on another schooner, the *Simmons*, and on to the Scottish Whaling Station at K'exerten Island, where he aimed to pursue his topographic studies. The local Inuits understood English so communication was fairly straightforward.

Boas participated and learned. He arrived armed with instruments and goods as well as theoretical training, but he knew only full immersion would do. He first lodged in a comfortably warm room, he reported to his family in early October, and while supplies lasted, it was possible to "prepare excellent meals" with Mutch. Coffee, tea, bread, and tobacco remained available as well, and these were readily consumed by the locals—in fact, they were also routinely used by visitors such as Boas for barter purposes to procure dogs, sleds, clothes, and so on. But he had his first taste of raw seal liver and roast seal meat around then: "It tastes not bad, but I have to overcome a certain repugnance." Eventually, and inevitably, he would get used to it, as well as to episodes of hunger. He ended up appreciating the meat of seals as well as that of birds, which "tasted superb." (Eskimos ate only the meat of seals, as he was careful to explain to his family: "No Eskimo eats blubber," which was used only to "keep the fire burning.")[6] He also became appreciative of igloos, eventually welcoming the comforts they offered. Similarly, while he described the language as "quite abominably difficult!" in an early letter to his parents and sisters, he would be learning it over the year, cataloguing words and insisting on the importance of using the Indigenous names for places, a practice that would prove highly influential within the development of anthropology. In fact, by the end of his stay, he had set down the Inuit names of 930 places. As he wrote: "In one respect, it can truly be deplored if Indigenous names get lost because these are so fitting like the Eskimo ones; but then I have experienced considerable anger, annoyance and inconvenience by the numerous English names and the missing of indigenous names." He deplored that Frederick Schwatka, an American traveler to the area who believed that names should be first and foremost pronounceable, "shares with almost all Americans and Englishmen the fancy to baptize all places anew; otherwise it would be possible to obtain a somewhat clear outline of the coast from different sources provided by the natives."[7] This effort to reinstate local names yielded today's Inuit nomenclature, which combines abbreviated Inuktitut with the previous European names.

This explicit analytic attention to local culture was of a piece with the attitude he developed in Baffin Island. In an article he wrote about his sojourn, he reported how he listened to "the natives who told me about the configuration of the land, about their travels, etc. They related the old stories handed over to them by their ancestors, sang the old songs after the old monotonous tunes, and I saw them playing the old games, with which they shorten the long, dark winter nights."[8] He followed the experiences of Schwatka as well as of the late explorer Charles Francis Hall, and had written one of his articles for the *Berliner Tageblatt* about the latter's expedition, emphasizing that, in Hall's case, "There was no other recourse but to live as an Eskimo with the other Eskimos, to go hunting and fishing with them— in short, to adapt fully to their customs," sharing foods, habits, emotions.[9] Quite quickly he too adopted the Eskimo way of life. As he would recount in his "A Year among the Eskimo," published in 1887, the Eskimos "were my companions in all my journeys. I used to travel from village to village, and thus their fortunes were my fortune. The little adventures of their life were my adventures." And indeed, from his arrival on, he observed how things were done in this part of the world—how, with the approach of winter and the rapid formation of ice, "the Eskimo had built snow huts and stone houses, which were covered with shrubs and turf. Large lamps were burning inside, affording light and heat. The ice-floes had consolidated under the shelter of the land, and the men went out every day to hunt seals at the edge of the floe. There they stood waiting for a seal to rise. As soon as the hunter sees it the harpoon is thrown, and the carcass drawn upon the ice." Soon he would be hunting as well, just as he would learn how to drive the dog sleds—but as he noted, his dogs and sled were of better quality than the ones of the Es-kimo, who would thus "gladly" agree to accompany him on his travels from village to village, once "the sea had sufficiently fro-zen over for travelling," from December until the end of July. [10]

All these "little adventures" became the substantive stuff of anthropological knowledge once Boas had gathered and writ-ten about them, basing his telling on his deep experience as well as on surveys, readings of previous explorers, and the Inuits' own knowledge. He was bringing to bear the geographical tools he had learned academically on his extensive analysis not only of migration routes but also of material, social, spiritual, and artis-tic culture. Admittedly, it was a physically harsh time. After an epic twenty-five-hour walk in December with their Inuit guide Ssigna to Anarnitung, on the northeast shore of Cumberland Sound, Weike became severely frostbitten. His toes, possibly his very foot, were saved thanks to the ministrations of Ssigna and another Inuit, Ocheitu, as he and Franz finally reached the warm, comforting igloo at the end of their expedition. As a consequence of this episode, however, Weike was unable to accompany Boas until April 1884. And even without frostbite, walking in the soft snow was challenging, as Boas reported to his family early on, in October 1883. Most distressingly, at around the same time, a diphtheria epidemic started raging among the Inuit in the settlement of Imigen on the west coast of Cumberland Sound—brought in with the foreign whalers, as had been the case with syphilis. There were many deaths, of adults as well as children. Boas, as a European visitor, was first viewed as a *Doctorádluk,* "big doctor," who tried to provide basic medical help. But inevitably he was unable to save lives. Eventually, perception of him changed: he became the intruder responsible for these deaths. This was the determination of the authoritative *angakut* (or *angakoq*), a shaman whose "principal office" was "to find out the reason of sickness and death or of any other misfortune visiting the natives," as Boas later wrote in the section on religion in his major report *The Central Eskimo,* which he published in 1888.[11] That year also saw the birth of the Washington-based journal *American Anthropologist,* the first one, as Charles King observes, to use the term as its title.[12] Boas was riding a wave as well as participating in its rise.

In his report, Boas told of the foundation myth of the Inuits, in particular the legend of Sedna. She was the fearsome and powerful goddess of the sea and "mistress of the underworld," the frightening figure of children's nighttime stories. The myth is complex and there are multiple versions. But in all of these, Sedna's father saves her from her husband, an abusive bird-spirit, or *fulmar.* Along with other bird-spirits, he pursued the kayak into which he had taken her and created a storm. To save himself, her husband threw her overboard, giving her up to them. As she tried to clamber back into the boat, the husband cut off her fingers—the first joints, which became seals once they reached the bottom of the sea, then, as she clung on, the second joints, which became ground seals, and then her finger stumps, which became whales. Sedna is the angry, vengeful mother of the sea mammals on which the Inuit rely for their very survival—

for everything from food to clothing. She hates the Eskimo, as Boas explained in his essay "A Year among the Eskimo," since "they hunt and kill the creatures which have arisen from her flesh and blood. Her father, who can only move by creeping, appears to the dying; and the wizards often see his crippled hand seizing and taking away the dead. The dead have to stay a year in Sedna's dismal abode. . . . Only those who have been good and brave on the earth escape Sedna, and lead happy lives in the upper land of Kudlivun. This land is full of reindeer; it is never cold there, and snow and ice never visit it."[13] Sedna is intolerant of any infringement of hunting customs, and she must be propitiated if one wants to ensure good weather and a successful hunt. As death corresponds to Sedna rising up from the underground, the *angakut* must spring to action to invoke the good spirits against the spirits of the dead, or *tupilaq.*

The *angakut* who had made the determination that Boas was responsible for the deaths, a man named Napekin, forbade Franz from entering the homes of his people, ordering the community to deny him the help he had been receiving from them in the form of logistics, clothes, dogs, and more. In response, as Boas himself recounted in his "A Journey in Cumberland Sound," he stood his ground: "I visited the settlement and told the men that every trade between myself and them would stop until they would invite me into their huts, even if I saw them in a starving condition I would not give them a piece of bread." (He had indeed been helping them out with food.) He was determined to have his way, despite what he reported on the *angakut*'s role as one who oversaw the observance of taboos related to Sedna. And he could afford to menace the shaman with ceasing all cooperation, since the latter needed a functioning rifle and ammunition for his own journey.[14] Six weeks later, Napekin did seek reconciliation—with a gift of seal pelts and a promise to help Boas, as indeed he did that summer on Davis Strait.

The way in which Boas navigated the situation is an exemplum of the complex status of the visitor, however ensconced within the daily life of the inhabitants. At once observer and observed, at once engaged participant and temporary guest, at once embedded and detached, Boas could of course never become an Inuit himself. There were limits to the sense of belonging he felt he could cultivate. Traditions were to be studied but he could not be allowed to trespass on what he needed in order to study these traditions in the first place. In this instance, communication was maintained within the conflict. After the standoff, Boas wrote, "one of them asked me to stop with him, and sometime afterwards the others came to Kikkerton to regain my goodwill by presenting me with a few sealskins." Clearly, the community for whose interests Napekin claimed to stand wasn't entirely convinced. Some resistance remained, however, as Boas recounted. In February, when he returned to the settlement, the diphtheria epidemic was still raging, and children were still dying. "I will suffer seriously from the sicknesses that are prevailing here, since I know that many Eskimos only reluctantly have any dealings with me, though they dare not express it to my face. Now none of them wanted to lend me any dogs, but when I asked for them, they did not dare refuse."[15] As Zumwelt writes, "Boas was balancing on a fulcrum that required the cooperation of the Inuit and, at the same time, that acknowledged the Inuit view of him as bringing disease to their families and their dogs" (the dog population too was ravaged by an epidemic).[16] Boas wanted the dogs and the sealskins: he needed to continue his work, no matter the conditions. Cultural differences could become barriers. This was precisely the challenge that Boas faced—and, to some extent, resolved over the year of his stay.

By the end of this sojourn, Boas had managed to survey a good twenty-four hundred miles of this massive island (the fifth largest in the world), using merely local means of transportation besides walking—dog sleds and boats. With the help of the locals with whom he lived and worked, he amassed an impressive amount of geographical data.[17] He did the science, the cartography, and the meteorology, and he studied, as he had planned to do, the routes used by the Inuit population—where they came from, where they met, and where they migrated—discovering, inter alia, that the vast majority of inhabitants of Cumberland Sound had never been to the west coast. He managed to conduct a census of those inhabitants, igloo by igloo, registering their names, ages, gender, place of birth, residence, and kin, as one does in any census.[18] There was also the collection of artifacts—human and natural—and maps, many of which he donated to the Royal Ethnographical Museum in Berlin. After all, he had come to observe, record, translate, and indeed transmit.

But all these achievements aside, it was his encounters with actual people that would revolutionize his outlook, his thinking and, by extension, the history of Western thought about its own nature. Boas never did resort there to the craniometrical studies Virchow had prepared him for, ensuring he had with him the equipment they required, or, for that matter, to surveying the menstruation cycles of Inuit women. He was aware that some of the methodologies he brought with him did not sit well with actual interactions with the living, breathing, feeling people he was slowly getting to know and understand. He knew that removing skeletons and skulls from graves was not a welcome act, and he resisted the temptation to do so—a temptation whose ethics he did not, however, question, bred as it was by the emphasis on the craniometry that had been one aspect of his training, and on the belief that such a practice was necessary for the advancement of science. "Unfortunately I cannot take away the skulls that were in the graves, because of my Eskimos," he wrote to Marie in late May 1883. Here, instead of measuring the populations from a remove, he gradually learned how to *live with* them and, in his words, how to "translate himself in to the views and modes of thought of the people."[19]

Of course he made detailed observations not only of the

daily life he came to share with the local inhabitants, but also of the rituals and practices he could not partake in as a native would—in true ethnographic style, but with great admiration, even love, for this culture, whose complexities he knew it took time to start comprehending. So, for example, he described at length the role and dramatically theatrical performances of the *angakut*, writing, "Some pierce their bodies with harpoons, evidently having bladders filled with blood fastened under their jackets beforehand, and bleed profusely as they enter the hut." He wrote at length about these practices, recording the "archaic" words that constituted the "sacred language" used by the shaman, the taboos and regulations related to the rich Sedna tradition, and more. He wrote about Inuit arts, poetry, painting, and music, about the people's in-depth knowledge of geography— he used their maps, too, which the Inuit drew for him. In "Poetry and Music of Some North American Tribes," published in 1887, a year before his *The Central Eskimo* appeared, he wrote that the examples of the arts he had surveyed "will show that the mind of the 'savage' is sensible to the beauties of poetry and music, and that is only the superficial observer to whom he appears stupid and unfeeling."[20] He also wrote eloquently about "how calmly the Eskimos look death in the face, although they are unbelievably afraid of the dead and even death, as long as they are healthy, and I have also seen such protestations of inner love between parents and children. I shall never forget coming into a small snow house in which a mother was sitting with her sick child which barely gave any sign of life, but still was voicing the most tender endearments to her child! And I'll always remember how Joe, who is dead now, told me that thinking of his son, who had died the previous spring, made him so miserable." He continued: "These are 'savages' whose lives are supposed to be worth nothing compared with a civilized European. I do not believe that we, if living under the same conditions, would be so willing to work or be so cheerful and happy! I have to say that as regards character I am totally contented with the Eskimos."[21] By the time of his departure, Boas had gotten attached to his "Arctic friends" and was sad to leave them, as he wrote in his essay "A Year among the Eskimo," which ends with these words: "I had seen that they enjoyed life, and a hard life, as we do; that nature is also beautiful to them; that feelings of friendship also root in the Eskimo heart; that, although the character of their life is so rude compared to civilized life, the Eskimo is a man as we are; that his feelings, his virtues, and his shortcomings are based in human nature, like ours."

This was a time when "savage" was not a questionable category within the European and American establishment, when indeed it seemed a given that only one form of society, with one set of values, could be called "civilized." Boas's in-depth, first-hand experience of what it means to be human within an entirely different context far beyond his own western, cosmopolitan, bookish comfort zone, made him realize how absurd was the mere existence of such a binary divide. A progressive today would want to think this a self-evident truth, but cultural context does determine outlook, as Boas was learning and would show the world. And since we all come to an experience from our own, culturally conditioned perspective, it is in fact difficult to escape one's comfort zone in a way as radical as Boas did during that momentous year of travel. Anthropology as it developed from Boas onward factors in and parses this perspectival difference with honesty—with an open mind and open heart. This was the *Herzensbildung* with which Boas was gifted by his sojourn in the Arctic: as he wrote to Marie from there in December 1883, the trip enabled "the strengthening of the viewpoint of the relativity of all cultivation [*Bildung*]" and revealed "that the evil as well as the value of a person lies in the cultivation of the heart, which I find or do not find here just as much as amongst us, and that all service, therefore, which a man can perform for humanity must serve to promote truth." He really did view his mission in strongly ethical terms. Shortly later, in January 1884, he wrote to Marie: "What I want to live and die for, is equal rights for all, equal possibilities to learn and work for poor and rich alike! Don't you think that when one has done even a little towards this, this is more than the whole of science together?"[22] In this, at least, he was very much his mother's son; she also fought for social justice. As Isaiah Lorado Wilner puts it, he awakened during his sojourn in Baffin Island "to the radical variety of human practice, the universality of human experience, and the sordid power performances involved in extracting information about both." Science could not just be about collecting data and deducing theories from it. Following a Kantian view of epistemology, Boas was convinced that, in Wilner's words, "The 'effective' search for the inner nature of the thing itself, rather than the way one might define it from the outside, could reveal a different form of truth."[23] His investigations could not be mechanistic. They had to involve communication, what rendered alive the artifacts he collected, such as masks, which were meaningless without their creators, owners, and users. The masks were all aspects of stories, incarnations of creatures spun out of collective imagination, intermediaries between the real and the mythical, the material and the transcendent—and between the present and the past, without which there was no future.

Boas and Weike left Kikkerton and Cumberland Sound in early May 1884. They drove one sled, and three Inuits another, pulled by two dozen dogs. Driving through wind and snow, it took them two weeks to reach Davis Strait, a terribly arduous journey through melting snow, fog, and snowstorms, during which they shed many of their goods and ran out of food. Boas also lost most of his precious photographs. The plan now was to survey the east coast of Baffin Island, and Boas spent the Arctic summer doing that. He would not be entirely happy with the result but, as he wrote Marie, "at least I have travelled and mapped a substantial stretch of country here."[24]

By this point, homesickness had set in—and the time had come to return. Boas and Weike awaited a boat from K'ivitung to start on the southward journey. By late August, almost exactly a year after first arriving in Baffin Island, they boarded a whaler bound for St. John's in Newfoundland, where they took a passenger ship to New York via Halifax.[25] From here Boas wrote to his parents: "All my thoughts are now centered on my reunion with Marie, as you may well imagine. I am so glad that she knows that I am back and that I can write her. How happy I will be when I shall have her again! And you dear parents must also be happy although I cannot come to you immediately." As arrival in New York approached, far too slowly, so grew Franz's trepidation at seeing his fiancée again: "Patience, a few days more and I shall be with you and may kiss your lips for the first time," he wrote to her, regretting terribly that he couldn't go to see her immediately: she and her family were upstate at Alma Farm on Lake George, the country house owned by the Krackowizers, who otherwise lived in New York City, where Marie had grown up. The boat arrived in New York on the morning of September 21. "Naturally I had hardly slept at night and was astonished by the wonderfully beautiful display as we passed by this Giant City under the enormous Brooklyn Bridge and rode into the wharf at 6:30." He had arrived in the city that would become his home—though he did not know that yet. He took the ferry, looked up the address of his aunt Phips Meyer (his mother's sister), and arrived at their house just as the family was sitting down to breakfast.[26]

The return to his urban modern life was a welcome one for Franz—and not just for its material comforts, which he had begun to miss, especially over the last months in the harsh north. There was Marie, of course. But also an urgency to kick-start his career in America, the one country where he felt he would find professional fulfillment. He was keen to make his way forward pragmatically, and programmatically: to make a living, to make a name for himself, and indeed to be able to marry Marie. All ordinary ambitions—and indeed the oft-told story of Boas's academic career from here on is fairly ordinary, given how common even today are the obstacles and frustrations that he faced, often impatiently—though of course the outcomes of his choices would be far from ordinary.

The couple was finally reunited at Alma Farm. But Franz was restless. After a week of joyful romance in that magical setting, he returned to New York. His priorities were clear: he could not even envisage marrying his beloved without a living wage. He knew whom he loved, and he knew what he wanted to do with his life. Now he had to ensure he would succeed. He wanted a job, he wanted to write his book on the Eskimos, he needed to publish articles. Eager to get back to work, he met with Jacobi to discuss his future, set about gathering his scientific notes, and prepared to give a talk, in German, at the Deutscher Gesellig-Wissenschaftlicher Verein von New York (the German Social-Scientific Association of New York). Jacobi suggested he go to Washington, which he did. Here, notably, he met with Otis T. Mason, who had just been hired as the curator of the Department of Ethnology at the National Museum at the Smithsonian Institution. Boas was able to examine the—extremely disorganized—Inuit collections there. He met fellow Arctic explorers, including, notably, Emil Bessels. (Bessels's trip there in 1871, as the onboard physician, had been ill-fated: he was suspected of having poisoned, and killed, the commander Charles Francis Hall with arsenic. Bessel would himself die young, aged forty.) Boas began commuting between New York and Washington, eventually taking a room in the residence where Bessels lived. He also had his first encounters with the powerful John Wesley Powell, director of the Bureau of American Ethnology, or BAE, at the Smithsonian Institution—a geologist, explorer, and devoted student of Indigenous American cultures, as well as a follower of evolutionists Herbert Spencer and Louis Henry Morgan. Boas was hoping he might be able to get a salaried position at the BAE, but other than an offer to publish his ethnological research in the BAE journal, no employment was forthcoming yet. Not insignificantly, Boas's English was still rough. He spoke mostly German with Marie, which didn't help. She and his aunt helped him prepare his first lecture in English, which he gave at Columbia College: his delivery of the first of two was so poor that the second one was barely attended by anyone, but he persevered. He wrote his pieces for the *Berliner Tageblatt* as well as for New York's German newspaper the *New Yorker Staats-Zeitung* and a few other periodicals. Jacobi, on his end, did all he could to help Boas find a job through his multiple connections, managing to arrange a meeting between Boas and the president of Johns Hopkins University in Baltimore. But nothing came of that either.

Meanwhile, his family was pressuring him to return to Germany. Boas felt torn, certain that Germany would not offer him what he needed, and feeling a strong attraction to the freedom and opportunity that America seemed to promise, however difficult he was finding it to integrate there as a newcomer. He knew what he wanted, he knew what impact he could have, especially as geography needed to be developed in the United States, whereas the field was saturated in Germany. He saw himself, as he wrote to Jacobi, as capable of fostering Arctic studies there.[27] Becoming a professor in Germany would be a sad compromise. It would require him to obtain a qualification, and even then there were few well-paying jobs available, especially for young men, and certainly nothing without a long wait, even if he were offered a position eventually.

Germany was also increasingly anti-liberal under Bismarck. Boas disliked the political scene there, as he wrote to his parents in January 1885.[28] Germany had just become a colonial empire, despite Bismarck's long-standing opposition to the colonial enterprise. Anti-Jewish sentiment and discrimination was on the rise—and likely to work against his finding a post at all. But Franz's sister Toni asked Theobald Fischer to persuade Franz to give Germany a chance all the same—the family wanted their Franz back. And so, only half believing Fischer's assurances that his Jewishness would not be a hindrance to the pursuit of an academic career in Germany and that the Prussian ministry paid no attention to religious confession when selecting professors, Boas reluctantly gave in.[29] Obviously he was sad to have to leave Marie again. But for now he didn't really have a choice. He crossed the Atlantic in March 1885. After a week at his family home, where he was welcomed like a returning hero, Boas traveled to Hamburg, where he delivered a paper, "The Eskimos of Baffin Island," at the annual congress of German geographers. Much to his surprise, he found he already had a reputation—at least partly based on his publications, but also thanks to his connections with the likes of Bastian and Virchow—and seemingly was "known everywhere," as he wrote to Marie.[30] His paper was warmly received. The Hamburg congress boosted his morale. But not for long. The situation in Germany was increasingly nationalistic and jingoistic. Over the years, his friend Karl von den Steinen would regularly send news to Boas of job opportunities in Germany, each of which required of any Jewish applicant that they convert.

He remained as active as he could, however, continuing to explore his options, fully intent on pursuing the investigations that he had begun in Baffin Island. His thoughts were maturing, and by now he knew it was peoples and their history, rather than terrain, that he needed to continue focusing on in order to understand cultural variations in the human psyche. He gave acclaimed lectures on the Eskimos at the Berliner Gesellschaft für Anthropologie, Ethnologie und Urgeschichte, and at the Gesellschaft für Erdkunde, and was congratulated by Bastian and Virchow. Back in Minden, he wrote up his studies on Eskimo folktales, *Die Sagen der Baffin-Land Eskimos*, published in 1885, as well as a work on Baffin Island that became his *Habilitationsschrift*, which he could use for the process of habilitating as a university teacher. Advised by Fischer, inter alia, Franz chose to undergo this process in Berlin, at the Friedrich-Wilhelms-Universität. Despite the efforts of a famously unpleasant professor, Heinrich Kiepert, to undermine Franz's efforts, he gained his habilitation in geography in June 1886, presenting a talk on "Ice Conditions in the Arctic Ocean," and announcing courses for the next fall—which he would never teach, because, as we know, he would never become a professor of geography in Germany.

And even now there was more to keep him busy than academic work. In September, Bastian had offered him a temporary position as one of many assistants at the Royal Ethnological Museum, to oversee its move to a new building, catalogue Jacobsen's chaotic collections of artifacts from Alaska and British Columbia, and prepare an exhibition based on them, about Indians from Vancouver Island on the Northwest Coast. These few months in what was an "anthropological hothouse," as Douglas Cole puts it, would prove crucial.[31] Here he was surrounded by brilliant peers and able to engage with rich materials, notably Tlingit "grotesque" dance masks and "elaborately decorated utensils," whose contrast with the "severe sobriety" of the Eskimo inspired in him new questions regarding the nature and causes of cultural difference. In the winter of 1886, encouraged by his friend the geographer and ethnographer Aurel Krause, he worked with nine Nuxalk members of the Bella Coola nation from British Columbia. Entrepreneur Hagenbeck had both Adrian Jacobsen and his brother Fillip bring them over for another one of the *Völkerschauen*—just as he had them bring over the Inuits who had died of smallpox some years earlier. They toured zoos, hotels, and amusement centers in Germany for over a year. In an article he wrote about the Bella Coola's tour for the *Berliner Tageblatt*, Franz expressed major reservations about this practice, questioning "the admissability of such exhibitions . . . when some individuals are gazed at more in wonderment for their striking bodies than because they represent a vivid representation of the manners and customs of their people." But he was transported by the ceremonial rituals, arts, and artifacts that he witnessed—"a wonderful technique in the use of carver's knife and paintbrush and a finely developed artistic sense," the "outstanding regularity" of the dance forms, the masks, the scars on their arms left from their initiation rites, and the "unique music on which they are based" as well as their stories and their language, which he set out to study, notably with one man named Nuskilusta.[32] Franz, happy to publicly expand his range of expertise beyond the Eskimos, found himself increasingly drawn to the cultures of the Pacific Northwest and "the high cultural state" of the Bella Coola.

Boas felt it was increasingly urgent to investigate the Indigenous cultures there as they would soon be wiped out, he was certain, especially given that a new rail line was being built that would make their lands easily accessible. He also still needed proper employment, however. Discussions with his family had continued—they remained keen for him to remain in Germany, suggesting that Marie come to him rather than he return to America. But he was convinced that he would be able to conduct much more useful work in the United States. He returned to New York in July—via a stop in London to visit the Colonial and Imperial Exposition. He went to Washington, to the Smithsonian, to edit his *The Central Eskimo*—quite typically, he didn't appreciate the many editorial changes to the manuscript.[33] He then traveled to Buffalo, where he was well received at the meeting of the American Association for the Advancement of Science and by its secretary Frederic Ward Putnam—though he refused to give a talk because his English was still too poor. Back in New York City, he learned that the American Museum of Natural History was searching for a curator of anthropology. Jacobi's friend the distinguished Carl Schurz was a good contact for Boas, who was also counting on such connections for the position he wanted and needed, given that merit alone had not yet secured proper employment. For now, though, he had to wait, though he did meet with Spencer Fullerton Baird, the new secretary of the Smithsonian, with whom Bastian was also in contact, in particular over the possibility of exchanging collections— a process that Boas would become involved with upon his return from his trip to British Columbia, a part of which Schurz helped arrange.[34] Jacobi and assorted friends helped with financial support. By September, Franz was on his way to the Pacific Northwest. He'd canceled his Berlin classes, of course.[35] In January 1887, shortly after his return from his three-month stay in British Columbia, he resigned from the university—and as we will see he became assistant editor of geography for *Science*.

His overall study plan was very clear. It consisted of fieldwork to understand in depth the customs, mores, history, social structure, religious, myths, stories, artifacts, and language or languages of a tribe. And then in the comparison of the characteristics of that tribe with a neighboring one so as to gauge geographical and historical factors in the development of each respective culture, with an assessment of common traits, ideas, and beliefs and of their variations over time and within a geographical area. This systematic comparative method of study would, he thought, yield insights into the psychic laws of humankind, which in effect was what most interested him ever since he had engaged with psychophysics. This is what he explained to Bastian in January 1886, transmitting to him—"father of all ethnographic studies," as he put it—a letter from the Ethnological Aid Committee, which indicated that it wasn't yet ready to grant Boas's request for financial support. He explained in his letter why he had wanted to undertake these travels at all, thus making good on Bastian's request that he come up "with well formulated and financially assured plans." Boas outlined a four-year program: he was to spend one winter in Labrador with the Naskopi and Eskimos, another in the Chesterfield Inlet, another in Alaska, and a fourth in Vancouver: "My chief idea," he went on, "is that these tribes must be studied in relation to one another and that only someone who understands the East will be able to thoroughly understand the West." In other words, his knowledge of Baffin Island was excellent preparation for the study of the tribes of British Columbia—and he "would not again make one isolated trip, but can only consider it worthwhile if the whole thing can be done as a related unit."[36] He also noted here that, in his opinion, Jacobsen's growing collections in the museum needed to be supplemented because many elements were lacking.

The sojourn in Baffin Island had showed him the way, as it were, and his vision was steady: his travel experiences could only consolidate his long-term intellectual mission. In June 1887, after his return from British Columbia, he wrote a cover letter from New York presenting his "plan of publication" to John Wesley Powell, the director of the Bureau of American Ethnology who had been long studying Indigenous American cultures while holding evolutionist views. Here he explained that he wanted to understand whether it was "possible to apply the methods of natural science, more particularly of physics to psychology. This led me to researches on psychophysics and induced me to follow a certain method of ethnological researches. I believe the fundamental question is: How far does an influence of the surroundings exist? In studying this question I found it necessary to limit my inquiry to a study of the influence of geographical surroundings upon migrations and certain classes of ideas. Even these I found extremely complex, and began to inquire into their psychological elements. Studying the literature from this standpoint, I found that I could not understand the questions and facts without practical experience; I considered it necessary to study on the spot a people living in a wide area of uniform character." Hence his travels. Since his trip to Baffin Island, he had become ever more "convinced that the phenomena such as customs, traditions and migrations are far too complex in their origin, as to enable us to study their psychological causes without a thorough knowledge of their history. I concluded it necessary to see a people, among which historical facts are of greater influence than the surroundings and selected for this purpose Northwest America."[37]

We know today how fertile this program would prove. It also bears consideration how utterly "other" could seem these cultures he chose to study: as we follow Franz on his geographical and intellectual journeys, we should remember what and where he came from, a Western-educated German rooted in post-Kantian, post-Enlightenment *Bildung*, yet a secular integrated Jew whose own identity could nevertheless never align with that of the land he and his forebears called home. Herder's notion of *Volk* was alive in that land, defined as "any culturally distinct nation or people, all of whom, Herder argued, called for recognition and conservation as unique forms of human diversity," in the words of anthropologist and historian Leonard Glick. "But," Glick continues, "embedded in this positive valuation of individuality was the clear expectation that each people should and must develop along its own particular historical track in order to maintain not only its individuality but its very existence. (It is worth noting, incidentally, that when Herder first used the term, in an early essay on the origins of language, he concluded that the definitive feature of a *Volk* was a common language, and cited the Jews and the Hebrew language as a signal example)."[38] The double-edged definition of a *Volk* as that which stood in relation to another corresponded, one might suggest, to the ambivalence inhering in the notion of "identity." Affirming the existence of a "Jewish identity" begged the question of what could constitute identity in the first place. Certainly, Boas would not have espoused a nativist view of it in the way in which Germans were increasingly embracing a nativist, blood-based definition of themselves as one united *Volk*. Rather, his would be a cultural definition, based on what he called the "shackles" of tradition, as well as a negative one, based on the Jews' status as outsiders within their own land.[39] The existence of such a difference, which Germans had been affirming for decades now, in turn begged the question of how cultural difference aligned with perceived identity, and beyond that, of what commonality united humankind beyond perceived or felt difference. Boas was keen to define identity in cultural terms as opposed to racial ones, precisely in order to seek commonalities. Or rather, to understand how and why cultural differences emerged out of the self-evident psychic unity of humankind. Biological unity birthed cultural diversity. This vision stood in sharp contrast with the increasingly chauvinistic, nationalist ethos that prevailed in the Germany he was keen to leave behind. It was at once the premise for and the point of departure from his own culturally ambiguous provenance and relation to roots. The ambiguity, in other words, set him free to explore.

Boas was an organized, intrepid, and confident traveler by now. His accounts of this first trip to the area in that fall of 1886, and also of his later trips, are published in a volume called *The Ethnography of Franz Boas*, so we know where he went and what he saw, or at least what he noted and recalled of what he saw, and what he deemed worth recording.[40] This initial trip to British Columbia was of course epochal and thus bears recounting here too. Boarding at New York's Penn Station, Franz arrived first in Tacoma—in Washington State—and traveled from there to Victoria, capital of British Columbia. Aware of how limited his time was, he knew he had to "have as many co-workers as possible." He first called on a Tsimshian with whom he wanted to work, who told him "more than I expected," communicating with him in Chinook. He went to see the Songis tribe, observing the "very old" houses, and witnessing mourning rituals as, sadly, the chief's child had died that very morning. To wade into the language, which was always "very hard work" at first, he began with "the pronouns and a few verbs"—a methodology that clearly bore fruit, as he had an extraordinary gift for unraveling the structure and morphology of languages. He found first Alkinous and then Itlkakuani, two of the Bella Coola members he had met and befriended in Berlin. He was mostly curious about the related languages spoken here, and he managed to communicate in what he had remembered of Bella Coola—which he would continue to improve. He observed the presence of many Chinese, Indians, and African Americans in Victoria. He went to the Songish settlement, "whose inhabitants all seem to be terrible drunkards." He tried to learn about the Comox and Cowichan, confessing that he was overwhelmed by the new material and the "confusion of dialects and languages." He heard folktales. His Tsimshian friend Matthew told him a story about "the origin of the cannibal." Within a few days, his Bella Coola was good enough that he was able to understand their stories as well, which he listened to with great attention. He started to see "certain traits characteristic of the different groups of people. I think I am on the right track in considering mythology a useful tool for differentiating and judging the relationship of tribes." He continued learning from the Bella Coola, noting that "these people have a highly developed religious system," and wondering how it was that, "in spite of the great differences in language there should be so great a similarity in the myths and beliefs." He was starting to see patterns. He realized, too, that he wanted to find out more about the neighboring Kwakiutl (or Kwakwaka'wakw, to use the name used by the communities today).

He was enjoying the fall weather, the gorgeous landscape, the abundant nature. And soon he prepared to travel to Alert Bay. He boarded a schooner on October 5, "taking only one box of books, a case of tobacco, and a bolt of cotton for the Indians;

the rest money. In this way I expect to get a lot, at least what I want." It was a "beautiful evening. The moon shone and the stars were mirrored in the cabin waters. The ocean glowed as the ship cut through, and a faint streak of light showed where we had sailed. In the moonlight the hills of Vancouver Island and the small islands, which leave only a narrow channel, stood out wonderfully against the night sky." The boat arrived in Alert Bay the next day, and from there the party made their way to a village near a place called Nawiti. Franz requested to be taken to an Indian home, "and so we were taken to the home of the chief," which was "fifty feet long and is built of heavy planks. The rafters are held up by beautifully carved supports." He observed everything, taking notes systematically. "All day long the natives sit here on mats and gaze out to sea or converse with one another. The women wear the same kind of clothes as the men." A room inside the chief's house would be his home here during his brief stay. He knew what he needed—as much material as he could amass—and he wasted no time. An old man soon told him some stories "and showed me the accompanying masks, which I intend to buy." His collection of artifacts would soon grow to about seventy pieces.

Most notably, he witnessed his first potlach festival, which was taking place in the house next door—the all-important ceremony by which a chief and clan affirmed status and distributed property, at once a social and an economic investment, using Chilkat blankets as currency. In fact Boas was more than a witness to the event; he became a participant as a "chief," by dint of being a newly arrived outsider and stranger. Everyone—mostly men, though also a few women—sat in one large space, a huge fire at its center. Fish oil and halibut were cooking in a kettle, which a man—the host—stirred. Another man sat "holding a large drum on which the sun, the crest of the host, was painted. It all looked very weird lighted up by the wood fire." The participants sang and clapped their hands to the drum's beat. Soon it appeared that he, Franz, was the subject of their speeches. He was first taken for a priest, then briefly for "a government agent come to put a stop to the festival." Canada had made the potlach illegal in 1884—missionaries believed it hindered the assimilation of Indians into the Christian fold. The First Nations ignored the ban, and obviously remained suspicious of the motives of any visiting European. A government agent had already visited these shores, threatening to "send a gunboat" to the community. Franz, the lone "white man" there, rose to the occasion, making a "beautiful speech" that was received with "joy"—stating confidently that he had come from far away to learn about their ways and beliefs. In response, they held a celebration for him the next day, calling him a "chief": "The chief came to me and said: 'When a chief comes to visit we do not celebrate with a dance but because the chief from a distant land came to us, we shall hold a dance. Go to your house and await us." Boas devoted a few pages of his diary to describing this elaborate ritualized dance, the costumes and movements, as well as the potlach he held to "pay" for the dance—the songs, cooking, eating, speeches and, most crucially, the exchange of gifts, especially Chilkat blankets. "A few figures of the dance were really beautiful," he wrote. "For example, the leader leaped forward, and following his lead the group, arms spread out above their heads, danced to the right, then to the left. Many of the dance forms end in a deep growling sound while the dancers bend their bodies toward the ground." The women's "hands are raised to the height of their heads, the palms turned outward. While dancing, both men and women jerk their heads from side to side in a lively fashion." This was a particularly popular dance, so catchy that the onlookers tended to join in.

There was still time for a lot of storytelling, during which "the women prefer to rest on their knees and elbows, with the heads propped up." Boas would feverishly write down these stories as soon as he could after hearing them. He sketched the houses and totem poles, and he bought masks. All this material constituted the stuff of his investigations into cultural transmission with which to mold his thoughts about the nature of culture itself. His findings were not mere ethnological data, curiosities about the ways of others: rather, they were insights into how each particular culture is but an instance of the ways in which humans generally build their collective lives in a particular place: the intricate tissue of social, familial, architectural, aesthetic, gastronomic, and bodily propensities and rules, all of which manifest aspects of the human psyche. Potlatches, for that matter, a frequent occurrence on these shores, merited the close examination that Boas accorded them: they were an essential part of social life, order, rituals, bonding, and concord, hosted to show wealth and power, exchange titles and goods, and assert or repair one's reputation, with attendants seated according to rank. To give or even entirely destroy a good was a way of affirming one's status over and against another chieftain, clan, village, or nation—and so the more gifts a chief distributed, the more power he (always a he) accrued. This is also why Franz was asked to "pay" by hosting his own potlatch.

Franz left Nawiti in mid-October, traveling through memorably stormy seas back up to Alert Bay and to a small Kwakwaka'wakw settlement there. Here he collected several stories, wrote numerous notes, and purchased more masks and a rattle, all objects of value insofar as they were connected to the long stories, though he also intended to use these purchases economically: he needed to cover his travel costs and hoped to net $500 from them. Buying artifacts from the locals and then selling them at profit to finance research costs was a common practice. Boas was unusual, however, in the depth of his knowledge, already remarkable. Others on the ground did not have the wherewithal to comprehend as much as he did. For instance, he interacted with the local missionary, a Mr. Hall, who, he realized "had no conception of the methods and aims of ethnological work," and knew far less than Franz about the locals or the language: he hoped that their time together would inspire him to find out more and "make a number of studies." He was an expert insider now—as opposed to the missionary, who had come with that old "civilizing mission," armed with the epistemic paternalism and concomitant ignorance of local ways that, for so long and in so many places, guided many seemingly well-meaning, but myopically arrogant European colonizers.

As soon as he could, Franz boarded the steamer to return to Victoria, where he spent more time with the Bella Coola. He had almost mastered their language by now, he wrote to Marie, and indeed he would remain fascinated by it for the rest of his life. He found a woman who could assist him with translation and transcription. He also transcribed Tlingit tales he had gathered from a woman there before stopping in Somenos, observing on the way how "the natives were occupied in catching salmon" from the Cowichan River. He noted while listening to stories from an old man there how "screaming, dirty children run about, sometimes a meal is eaten. Dogs and chickens force their way between the people; the fire smokes so badly one can scarcely see. The old man watches to see that I write down every word he says, and, if I fail to do so, he takes it as a personal insult and holds a long speech of which I do not understand a word." Franz was by turns amused and annoyed, interested and critical. But regardless of his own reactions, he felt that everything was worthy of observation.

The next stop up the coast was Cowichan, then Nanaimo, where he found a group of people speculating about this "Boas" visiting them. Then, onward to "the much-talked-of" Comox. Linguistically alert as he was, he realized that the Comox and Pentlach languages had combined—and in fact that there was only one Pentlach family left. The Lekwiltok settlement was nearby; they were "formerly open enemies" of the Comox, whom they had "sold to the north as slaves." He had an altercation with a man there who demanded payment for the photographs Franz took of his house, using a camera he had borrowed from a photographer—he refused, sensing that paying inhabitants in such a way would greatly complicate his work. His diaries reveal how quickly he had become good at organizing his time, finding the materials he needed, interviewing, listening, and interacting, all the while standing his ground and keeping to his well-defined program of study. He also managed to obtain skulls from the burial ground in Comox. As we have seen, this was a practice he had tried to engage in while on Baffin Island as well, and in his view it was no different from collecting tales, artifacts, and indeed languages.[41] We will return to this.

By this point, he wrote to Marie, he had pretty much "covered all tribes of the seashore between Vancouver Island and the continent."[42] Many of the seventy tribes he found, "with the greatest difficulty," were even unnamed, as he noted in his diary, and he had had "to arrange them according to language and dialect and determine their locations"—an instance of Ratzel's anthropogeography. After all this intense linguistic effort, he was happy to be able to speak German again when, quite by chance, he encountered Jacobsen venturing out onto the pier at Comox, alighting from the very schooner that had taken Boas to these parts a few weeks before: Jacobsen was on his way back to the Bella Coola settlement where he was staying. Like Boas, he was passing through—an explorer does not "go native." And in Boas's case even more than in that of an explorer and collector like Jacobsen, visits to these lands were empirical and clearly situated attempts to understand human nature. The task implied collecting all that was left of cultures and languages rapidly disappearing due to the impact of the material goods, cultural ways, and diseases of the modern Western world—yet still offering insights into very particular modes of relating to self, others, emotions, traditions, nature, and artifacts. Anthropology entails distancing. It takes on board and parses difference. It constructs comparison. It requires a resistance to belonging, even as it enables participation and empathic understanding.

There is in fact a paradox inherent in the anthropological drive: to understand the world of another, one needs to stand outside it. Only then can one examine those whose likenesses with and differences from self one wants to enumerate. Intent on overcoming the old division between the *Naturwissenschaften* and the *Geisteswissenschaften* to understand the human mind as naturally cultural, Boas knew that he had to preserve the critical distance that enabled him to travel as the scholar he really was. This is what underlay his admittedly repugnant practice of digging up skulls, and what seems to us his blindness with regard to the paradoxical nature of the anthropological enterprise, which relied on human remains and on informants who were viewed primarily as useful interlocutors rather than as equal friends. "Indigenous people," as King writes, "were not just the subject of anthropological research—they were the reason for its existence." They constituted "a silent procession of the unnamed and unburied . . . : people whose words, belongings, and bodies were the evidence that shaped an entire science of humankind."[43] Similarly, Matthew Vollgraff writes: "Even the more self-critical figures of twentieth-century anthropology in America—like Franz Boas and Alfred Kroeber—tended to repudiate the modernity of the people they studied, focusing instead on preserving their supposedly unchanging folkways, legends and implements before they vanished for good. Salvage anthropology thus placed a perhaps disproportionate stress on museum collecting as a means by which the escalating loss of human diversity could be objectified and preserved."[44] Though Boas professed friendship and related deeply to the people he studied, it still was the case for him too that all sources of documentation, whether tale, myth, house, dance, song, language, mask, or indeed skull, were of value in relation to his mission to preserve, study, and measure. All were part of building a science of man, an anthropology that would reconstitute with sensitivity specific beliefs, ethics, and artistic worlds in the name of universal aspects of human experience.

Although frustrated by the limited amount of time he had, Boas was by now eager to get back to his life. In December, he returned to Victoria, where he gathered his plentiful material and prepared to embark for the trip back to New York. He wrote to his parents on the 16th, "When you get this letter you will probably have received my telegram from New York, perhaps even a note of greeting from there." He described to them Vancouver, where he had gone before returning to Victoria, and his words merit a lengthy quotation: "Vancouver makes a very strange impression. It is scarcely a year since the city arose from the wilderness, the moment it became known that the Canadian Pacific would have its terminal here. Where there are no houses, even in the middle of the city, there are burned or burning tree stumps. People from all lands, no one really seeming at home, swarm about the streets, which are covered with wooden planks. The streets are not yet completely finished, and where there are no wooden side streets, as well as other streets not covered with wood, there is nothing but impassable swamp. A white collar is still an event in Vancouver, but all this seems to be disappearing rapidly. The landowners believe the city to be a second San Francisco, but I am afraid they are mistaken. . . . The city will soon become important, however, as a harbor city and railway terminal." The local Squamish did not live in the Indian settlement, which instead was peopled with "a mixed company from this district together with white and Negroes. I find it very unpleasant to visit this kind of place. Nowhere else is there so much dirt, dirt of all kinds. . . . Picture to yourselves a number of wooden huts, crowded together along the shore, some deserted and some in ruins, poorly put together, all the rubbish heaped in front of the houses, the ground so swampy that one must balance oneself on boards carelessly strewn about, and you have a picture of this place."[45] He was witnessing the birth of a new world on the grounds of a much older one, whose first inhabitants were displaced and dispossessed—and it was a painful, messy process. Yet Boas knew that this new world, of which he would become a part, was inexorably advancing, and that it would succeed in fully wiping out the ancient cultures he felt it was his role to record, as a way to redefine the ambit of what was known as "civilization."

It was late December 1886 when he was back in that multicultural hub that is New York and reunited with Marie. He worked on his paper "The Study of Geography," which he had begun eighteen months before and which, as we saw earlier, would be published in *Science* in February 1887. Here he developed his revised thoughts on the subject for which he had trained, positioning it in between the general and the particular, the need to arrange phenomena and the need to find laws, the nomothetic and idiographic, physics and cosmography or history. It read as a tribute to a field he knew was underdeveloped in the United States, a field he felt he was in a position to nurture, though it also marked the end of his self-definition as a geographer.[46] The paper bore unexpected and very welcome fruit. When Franz delivered it by hand to the editor of *Science*, N.D.C. Hodges, the latter suggested to Boas that he become the journal's Berlin correspondent. When Boas told him, over dinner, that he intended to stay in the United States, so Berlin wouldn't be a possibility, Hodges asked him if he knew how to draw maps. Franz's affirmative clinched an alternative offer from Hodges: a position as assistant editor for geography at *Science*.

Franz could stay in America. Now he would officially request to emigrate, renouncing his German citizenship and thereby avoiding the draft in a country that was becoming ever more militarized and chauvinistic. Finally, Franz had found a viable position, a job that would give him the chance to do what he dreamed of doing. Finally, he and Marie could marry. And so they did, not long after, on March 10, 1887, at the apartment of Marie's parents. The couple moved into a walk-up on Third Avenue, between Seventeenth and Eighteenth Streets. There was a lot to look forward to, and a lot to hope for.

3

Exploring Minds

IT HAD BEEN a long, pivotal few years. Franz had a reputation by now, reinforced by his new position as geographical editor at *Science*. He used it well. He set about reorganizing the American Ethnological Society and helped found the American Folklore Society along with its accompanying journal. Ever keen to move on, however, he did not see himself holding the *Science* job for too long. He even pitched to publisher Charles Scribner's Sons a plan to create a new travel journal. But the pitch was unsuccessful. So he plowed on. In the meantime, he continued to work on the vocabularies of the Kwakwaka'wakw, the Salish, and the Kootenay.

He also got entangled, via an article in *Science*, in a controversy with Otis T. Mason, and then with John Wesley Powell, over the classification of objects in the Ethnology Department of the National Museum in Washington, of which Mason was the curator. (A few years later, in 1893, Mason would become head of Harvard's Peabody Museum.) The debate, ultimately involving how to explain "similar inventions in areas widely apart," took place against the background of Boas's hesitation to hand over some of his collection to the Smithsonian, including especially those that Mason thought of as "duplicates."[1] Much has been written about this episode because it was an occasion for Franz to state his views on how cultures were formed, and for Mason to advance public awareness of the stakes and arguments involved.[2] Boas's letter to Powell of June 12, 1887, in which he outlined his "plan of publication" (quoted in chapter 2) was intended as an explanation of "the foundation of my criticism of Mason's method," which he announced he would "set forth more fully in the next issue of *Science*." In turn, this article was a response to an article by Mason published in 1886 in *Science*. Certainly, it was an expression of still youthful authority.[3] Boas took the step of boldly critiquing Mason's belief that—and this is Boas quoting Mason's words—"like causes produce like effects." As a result, Franz wrote, Mason had "arranged the ethnological collections of the national museum according to objects, not according to the tribes to whom they belong." The objects were decontextualized, their meaning lost, because "the art and characteristic style of a people can be understood only by studying its productions as a whole." Indeed, each tribe had its style. Mason was wrong to classify the objects as if they were biological kinds, subject to the laws of nature as living organisms are, thereby introducing "the rigid abstractions species, genus, and family into ethnology," as if "a connection of some kind exists between ethnological phenomena of people widely apart." It did not. On the contrary, Boas wrote, "unlike causes produce like effects. It is of very rare occurrence that the existence of like causes for similar inventions can be proved, as the elements affecting the human mind are so complicated; and their influence is so utterly unknown, that an attempt to find like causes must fail, or will be a vague hypothesis." And so he advocated studying "each ethnological specimen individually in its history and in its medium," according to what Bastian had seen as a "geographical province." More: "In ethnology all is individuality," he affirmed.[4]

It was clear to him that one "must refer to the history and development of the individual form, and hence proceed to more general phenomena." The best method of study, in other words, combined "physical science and cosmography," the deduction of laws from phenomena and their description, so as to understand peoples "in their historical development and geographical distribution, and in their physiological and psychological foundation." Only so could one understand "the occurrence of similar inventions in regions widely apart, and without having a common origin." Mason was using a purely deductive method, Boas pointed out, comparing phenomena and drawing "conclusions by analogy." Boas believed instead that one should use an inductive method, "study phenomena arising from a common psychical cause among all tribes and as influenced by their surroundings; i.e. by tracing the full history of the single phenomenon." And so, "the tribal arrangement of museum specimens" was alone the "satisfactory one, as it represents the physical and ethnical surroundings" of the objects, which Boas viewed as "researches on psychology," no less.

As Herbert Lewis highlights, and as we know, Boas did embrace Darwinism: "He noted that evolution operates on individuals and that the episodes of evolution are historical in nature, wholly dependent upon location in time and space and upon the history of the organism."[5] It was thus not only possible but necessary to combine Darwinian evolution with a now fully affirmed historicism. In 1909, Boas would give a talk—unpublished—to celebrate the fiftieth anniversary of Darwin's *Origin of Species*, "The Relation of Darwin to Anthropology," in which he fully took on board Darwin's rejection of deistic theology and his notion of variation and random natural selection as the motor for "unconscious" cultural and linguistic change, bolstered with the time's still fresh archaeological finds that continued to push the origins of humanity back into geological time—and with a nod to Haeckel's "bold attempt" to "reconstruct the whole phylogeny of man."[6]

As Cole writes, "Boas's conversion to the historical and the individual did not mean that he rejected any search for generalizing principles or for social and psychological laws."[7] For Boas, and Lewis cites him here, "one of the greatest achievements of Darwinism" was that it brought to light how past events "leave their stamp on the present character of a people," thereby enabling "a physical treatment of biology and psychology." For him, "the physiological and psychological state of an organism at a certain moment is a function of its whole history."[8] Historical research was the ground from which to explore the general laws at work in the development of humankind. To be complete, however, it needed to be carried out in association with "the comparative method based on careful correlation of phenomena observed among a great number of tribes," since societies were not only made out of the *Elementargedanken* shared by all of humanity but by variations in the "laws of development," in the structures of family, religion, ritual, gender relations, class, and so on.[9]

The senior scholar responded, of course—immediately, and with a tone of courteous irony, opening his letter with this statement: "I think that Dr. Boas honors me overmuch in giving me the entire credit for a system which had taken possession of some men's minds before I was born." The stuff of his objection was substantial, however. He first defended the notion that museums could adopt any of many principles of classification, depending on what the exhibit's aim was, and assuming therefore that the context did change an object's meaning. And he objected strongly to Boas's argument that like effects did not have like causes:

> As regards similarities in the products of industry of areas widely apart, I think Dr. Boas's suggestion about superficial similarities from unlike causes a very ingenious one, but it has nothing to do with the case. Except in a general way, his affirmation that similar effects proceed from different causes will hardly meet with acceptance, in the face of the axiom that "like effects spring from like causes."
>
> In another place I have sought to show the gradations of similarities. Superficial, formal, or functional similarities in nature may spring from diametrical opposite motives, as in the case of mimicry. But according to the doctrine of chances, the possibility of similar effects diminishes with the complexity of the organization and the number of co-operating factors.
>
> The perplexing question is this: Can these similarities be made to throw any light upon the migrations of men?[10]

Answers to this question were actually not so clearly given. Unwilling to let go, Boas tried to convince Mason again.

And it was Powell, the director of the BAE, in that capacity highest up in the hierarchy of the discipline's establishment in the United States, who responded to Boas's response to Mason. He notably stated: "As there is and can be no ethnic classification of the tribes of America, so there can be no classification of their arts on that basis." This, in fact, was a clear defense of evolutionism, as Stocking notes:

> In attacking the possibility of any ethnic classification, Powell in effect rejected the idea that those evanescent tribal groups might each have had "a culture"; culture, for him, would seem instead to be a singular phenomenon that inhered in the overall classic sequence of "opinions or philosophies." In contrast, what might appear in Boas's defense of tribal museums as an essentialization of human differences reflects instead

the Herderian interest in "the genius of a people" which led in his case not to "race" but to a pluralistic anthropological view of "culture." . . . For Mason and Powell, the goal of museum exhibitions was to demonstrate progress: the progress of anthropology, the progress of science, the progress of human culture, especially manifest in that of late Victorian Euro-American civilization which had replaced all those evanescent "tribes" which for the three centuries since "the discovery" had wandered over the American landscape without ever establishing themselves as permanent "bodies politic." For Boas, in contrast, the goal of museum exhibitions was to demonstrate for late Victorian Euro-Americans that "civilization is not something absolute, but that it is relative, and that our ideas and conceptions are true only so far as our civilization goes." If his notion of the tribe implied a certain essentialization of the culture of each ethnic group, it was to the end of defending a diversity of human value orientations that could not easily be arranged in a progressive sequence.[11]

A lot was at stake, then, in this debate. Boas knew that. But given the powerful position of Powell, who took Mason's side, and despite a letter from Bastian defending his protégé, Franz let Powell's letter be the last word on the matter—for the moment. He was pragmatic: he couldn't afford to alienate the establishment if he was to establish himself one day. But he stuck to his views.

And it was for and via his views that he wanted to become established. He knew how to hold his ground. True to his ideas, he was developing as a theorist as well as an empiricist, aiming for the general laws while collecting and analyzing ethnological data in the finest detail. His fieldwork continued—as it would for many more years. At the end of 1887, in December, he received a letter from Horatio Hale inviting him on behalf of the Committee of the British Association for the Advancement of Science (BAAS) to return to British Columbia to draw up a report on a dozen tribes, a project that would take two or three months. Hale was an American-Canadian ethnologist and law-yer who had made important contributions to the study and analysis of American aboriginal languages and their distribution. He expected Boas to conduct the anthropometric measurements that had been established by Virchow—and that, we remember, Boas had not conducted during his first sojourn—and to pro-vide descriptions of "the complexion, features, and general ap-pearance of the natives of the various tribes in ordinary lan-guage, noting their difference if any." The committee, he wrote, wanted "a general report from you in the ethnology of the whole Province." Hale was in his seventies and could no longer travel himself, and by all accounts, it quickly became clear that he saw in Boas a less established young man who could be sent off on a fieldtrip that Hale wished he himself could have under-taken. (He had done research especially in Oregon.) As a result, he loaded the younger man with expectations and instructions as well as requests that Franz follow his instructions exactly. Franz found the patronizing tone and attempt at control in-creasingly irritating and invasive.[12] He may have been young still—not yet thirty—but he was more and more assertive. He knew his worth. And yet he did need sponsors. He was a man with a clear vision who did not like to compromise, however much he had learned how to by now. When confronted with obstacles or blinkered reactions, or indeed with mediocrity in general, he could become frustrated, impatient, and quite en-raged. But on the whole, he was fair—and always pragmatic.

Marie was six months pregnant with their first child by the time he left for his second trip to British Columbia, on May 25, 1888. (He wrote how deeply impressed he was with the beauty of the Rocky Mountains and Selkirks on the way—he had "never passed through a high mountain before.") This would be the first of three annual trips he undertook under the aegis of the BAAS and the controlling directorship of Horatio Hale. He set to work immediately and efficiently, as was his wont, meeting soon after arriving in Victoria a Tsimshian woman from whom he "learned a great deal," as he wrote in his diary.[13] He also helped himself to "a complete skeleton without head," he wrote on June 6, as all the skulls had been stolen from that site. "I hope to get another one either today or tomorrow. It is most unpleasant work to steal bones from a grave, but what is the use, someone has to do it." He also regretted that he did not have "more Tsimshian skulls"—he even had a photographer go to a nearby village to distract the inhabitants' attention in order to try to get another one.

One may easily find issue with his zeal for old bones, and with the notion that he *had* to undertake this admittedly unpleasant work: from today's vantage point, its ethics are more than questionable. Boas felt there was a justification for participating in that market—only buying, however, as he left the selling to others. Not only was it necessary for his economic needs, since research funds were not easy to come by, but he also did believe that bones were legitimate research material: anthropometry was still a fundamental part of physical anthropology. (And in fact he would make use of this for the rest of his life.) Besides, the market was very active even without his input: "I wrote to the Museum in Washington asking whether they would consider buying skulls this winter for $600; if they will, I shall collect assiduously." He visited a man from Cowichan called William Sutton who, together with his brother James, had robbed so many graves that they now had a large collection of skulls: the BAE approved Franz's request to purchase them. They pursued "phrenologie," as Boas observed, using quotation marks, and "of course I refrained from saying anything about the nonsense of phrenology. In the course of years I have acquired the curious habit of listening to all manner of opinions without agreeing or opposing"—a habit that may well be a useful characteristic of all anthropologists. And so, without further ado, he first set to work measuring seventy-five of them. In fact, he found it was a "very instructive" collection because it unexpectedly revealed, he wrote, "that the individual tribes, speaking the same language, vary considerably from one another. I hope I shall have the occasion to investigate the Kwakiutl, to better understand this phenomenon." In other words, the diversity of skull shapes seemed to him to demonstrate that cultural unity did not signify or rely on any biological unity. As we know, Boas would soon be able to corroborate this insight with much more data, and to extract momentous conclusions from it and further research that would drastically challenge the biological arguments for racism.

By the time he returned to New York, he had eighty-five skulls and fourteen skeletons. Boas had asked the Sutton brothers, who were effectively looters, to find—to steal—other remains besides those he had purchased. The Cowichans resorted to a lawyer once they realized that their graves had been "molested," to cite the word William Sutton used in a letter to Franz about this business in January 1889, and the brothers expected "to have a good deal of trouble." They were eager to be rid of the spoils for fear of "the authorities confiscating them," and William shipped them to the United States at his own expense.[14] Franz would sell them in 1894, not to the BAE but to the Chicago Columbian Museum, which became the Field Museum of Natural History and where one can still see a good number of the artifacts that Franz collected—and he knew full well that he was collecting for posterity.[15] Again, he made use of the brutal deeds of looters for his own scientific ends—the bones were of a piece with his collecting artifacts, idioms, and stories. So, while he "obtained three, not-quite-complete skeletons" from a Stikine on this trip and hoped to obtain another skull once he was in the missionary town of Port Essington, he was able also to perfect his Tsimshian there. He got on with learning Haida, realizing that it belonged to the same language group as Tlingit and optimistic about being able to untangle the linguistic complexities he had so deeply delved into. Eventually, in July, it dawned upon him that their morphology was Asiatic rather than Indian—and this was an important realization, as we shall see. He happened upon a photographer and had him take photos of "five beautifully tattooed Haidas." He heard about "old customs and practices" from "a few old men and women." His concern was principally to learn about the relation between individuals and the social group and its traditions since, as he would later put it in his introductory chapter "What Is Anthropology?" in his *Anthropology and Modern Life*, published in 1928, "when discussing the reactions of the individual to his fellows we are compelled to concentrate our attention upon the society in which he lives. We cannot treat the individual as an isolated unit."[16] Again, Boas was not practicing as a psychologist would, precisely because he was interested in collectivity. But his goal was to create a comparative psychology. He had focused on geographical circumstance at first, but he no longer believed in a purely Ratzelian geographical determinism. The cultural environment was as causally powerful as the physical environment, which played only one role in shaping culture, along with other factors such as history. It was the human mind he was interested in, as a product and enabler of the collective. He took it as an important given that we are each the outcome and product of the complex, multilayered circumstances we are born into.

It was also during this trip that he met George Hunt, whom he first called in his diaries "my Kwakiutl" and who would become a crucial local informant for him as well as a friend. Hunt was half Tlingit, half English, though he had grown up among the Kwakwaka'wakw of Fort Rupert, where the Hudson Bay Company was stationed. He had also married into a high-ranking Kwakwaka'wakw family. He never felt he was a member of that nation, and in effect he spent his life in a border zone, between cultures and languages. In this sense, one might surmise that he had a relation to belonging that was analogous to Franz's, however different the context, and that this might be a basis for the understanding shared by the two men. He had worked for Jacobsen, helping him gather the Kwakwaka'wakw materials for his vast collection at the Royal Ethnographic Museum in Berlin. And over the years, until his death in 1933, Hunt would assist Boas similarly, assembling into a collection the artifacts, tales, stories, myths, customs, and laws of his adopted people: Franz would work on the Kwakwaka'wakw for a solid four decades, and throughout, Hunt was of invaluable help also in helping Boas transcribe or correct transcriptions of texts. His central role in preserving Kwakwaka'wakw culture would eventually be recognized.

Inevitably, this collection would also become a memorial, a displaced reconstruction of sorts, that paradoxically preserved a disappearing, minority culture within the dominant one. This remains also the paradox inhering in any scientific study of mind (individual or collective), which necessarily enacts a distance from the subject in order to understand it at all. It is in this sense, too, that anthropology is a sort of epistemology. The relation between empirically grounded fieldwork and theoretical construct remains an unresolved knot at the heart of the anthropological project and discipline. The catalogued data becomes a new object rather than a mirror image of the data. But it remains a crucial source, even today. As Regna Darnell explained,

> Boas developed a mode of fieldwork that emphasized culture as a body of knowledge in people's heads rather than a thing that could be observed directly. He argued that language, thought, and reality were inseparable and that the best route into "the mind of primitive man" or "the native point of view" was through written texts based on the spoken words of native speakers in their native languages. The categories of Indo-European grammar and mainstream North American cultural assumptions could not be imposed without distortion. Collaborative research methods and recognition of the expertise of the "informants" arose naturally from these assumptions.

Such fieldwork took, and still takes, a long time. Many of the texts Boas and Hunt collected were never translated. But they remain accessible to contemporary use because they were recorded. The meaning encoded in them, both form and content, is itself the primary evidence—not the analysis of the outsider anthropologist or linguist.[17]

For his linguistic cataloguing, in particular, Franz drew on a philological tradition that was well established in Germany, owing as it did a lot to Herder, and where it was deployed for the study of classical languages and the investigation, or rather reconstruction, of their Indo-European roots. It was also a mapping, and in this sense, the Ratzelian mode remained. This cataloguing of linguistic data could also be understood as a necessary distancing from the pragmatics of communication, although, as Boas put it in the same introductory chapter in which he defined the tenets of anthropology, "The anthropologist is more deeply interested in the social aspect of the linguistic phenomenon, in language as a means of communication and in the interrelation between language and culture." By contrast, students of linguistics were concerned with "the mechanical processes that give rise to phonetic change; the psychological attitude expressed in language; and the conditions that bring about changes of meaning."[18] Franz would in fact pay a lot of attention to these as well—he was very interested in those "mechanics" underlying the "social aspect of the linguistic phenomenon." Indeed, as we saw earlier (in the introduction here), in his painstaking transcriptions of Native American languages he employed the notions and techniques he had gleaned from his study of psychophysics: he was acutely aware of the biases inhering in the apperception of new sounds, which are always filtered by known ones.[19] The phonetic texts, his last student Marian W. Smith writes, "were taken down verbatim, and the interlinear translations were made with the assistance of the informants. These come close to being exact samples of a people's thought. Boas was conscious of distortions which could occur through the introduction of a foreign or a sophisticated collector."[20] From the very start, he had resorted to the law of differential thresholds, in particular in his article "On Alternating Sounds," published in *American Anthropologist* in 1889, to explain the phenomenon of "mishearing" that was so current in the philological exercise of transcribing Indigenous languages—and it is possible that his musical sensibility increased his attention to this phenomenon. The nationality of the hearer, he noted, could be gleaned from the errors made, which were all "due to a wrong apperception, which is due to the phonetic system of our native language." He reasoned, then, that "alternating sounds are in reality alternating apperceptions of one and the same sound," because "classification is made according to known sensations," and "a new sensation is apperceived by means of similar sensations that form part of our knowledge."[21] Sense perception is shaped out of prediction—and Helmholtz had held a similar view.

This is how the psychophysical framework helped to dissolve the boundary between *Naturwissenschaften* and *Geisteswissenschaften:* it enabled the study of culture via the natural processes underlying differences, thereby going some way to solving the problem of the psychic unity of humankind, and with it, dismantling the very bases of a biological definition of race. It helped explain how we are biologically cultural, that is, naturally given to create and live within cultures. And it justified Boas's stance regarding methodology: he could be a scientist, a Humboldtian "cosmographer" in search of general laws, regardless of whether he would ever find them, as well as a historian focused on individual facts. And by dislodging these divisions, one could undercut the use of ideas informing biological reductivism and racist beliefs—themselves the outcome of culture as well as evolution.

Boas would spend a lifetime developing these ideas. He was intent on parsing the interrelation of individual and environment on the basis of the observation of all that pertained to the societies in which individuals are inevitably embedded. And of course his collecting of material data was directly relevant to this project. Charles Briggs and Richard Bauman cite these following words of Franz, written in 1897 for Hunt to read out on Franz's behalf to the Kwakwaka'wakw community to persuade them to let go of artifacts: "My friend, George Hunt, will show you a box in which some of your stories will be kept. It is a book that I have written on what I saw and heard when I was with you two years ago. It is a good book, for in it are your laws and stories. Now they will not be forgotten." And the authors comment: "The Boas-Hunt collaboration secured the removal of vast quantities of Kwakwaka'wakw objects and the creation of written texts, photographs, recordings, and artifacts. Boas's authority helped to enhance the legitimacy of Hunt's employment as a collector at the same time that the Kwakwaka'wakw and particularly George Hunt were being socialized into a process of constructing texts in Kwak'wala (the language spoken by Kwakwaka'wakw), putting them in 'boxes' that could be likened to the shaped and carved wooden boxes in which the Kwakwaka'wakw cached their treasured objects, and contributing to their storage and preservation. . . . Boas played a crucial role in determining what would be rendered as 'laws and stories,' the form and content of the corpus, the discursive frames in which it would be placed, and what sorts of authority would accrue to the texts."[22] With each trip and with each interaction, as Franz's knowledge of the languages, histories, and communities deepened, so did his vision of culture take shape, transcending the mere ethnological data about "others" that constituted the collections to become cultural anthropology—now redefined as the study of how human nature was universally acculturated and as a discipline that was entwined with psychology. The masses of empirical data and of artifacts he accumulated from here on and over the next decades were not an end in themselves but served that deeper purpose of his—to find, as we saw at the outset, "the laws governing the activities of the human mind" as these were made manifest throughout the cultures humans have created. As Cole writes, his "conversion to the historical and the individual did not mean that he rejected any search for generalizing principles or for social and psychological laws."[23] There were generalizing principles—such as *Elementargedanken*. But the particular stuffs and objects of each culture were irreducible to these principles, however much they may also have been an expression of them.

The objects that he and Hunt had put into "boxes" were no mere exhibition artifacts: they contained multiple meanings and stories that it was the job of the cultural anthropologist to interpret. A strange irony, told by Wilner, was that when Franz had been working at the Berlin Museum in 1885, one of his assignments had been to catalogue a mask that Jacobsen had bought. He would find out many years later, in 1920, that this mask had in fact belonged to Hunt's wife, Lucy Homiskanis, or T'łaliłi'lakw. A powerful story was associated with it:

> As a teenager Lucy had disappeared while digging for clams, leaving only a pile of clothes on the beach. For a month she was thought to be gone—until the winter ceremonies when the dance leaders of Fort Rupert called the people to their secret spot in the woods to compose two songs for the supposedly vanished girl.
>
> That night a Killer Whale dancer appeared in the house, spouting water from his blowhole. Suddenly he pulled a hidden string, splitting his face in two and revealing the form of a supernatural Monster Fish said to have taken the girl away. Following this transformation, and shocking those who thought her gone, Lucy emerged to dance, enacting her role as a bearer of wealth for her family.[24]

It was a personal story but also one that grounded the heroine within her clan. Most compellingly for Franz, the mask was vitally connected to Hunt—who, it turns out, had been the one to send the mask to Berlin. Hunt was the go-between who brought life to knowledge and knowledge to life—this too made him a crucial friend to Boas as well as a co-author.

Now that we find Franz launched on his career and intellectual path, and that we have met many of the important individuals in his life (not all, of course), we can let the years whiz by at a progressively accelerating pace, much as it does in life. It did take a while longer, however, for him to find his definitive professional footing; ahead there lay a few more years of temporary jobs and frustrating travails. The employment at *Science* was not made to last: funds for the position were short, and when Franz arrived back in New York in the middle of summer, Hodges announced that he had to terminate the appointment six months hence. Franz would have to find other sources of income. This was all the more urgent because Marie was eight months pregnant by now; she and Franz were starting a family. He continued making connections, hoping for as well as creating new opportunities. He presented a talk, in English and without incident, at the meeting in Cleveland of the American Association for the Advancement of Science, to which he was elected a fellow. On his way there, possibly on the train and certainly by happenstance, he met the president of Clark University, the psychologist Granville Stanley Hall. (Hall was interested in the biological underpinnings of development. He had studied under William James, obtaining the first-ever PhD in psychology awarded in the United States. In 1904, he would publish a study of adolescence, now well known. He also was the one who in 1909 invited Freud to give the first talks beyond European shores.)[25] Franz felt he was becoming established, and that his voice was heard: the AAAS approved his proposal to catalogue ethnological collections in the United States, as well as his suggestion to improve the teaching of geography in his adopted country (never a national forte, then as now). He proposed to

Hale further fieldwork trips for the BAAS, and was in touch with Mason. Hodges then offered to prolong the *Science* contract. Powell got the BAE to pay Franz for drawing up a report of his findings on Indigenous languages in British Columbia. Franz became secretary of the Gesellig-Wissenschaftlicher Verein, another paid position. He was not curator at the American Museum, and he was not doing all he had hoped and imagined he would be able to do. But all the same, things were looking up. He planned his second trip to British Columbia for the BAAS.

On September 10, 1888, Marie gave birth to their daughter Helene. Uncle Jacobi was the midwife. Franz relished fatherhood. But he managed to work hard—and he had to. He gave a talk at the New York Academy of Science. He finished his reports. He and Marie decided to visit family in Germany with little Helene: they left in May 1889 for Berlin, where his parents had settled. There was a lot to do there too, writing, revising proofs, and visiting again Virchow and Bastian's museum to look at the collections. Marie and Helene stayed on in Germany when Franz left again a few weeks later for New York (via England, where he met with E. B. Tylor in Oxford) in time to set out for his third journey to the Pacific Northwest. From Victoria, he responded to a letter from his "Sweet Wife" that their "little Bublichen"—one of their nicknames for little Helene—"finally has one, or rather several, teeth." He disliked being away from his family. In the meantime, Hale continued to be patronizing and to direct Franz away from his wish to continue studying the Kwakwaka'wakw—Hale wanted a study of the Nootka, who were of no interest to Franz. He wrote to Marie from Victoria, where his boat was frustratingly stuck for a while, "You cannot imagine how angry I am with Hale's instructions. Apparently he is not familiar with the existing literature on the coastal tribes, otherwise he would not state that the tribes of the west coast are the least known. The opposite is the fact. The outcome of this trip will be very meager, I am afraid, just because I have to follow useless instructions." Yet of course Franz was attentive as ever, discovering, for instance, that "the shamans here also use a special language." He managed to progress in his research especially on the Kwakwaka'wakw, meeting with George Hunt at Alert Bay. He also made "the interesting discovery that Nutka and Kwakiutl belong together. This is even clearer than the connection between Haida and Tlingit." He understood better and better the morphologies of these languages, their mutual borrowings and their genetic similarities. As we have seen, and as was evident in his debate with Mason, his genealogy of culture, including languages, had by now taken a strongly historicist turn. And this historicism, as we have seen and as Cole noted, itself owed a lot to recent developments in post-Kantian thought about the nature of historical knowledge, even preceding chronologically Windelband's distinction, mooted a few years later in 1894 between the monothetic and the idiographic, general laws and contingent facts, the natural and the social.[26] Boas, again, was intent on combining these. As pointed out earlier: he favored induction from contingent, particular facts to a broader picture, not the deduction of putative truths from a priori principles. This was how empirical research—whether scientific or historical—could be a bulwark against ideology rather than a servant to it.

This approach is called historical particularism. As emerged from the debate with Mason, it privileges the use of empirical evidence over the long term, rendering untenable a priori classifications such as those characteristic of the evolutionism inherent in racist theories. All cultures, on this approach, are constituted of their history, which is itself replete with myriad causes. Each story is different, each culture different. One might compare this view with the individualism inherent in humanist medicine: while all persons are made of the same anatomical and physiological stuff, all differ, all are unique, and each patient's story is irreducible to that of another. This was the ultimately humanist approach that Boas was defending and practicing. He hoped that, by delving deep into the particulars of history, he would eventually retrieve general laws regarding the functioning of the human mind—and again, reconcile the notion of a psychic unity of humankind with the multiplicity of its cultural expressions.

Over the years, he would develop this view, which informed his accumulation of as many material objects of a culture as possible—as well as immaterial objects such as languages, songs, and so on—in order to preserve and understand that culture. This is the context within which to make sense of his acquisitions of countless objects as well as his tomb raids. Today, any such justifications fall apart. For Boas, however, there was no ethical quandary, especially as, again, foremost for him was the demonstration of cultural equality. In his BAAS report for 1898, he listed "the three methods of classifying mankind—that according to physical characters, according to language, according to culture," all reflections "of the historical development of races from different standpoints." Since "the historical facts do not affect the three classes of phenomena equally," one had to take all these factors into account to "reconstruct the early history of the races of mankind."[27] Stories and myths migrated and disseminated, changing tone and color as they were carried over to other shores, integrated with other mores, and translated into other languages. A noteworthy example of this was the Raven tale, popular throughout the North Pacific coast, whose variations he had precisely and statistically tabulated. He found that while variations diminished with greater proximity, there could also be breaks in transmission despite geographical closeness, that is, "lack of assimilation, which may be due to a difference in character, to continued hostilities, or to recent changes in the location of the tribes, which has not allowed the slow process of assimilation to exert its deep-acting influence."[28] The obverse held as well, with similarities despite geographical distance due to previous closeness. In other words, by now Franz wholly moved away from the more deterministic aspects of Ratzel's anthropogeography. So, in his *The Mind of Primitive Man*, which was based on lectures he gave in 1910–11 at the Lowell Institute in Boston, he stated, "No matter how great an influence we may ascribe to environment, that influence can become active only by being exerted upon the mind; so that the characteristics of the mind must enter into the resultant forms of social activity."[29]

Well before 1911, he had the opportunity to investigate and demonstrate empirically this interplay between environmental influence and "characteristics of the mind," or cultural psyche. When he had arrived in Victoria in early September 1889, he had found a letter from G. Stanley Hall offering him what in effect was his first academic position: a job as docent at Clark University. Named for its funder and founder Jonas G. Clark, it was a new university offering programs in the sciences, exclusively graduate, and focusing on research. It was located in Worcester, Massachusetts—a town where, it so happened, Marie had spent some time in her childhood. In a letter to Marie from Kamloops (where he awaited the steamer back to Victoria) announcing he had accepted Hall's offer even though he wished he "could have talked the matter over with you," Franz fretted a little: "I hope you will like it there and soon make friends. I hope they will be satisfied with me and that the position will become a permanent one. . . . Darling, how will you feel about going back to Worcester? Will you recognize the city again? Are any of your old acquaintances left there?"[30] It was a modestly paid position, but it came with the freedom to create his program in anthropology as he wished and to travel to the Northwest Pacific over the summers. Franz and Marie—she had returned from Berlin while he was still in the north—moved to Worcester with Helene in the fall, occupying a large basement flat, simple but pleasant. Franz was able to rent a piano, with money supplied by his ever-generous parents: music remained very important to him. He had a particular predilection for Mozart sonatas. He also played the violin. And he would find joy at Clark in playing chamber music with a few of his colleagues.[31]

Franz found himself teaching anthropology for the first time in his life. It was all novel for him. Lecturing was challenging, though fulfilling as well. Franz wasn't too happy with the disorganized nature of the place, or with the insufficient pay of $1,500 a year. Still, for a while life was significantly more settled than it had been until now. Franz managed to write and to return to British Columbia for the BAAS in the summers. And in February 1891, Marie gave birth to their second child, a boy they named Ernst.

Franz's colleagues were of high caliber. He and Marie befriended in particular pioneering neurologist and psychologist Henry Herbert Donaldson—and his wife Julia—who had been a doctoral student of Hall's (he investigated the sense of temperature) and was conducting at Clark what would prove important research on the growth of the brain, and on sensory deprivation via the once-famous case of deaf and blind Laura Bridgman.

From the start, Franz was eager to pursue physical anthropology in the small laboratory he had been able to install to that effect, to put to work the techniques of anthropometry he had been trained in—and for which he had gathered all those old bones, a collection he cared about and fretted over. In 1891, the Worcester school board agreed to his request to measure children there, in effect to start what would become a proper longitudinal study of these children. Endocrinologist and pediatrician James Mourilyan Tanner has recounted and analyzed Boas's contributions to this specific topic.[32] It was what one would call today an interdisciplinary endeavor: Franz had the help of a student in biostatistics, Gerald West, as well as of A. F. Chamberlain, who is on record as the first person in the United States to obtain a PhD in anthropology—on the subject of the heights and weights of these children from Worcester.[33] Another collaborator was a Harvard professor, Henry Bowditch, the first ever in America of physiology, and a doctor called Charles Roberts. Both Roberts and Bowditch had done work on adolescent growth, noting that it was affected by socioeconomic background—wealth as well as national provenance. American children from "lower socio-economic groups had a higher weight for given height than the upper groups." Boas focused on what he coined the *"tempo of growth,"* based on an assumption, in Tanner's words, that "the physiological status of the children is normally distributed around an average value," a distribution that is "assumed to be Gaussian."[34] Tanner notes that Boas not only started "the first substantial longitudinal growth study," he "produced also the first standards for height and weight for American children."[35] Boas would remain actively interested in the impact of heredity and environment on physical stature throughout his life, though his understanding of it would change. He certainly believed in the importance of measurements as an analytical tool, as long as they had "biological significance. As soon as they lose significance they lose their descriptive value," he would write a few years later, in 1899.[36] The conclusion of the Clark longitudinal study, which he wrote up in 1897, was "the relative independence of final adult height and the speed with which it is reached," as Tanner summarizes it. Boas noted that "the differences in development between social classes are to a great extent results of acceleration and retardation of growth."[37]

This conclusion was based on only one year's study, for his time at Clark was cut short, as was that of his colleagues. The *Worcester Telegram*, the local sensationalist and xenophobic paper, was bent against the university—it had earlier attacked it viciously over vivisection practices, for instance. And as soon as Boas's project became known, the paper opined it was a scandal that "children at school have their anatomies felt and the various portions of their bodies measured for no reason established by science, and by a man unknown to Worcester," to boot—a man with "scars on his face and head that would make a jailbird turn green with envy."[38] While the outrage did not discourage the university in its support of Franz's project, Hall became at best ambivalent, if not hostile, in large part because Clark, on whom the university depended, disapproved of it. Hall, moreover, was in no position to fight: tragedy had struck him in 1890, when his wife and daughter had died, accidentally asphyxiated, while he was away recovering from diphtheria.[39] Nor did he know how to see to the needs of his generally frustrated, underpaid faculty while placating the unpleasant whims of Clark. The Boas affair was just one source of tension. It got worse when Clark pulled out of the university in 1891, and Hall was neither forthcoming nor diplomatic enough to satisfy the demands of the faculty. Boas was not the only one to feel badly served by the president when he did not get an expected raise in his third year. The atmosphere grew sour, and two-thirds of the professors, including Franz, resigned. His anthropometric research was over at Worcester. But it would have to continue elsewhere.

It was a sad ending for Franz—those three years had been fertile, rich in friendships, and overall pleasant. Seven out of the nine faculty members who resigned, including Donaldson, were personally hired by the president of the then recently instituted University of Chicago, William Rainey Harper.[40] Franz too would go to Chicago—but not to the university, as Harper had decided not to hire him. Putnam, however, with whom he had remained in touch, asked him to be chief assistant at the World's Columbian Exposition in Chicago, whose Department of Anthropology Putnam was heading. This fair was being organized to celebrate the four hundred years since Columbus's arrival in the New World. Selecting Chicago as the host city, Congress had conceived it as a competitive response to the 1889 Exposition Universelle in Paris. It was to be about ten times the size of the French exposition, "an American fair, the grandeur of which would prove that American culture was not only equal to, but had surpassed European culture."[41] It was designed by the great landscape architect Frederick Law Olmsted who, along with Calvert Vaux, had designed New York's Central Park a couple of decades before.

Putnam's project, called "Department M," had a budget of $300,000 and consisted of curating the exhibits that would be shown in the Anthropological Building and the "living villages" that would be reconstituted on the grounds around it.[42] A lot was at stake for Putnam, who envisioned this massive project as an opportunity to centralize and synthesize the sundry aspects of ethnology and archeology—"a perfect ethnological exhibition of the past and present peoples of America"—and the department as one that would "illustrate early life in America from remote ages before historic times down to the period of Columbus."[43] Its motto was "To see is to know."[44] He had published his proposal for it in the *Chicago Tribune:* it was to be "a collection of the habitations of the dwellers in the Americas from Primitive savages up to the present time."[45] Franz had become involved in 1891, helping Putnam (for a small pay) to build up the section on physical anthropology, which included psychology and neurology, for which he contributed his ongoing measurements of the native populations of America as well as those of ninety thousand school-age children. As Cole recounts, he called on students from Clark—he was still there then—and Harvard, as well as on "a large number of missionaries, army and navy doctors, Indian agents, and even teachers measuring Indians from Greenland to the Aleutians, and from Nova Scotia to Arizona."[46] The people involved included, among many others, the Jacobsen brothers, who would provide a collection of Bella Coola artifacts, and George Hunt, in charge of the Kwakwaka'wakw. Boas decided that the latter's "standard tribe" was to be that of Fort Rupert which, he was convinced, was central to the whole region. He asked Hunt to deliver a copy of a village to be shown at the fair, on the shore of the South Pond in Chicago's Lincoln Park. The village would include houses, canoes, clothes, ceremonial objects, and so on. Hunt was also to bring over families from Fort Rupert who would live in the reconstructed houses and perform Kwakwaka'wakw ceremonies, from the dedication dance to feasts and orations. There were also Haida, Tsimshian, Bella Coola, Salish, and Tlingit houses.

All of these First Nations of the Americas were quite literally on display for the benefit of the new industrial America, at once entertaining exhibitions, educational displays, and "objects" of study. Visitors could take part in workshops and learn handicrafts—in a way that is not so remote from the kinds of hands-on exhibits one may find in ethnographic museums today. We still look at the artifacts left over from other eras and other places—even our own places—as somewhat distant objects we do not and will never own, rather than as elements that inhere in our lives and livelihoods. But the "tableaux vivants" that Franz took part in curating had a strongly exhibitionist element, however much, to the contemporaries, the very act of exhibiting these living peoples assumed that other cultures could be translated and understood—to a point. The fair was, mostly, a popular entertainment ground.

It took place over six months, until October 1893, during which some 27 million people visited. To work on his exhibit and curate his eight rooms in the building, Boas moved to Chicago, settling in Englewood with his family in late 1892 and returning to New York in the spring of 1894. Those two years were not easy for him or for his family. Zumwalt quotes Boas writing to his parents: "I do not have very good remembrances of 1893. A rushing rat-race, great uneasiness, and unsatisfactory work have been its watchwords," along with bureaucratic mishaps, institutional rivalries and personal unpleasantness. He vowed by the end "never again to play circus impresario."[47] The fair featured a plethora of uncoordinated exhibits, including the governmental one set up by Mason and Powell. Both Boas and Putnam worked unremittingly—the latter was "overworked and driven to death." The construction of what was baptized as the "Anthropological Building" was delayed and ended up being a simple box-like structure rather than ambitiously inspired by a Mesoamerican one, as Putnam had wished. Moreover, it was pushed to an obscure outer corner of this massive fair, a poor rival to the action on the Midway Plaisance, which Cole described as "a free-wheeling entrepreneurial sideshow that almost overshadowed the exposition itself," gathering peoples from all over the world besides the Americas—from Java, Samoa, Dahomey, and Egypt—replete with entertainments and merchandise under what was the original Ferris wheel, designed by civil engineer George Ferris Jr.[48] But relatively few people were drawn to that outer reach of the fairgrounds—not even the director of the fair bothered to visit. It was, all round, a disappointment.

From the outset, however, Putnam, ever the entrepreneur—whose background meant that he had contacts in the world of philanthropy—was determined to create out of this temporary exhibit a permanent collection. It would be housed in the Columbian Museum that the city of Chicago was to inherit from the fair. Despite the depression that struck America in 1893, slowing down investments, department store magnate Marshall Field pledged $1 million toward the realization of Putnam's vision. This is how the Field Columbia Museum was born, which we know today as the Field Museum. Franz had been counting on becoming permanent curator of anthropology there. But Putnam, unpopular with the local authorities as well as the university, was sidelined as director. William Henry Holmes came on board instead, from his post at the BAE in Washington. As a result, Franz was not offered the job—an "unsurpassed insult," especially as he only learned of Holmes's appointment indirectly.[49] Still, he accepted the offer of a temporary post, to assist in setting up the anthropological collections: he had no choice, because finances were still so tight. And the family was growing larger: on March 24, 1893, Marie gave birth to their second daughter, Hedwig, whom they nicknamed Hete.

The three children soon got sick at the same time with measles—then, that December, with flu and whooping cough. Helene and Heini recovered. But tragically, little Hete did not: she died on January 11, 1894, barely ten months old.

In the midst of the tension and grief, and saddled as he was with hefty medical expenses, Franz requested a proper curator's salary. When the museum committee turned it down, he knew that he and the family would have to leave Chicago. New York beckoned again. Putnam was hired as curator at the American Museum of Natural History (AMNH) there by its new president Morris K. Jesup—while keeping, for the time being, his position at the Peabody. (Jesup was a financier and philanthropist, as well as an art collector and patron, who had made his fortune in finance and railways before retiring in 1884 and devoting his life to art, culture, and science—and to the AMNH.) Franz, unfortunately, remained without a job and without an immediate prospect of one, despite an intercession with Harper by Donaldson to hire him at Chicago, and after a vain approach to the University of Pennsylvania.[50] He was shaken by those two years of stress and professional frustration—and, of course, by the loss of Hete. He would remain without a position for eighteen months.

But some important work arose out of this difficult time. Spending part of the summer of 1894 at Lake George, he prepared the address he was to give in Brooklyn on the occasion of his retirement from the vice presidency of the anthropological section of the AAAS. In his speech, entitled "Human Faculty as Determined by Race," which he presented before returning to Fort Rupert, Boas addressed head-on the most racist theories of his day. It still reads today as a powerful rebuke to those scientists, dead by then but still influential in the 1890s, who, convinced of the higher status of the white European, used the scientific method to justify their racism—such as anthropologist Arthur de Gobineau, who developed the notion of an "Aryan" superior race, or biologist and polygenist Louis Agassiz, among others. (As King puts it, "Race as a principle of political power energized the study of race as a scientific one.")[51] Boas made use here of the vast amounts of anthropometric and biometric data he had been accumulating and analyzing statistically as well as of his experience with the First Nations, patiently building the case that would topple the arguments for the "inferiority" of certain "races." Boas did use the terms *race* and *primitive* throughout his career, but as shortcuts to undermine the very notion of a hierarchy of population groups: the assumption that the "white race represents a higher type than all others" is based on the confusion of "achievement and the aptitude for achievement," he said in that 1894 talk.[52] He went on to show how environmental and cultural conditions determined achievements as well as the degree of "civilization": there were no biological bases for them, and no innate faculties. Variations in physical stature seemingly characteristic of whole populations could be attributed to environmental conditions that favored or disfavored growth, muscle mass, and cephalic index (about which he would publish a rigorously mathematical study in 1899).[53] Civilizations come and go, and it was clear that "ideas have been disseminated as long as people have come into contact with each other and that neither race nor language nor distance limits their diffusion."[54] There was "no satisfactory evidence that the effects of civilization are inherited beyond those which are incident to that domestication to which civilization corresponds."[55]

Indeed, this notion of humans as essentially a species that had domesticated itself around fifty thousand years ago was an idea that Franz would develop over the following decades, culminating in *The Mind of Primitive Man*. The idea appeared first in his 1907 talk at Columbia, published as "Anthropology," where he noted that what "has been recognized by a study of the morphology of the races is that man must be considered as a domesticated animal, and that even those tribes which are industrially the most primitive are somewhat removed from the anatomical conditions characterizing the wild animals."[56] In 1894 his description was still close to the notion of anatomist and anthropologist Gustav Fritsch, based on Fritsch's fieldwork in South Africa and his analyses of bone density, that the Europeans there were to domesticated animals what bushmen were to wild animals. In *The Mind of Primitive Man*, Boas would link the degree of vitality of a civilization to its degree of plasticity and instability.[57] These were a matter of lifestyle, since it had been shown "that a series of measurements which depend largely upon the functions of groups of muscles change very rapidly under the influence of practice. . . . Such differences must, therefore, not be considered racial but cultural features. The differences which cannot be explained by functional causes are few in number and they are not of such a character as to stamp one race as lower than the other."[58] Moreover, there were too many variations within peoples to establish racial distinctions. Racial essences were inventions—though at this stage, as Stocking observes in his introductory pages to this address, Boas "had not achieved a fully developed notion of the cultural determination of behavior as an alternative to the prevailing racial determinism."[59] And as Stocking wrote in his 1966 article "Franz Boas and the Culture Concept in Historical Perspective": "Most of the arguments against traditional racial assumptions that Boas was to use 17 years later in *The Mind of Primitive Man* are employed here." But there were "limitations" to his cultural determinism in his 1894 address: he took on board the view of his close friend Donaldson "that at adolescence there is a great divergence between 'lower and higher races' in their capacity for education, and that this is related to a cessation of growth in the cerebral cortices of the lower races." What Boas did not consider in following Donaldson was that this was "an inference from the observed, but, as we now know, culturally conditioned, fact that 'lower races' become difficult to teach in adolescence." In other words, "the idea of the cultural determination of behavior was not well enough developed in 1894 to cope with such a problem as the differential performance of various racial groups within the American educational system."[60] But Franz was on his way to developing this idea—powerfully.

Franz returned to British Columbia in September 1894. It was the last of the trips financed by the BAAS. He worked hard there, as immersed as ever in this northern world—the landscapes, the adventures, the encounters, as well as the challenges of continually studying the customs, stories, vocabularies, and grammars, taking notes, taking part, witnessing, relating, and reflecting. He also needed this break from his personal life, and the time to mourn the death of Hete. He wrote to Marie that October, "Darling, I could not sleep because I constantly thought of our little baby which we lost nine months ago. There is almost no day in which I don't think of the dear little one. It is so hard to get adjusted to such a loss."

But he wrote little else to Marie about his grief during that time, concentrating rather on the complex logistics of traveling, progress in his studies and measurements, the next steps he would take professionally, money issues, the family plans and comments on family news, requests for advice—and very concrete descriptions of day-to-day events, including the often unpleasant foods: "For three weeks I have had nothing but pigs feet, potatoes, and tea—and oatmeal at breakfast. Yesterday I had some deer meat, which was a nice change, and last week there was some leaf cabbage which did not look very good. Well, one just shouldn't look! So many things go through my mind during these nights. I wish I were finally back in Victoria! There will be five or six weeks until then. I wish I had some letters from you. I am honestly getting depressed." In late September, he added at the end of his letter to Marie a note to his children: "My dear little kiddies! . . . Daddy is now on the shore of a huge ocean, and in a few days he will go on a big steamer and return to you children. Will you be happy then? The Indians will tell me beautiful stories which I can tell you later, of the Raven and the Wolf and many others. Here is some space left for a kiss for each of you. Who will get the biggest?" (He wasn't returning in "a few days" but a few months later.) In mid-December: "Dear kids, Papa is so busy now that he cannot write you special letters. Every day the Indians tell me so many things that I don't have time to write you. . . . It is very cold here. The mountains are covered with snow and the rivers are full of ice. The wind is howling terribly. Are you cold too? Isn't it nice that little Ernst is going to kindergarten now and that Helenchen can talk to him now and then. Remember well everything that goes on at Christmas so that you can tell me when I come back. Goodnight! Today I send a kiss to each of you. Guess for whom each of them is. Your papa."

Franz missed his family, of course. But he was taking in a lot. He began with a trip to areas he hadn't been to before, in particular those of the Tsimshian and the small, disappearing tribe of the Tsetsaut. In November he returned to his old haunt, Fort Rupert, and reunited with George Hunt, who had six children by then, reported Franz, "two of whom are married and also living there, you can imagine that the house was very crowded." Despite this busy family life, Hunt helped Boas immensely—with measurements in particular—though he was not always reliable, and Franz had to adapt to his whims: "He is too lazy to think, and that makes it disagreeable for me. I cannot change this, though, and have to make the best of it." There were countless feasts here, one a day, which made his life irregular as "I don't want to miss any." He himself held one with "250 Indians in the house—men, women, and children. They were painted red and black and wore jewellery; each was dressed in his cedar bark cloak."[61] There were dances and ceremonials. For the first time, wearing blanket and headring, he witnessed the ritual of the Hamatsa secret society, held only in the winter, about the Cannibal woman of the Kwakwaka'wakw, and he described it at length—an elaborate ritual involving a meal of salmon and berries, a fire so hot "that the roof started to burn several times," speeches and songs, a team of Seals and one of Bears, spirit possession, and more.[62] Later, at the National Museum, he posed as the Cannibal in the Hamatsa ritual for a diorama. The photographs are still extant.[63] Hunt, one of whose sons, David, was a Hamatsa initiate, got into trouble for collaborating with Boas. Cole tells us that his "detractors claimed that Boas wrote that the Hamatsa still ate human flesh," among other unflattering things.[64] Despite his deep familiarity with the place and his personal ties, which had grown over the years, as well as his participation in everyday and ceremonial life, Franz would always remain an outsider looking in. The people there knew they were being studied, explicitly so.

This time, by the end of his three months there, Franz felt his "last weeks of work here are very sour for me."[65] He was eager to go home. In the meantime, he awaited publication of his Chinook book and was working on the songs that musicologist John Fillmore had written down while in Chicago, based on recordings taken with a phonograph. ("One of the songs very strangely reminded me of Chopin's Funeral March!" he wrote to Marie.) In December, he went inland to measure the Chinooks for the BAE—reluctantly, spurred by financial necessity. Here, however, he met with Charlie Cultee, a Chinook he had first encountered and worked with on his 1891 trip: Cultee had been a unique source of information, in particular for the Kathlamet dialect which, Boas surmised, was only spoken by three people, including Cultee, who now helped him further, so that Franz could complete this assignment for the BAE (he would publish

Kathlamet texts in 1901).[66] Franz would not be back in New York until January 1895, after spending a few weeks in California for more research.

He worked incessantly, learned constantly, witnessed, took copious notes, published widely—all along holding on to his passion, ambition, and sense of self-worth. But he was also increasingly worried about money and about the future. Admittedly, Franz was, in Cole's words, "a loose fish because he had, in part, willed it. He was unaccustomed to subordination and disliked the idea of restraints upon his scholarly choices."[67] Over the previous months, however, Putnam had been assuring Boas of his friendship and support in helping him find a professional footing. Yet Marie was skeptical, writing to her husband, "What do you owe him! For all the friendship which he harbors for you, he has always thought of himself first."[68] That was not quite true: Putnam, as Zumwalt notes, really did care for Franz, and knew his worth. And eventually he came through, as indeed he had done previously. This time, he saw an opportunity for his friend when Jesup became enthralled with "life groups" he had first seen in Paris that summer, asking Putnam to install them in the museum—a project that Franz would be perfect for, Putnam had assured Jesup. These life groups would illustrate "the people and some of their industries, and some phase of their home life with its proper surroundings."[69] Perhaps something more permanent would come of this project.

Franz was in Germany and England over the summer, working on the Kathlamet texts and on the massive tome that would appear later in 1895, *The Social Organization and the Secret Societies of the Kwakiutl Indians*, based on his recent trip and on Hunt's reports.[70] During that time, he received an offer from Powell at the BAE in Washington, but it was for a modest and poorly paid editorial job. Boas did contemplate it, however, telling both the president of Stanford (he would be ready to move there) and Putnam of the offer. This motivated Putnam's determination to accelerate things. He managed to persuade Jesup to offer Boas a post as long as it was combined with a lecturer position at Columbia. The process took a long time. In the meantime, Boas started working on the life groups. And eventually, Putnam convinced Jesup that having Boas on the team would guarantee the excellence of the Department of Anthropology.

In December 1895, Jesup, suitably impressed, offered Franz a proper job as "special assistant in charge of the Sections of Ethnology and Somatology in the Department of Anthropology for the year 1896." Franz had rashly and proudly turned down the initial offer of "Assistant in the Department of Anthropology of Natural History" because another curator, Mesoamericanist Marshall Saville, would have been above him, and "I consider that my place among American Anthropologists entitles me to more than a third class position," he wrote.[71] The revised offer meant that he would serve directly under Putnam, as he had staunchly requested. Meanwhile, Jacobi had long been petitioning the president of Columbia College, Seth Low, on behalf of his beloved nephew. In May 1896, Low offered to appoint Boas "Lecturer in Physical Anthropology in this University." Zumwalt tells us that Jacobi, and possibly another uncle, Kobus, had offered to cover the starting salary for this yearlong but renewable post, unbeknownst to Franz, "until Columbia could commit itself."[72] The Boas family moved into a three-story brownstone on West Eighty-Second Street, between Columbus and Amsterdam Avenues, just a few minutes' walk from the American Museum of Natural History. It was about time. Boas had become established. He and Marie could now safely call New York City their home.

4

A New Field

EVERYTHING THAT Franz had worked toward was finally coming to be. His position was secure, his place assured, his authority recognized. Still, money remained tight. Although he never was supposed to find out about Jacobi's input into his Columbia salary, he did get a whiff of it, and he had no wish to remain dependent on his family at his age. But at least this, the first lectureship that Columbia had given in anthropology, was a proper appointment. The subject had been taught there but had never before had its own department: Franz was inaugurating a new program. When, in May 1899, he became full professor of anthropology in what was actually named the Department of Psychology and Anthropology, Boas effectively created the first such professorship in the subject in the United States.

One of his first students was Alfred Louis Kroeber, who, albeit a first-generation American, was also of German origin and shared with Boas a thoroughly German intellectual background. He had arrived at Columbia four years earlier, aged sixteen, and so was in his senior year when he met Boas. In 1897 he obtained an MA in English drama. But he was drawn to Boas's weekly seminar on American Indian languages, which Franz taught at his home. There were only two other students then. The program included Chinook, Klamath, Salish, and Eskimo, the latter taught by a native speaker called Esther Bein, who would also translate texts for him.[1] For Kroeber, there was no looking back. The first student to be awarded a degree in anthropology at Columbia, he went on to take up the first anthropology professorship at Berkeley. Kroeber became known as a towering figure in cultural anthropology. After his death, his name became associated with his work with Ishi, the last member of the Yahi people of northern California, 120,000 of whom were victims of what is known as the California genocide that had occurred earlier in the century.[2]

For the present, dividing his time between Columbia and the National Museum of Natural History, Franz explicitly conceived of his university work as based on the museum materials and projects. He wrote to Low in February 1899 that, since Jesup too wished for "the fullest co-operation between the AMNH and the University," he presumed that "no obstacle will be put in my way in regard to giving the University a full equivalent in the way of instruction."[3] As he began his dual position, intent on injecting the field with dynamism and on centralizing research, he reorganized the American Ethnological Society in New York, setting up an Anthropological Club.[4] And he was extremely keen, as he would explain in 1901 to Zelia Nuttall—a distinguished archaeologist and anthropologist specializing in pre-Columbian art, especially that of Mexico, who was hired by Putnam at the Peabody—to "develop the collections of this Museum in such a way that they will ultimately form the basis of university instruction in all lines of anthropological research."[5] Developing collections was part and parcel of his intellectual project from the very start. In late December 1895, before his first classes began that following January, he had given a talk in Philadelphia before the American Folklore Society, published in 1896, "The Growth of Indian Mythologies." He addressed "the gradual dissemination of a myth over neighboring tribes. The phenomena of distribution can be explained only by the theory that the tales have been carried from one tribe to its neighbors, and by the tribe which has newly acquired them in turn to its own neighbors. . . . In this manner a complex tale may dwindle down by gradual dissemination, but also new elements may be embodied in it." Dissemination, not independent origin, explained the similarity of tales and myths across "geographically contiguous" areas. It was not inevitable that similar circumstances produced similar ideas.

In the famed paper "The Limitations of the Comparative Method of Anthropology" that he gave a little later, in August 1896 at the AAAS meeting in Buffalo, published that December in *Science*, he put it even more clearly: the similarity of "forms," "opinions," and "actions" of human societies "implies that laws exist which govern the development of society, that they are applicable to our society as well as to those of past times and of distant lands; that their knowledge will be a means of understanding the causes furthering and retarding civilization; and that, guided by this knowledge, we may hope to govern our actions so that the greatest benefit to mankind will accrue from them. Since this discovery has been clearly formulated, anthropology has begun to receive that liberal share of public interest which was withheld from it as long as it was believed that it could do no more than record the curious customs and beliefs of strange peoples; or, at best, trace their relationships, and thus elucidate the early migrations of the races of man and the affinities of peoples." As a result, he went on, "there are even anthropologists who declare that such investigations belong to the historian, and that anthropological studies must be confined to researches on the laws that govern the growth of society. A radical change of method has accompanied this change of views. While formerly identities or similarities of culture were considered incontrovertible proof of historical connection, or even of common origin, the new school declines to consider them as such, but interprets them as results of the uniform working of the human mind," going "much farther than Bastian himself," who talked of the "appalling monotony of the fundamental ideas of mankind all over the globe." Those *Elementargedanken* were not in question for Boas. But when there is, as he wrote, "an analogon of single traits of culture among distant peoples, the presumption is not that there has been a common historical source, but that they have arisen independently." And this was the notion he wanted to parse, and from which he wanted to salvage the historical approach, for "the discovery of these universal ideas is only the beginning of the work of the anthropologist": it was the job of the scientist to, first, investigate their origin, and second, to ask, "How do they assert themselves in various cultures?"

To the second question, one could quite easily respond that "ideas do not exist everywhere in identical form, but they vary," and that "the causes of these variations are either external, that is founded in environment . . . or internal, that is founded on psychological conditions. The influence of external and internal factors upon elementary ideas embodies one group of laws governing the growth of culture." The question therefore concerned "how such factors modify elementary ideas." To this end, there was the geographical method, such as Ratzel's, or the sociological one: "The mutual relations of tribes and peoples begin to show that certain cultural elements are easily assimilated while others are rejected." It was much harder, however, to answer the first question, and draw the *origins* of universal ideas. Bastian had in fact denied—and in this he had been "misunderstood," wrote Boas—that one could possibly "discover the ultimate sources of inventions, ideas, customs and beliefs which are of universal occurrence. They may be indigenous, they may be imported, they may have arisen from a variety of sources, but they are there. The human mind is so formed that it invents them spontaneously or accepts them whenever they are offered to it." And so, "anthropological research which compares similar cultural phenomena from various parts of the world," be they totems, masks, or geometrical forms, "in order to discover the uniform history of their development, makes the assumption that the same ethnological phenomenon has everywhere developed in the same manner. Here lies the flaw in the argument of the new method, for no such proof can be given. Even the most cursory review shows that the same phenomena may develop in a multitude of ways."[6]

Boas's point in both those papers, as elsewhere, was to combat the grounds for evolutionism in understanding the relation between culture and psyche. Rather than think, as did Tylor and others, of so-called "primitive" societies as chronologically prior, unevolved forms of a so-called "civilization" of a uniform shape, all of which obeyed universal psychical laws, one could only look at each people sui generis. Tylor gathered as one "mythic group" stories from all over the world as manifestations of a "mental law," as Christopher Brakken notes in an essay on Boas's notion of dissemination. For Boas, we now understand, the obverse held, that one phenomenon could "develop in a multitude of ways."[7] This applied, as he would synthesize later in *The Mind of Primitive Man*, to tools, pottery, metallurgy, agriculture and animal husbandry, art and design, religious beliefs and theories of the soul, ethics and mores, and so on: all arose in different ways for different reasons in different places, and not, contrary to the evolutionist belief, in a linear, uniform fashion.[8] Cultural similarity did not indicate psychic causality. In the Philadelphia talk, Boas had reiterated the need to "define clearly what Bastian terms the elementary ideas, the existence of which we know to be universal, and the origin of which is not accessible to ethnological methods. The forms which these ideas take among primitive people of different parts of the world, '*die Völker-Gedanken*,' are due partly to the geographical environment and partly to the peculiar character of the people, and to a large extent to their history. In order to understand the growth of the peculiar psychical life of the people, the historical growth of its customs must be investigated most closely, and the only method by which the history can be investigated is by means of a detailed comparison of the tribe with its neighbours." Only thus, asserted Boas, could one "make progress towards the better understanding of the development of mankind."

With this in mind, we can understand why he was so intent on increasing collections of artifacts, which he saw as contributing to a large-scale, geographically extensive investigation insofar as it consisted in gathering piecemeal, irreducibly individual data—data that then had to be displayed within their context (as he had argued in those exchanges with Mason and Holmes which, it must be said, did not make any dent in their views on evolutionism). The more data, the more fine-grained the picture, the more comparative study, the better the understanding of the mechanisms and possibly laws of cultural development. The data included materials from Baffin Island—from Cumberland Sound, via the correspondence that he maintained with James Mutch, who in 1898 sent him a collection of Eskimo folktales Franz then asked Kroeber to report on at the AAAS.[9] (Kroeber had the help of Esther Bein for the translations. She had also been the housekeeper for the ill-fated Smith Sound Eskimos.)[10] Intent as he was on purchasing more materials for the museum collections, especially given what he thought of as lacunae in its holdings from the Northwest region he knew so well, he did face resistance from Jesup, who insisted on being consulted for all acquisitions, and who also wanted to limit them, though Franz managed to acquire and install many more pieces during his full decade at the American Museum of National History.

For six of those ten years, he was involved with what would become known as the Jesup North Pacific Expedition, a large-scale venture that began in earnest in early 1897 and lasted until late 1902. It was announced in March 1897 as a mission to explore the east-west passage between Asia and America and interactions across it. Boas was convinced that mutually influential interactions across the continents must have existed, given "so many points of similarity between the tribes of this whole region."[11] And so he had argued to Jesup that discovering them through a widespread comparative study of peoples on the verge of disappearance—whose languages, mores, myths, and materials would soon be no more—would help understand the cultures of the New World. Jesup embraced enthusiastically "the theory that America was originally peopled by migratory tribes from the Asiatic continent," as he put it to the National Museum of Natural History trustees in December 1896, and he set out to execute the grand plan to map out these connections on either side of the Bering Strait.[12] As Franz wrote to Putnam that February 1897, for Jesup, the expedition he was spearheading to that effect would be "the greatest thing ever undertaken by any Museum either here or abroad," and would "give the Institution an unequalled standing in scientific circles."[13] Jesup would use it also to obtain from the New York state government a new wing for the National Museum of Natural History, as Cole tells us. Jesup put Franz in charge of North America, so he would be traveling again, due to leave in June. Others would travel to Alaska and Siberia. Franz saw this expedition as a proper study, "not a collecting trip," as he wrote in a letter to the German Humboldtian periodical *Globus* that May: "My plan is to make the relations of the neighboring peoples the leitmotif of the whole investigation."[14] Putnam was nominally the head of this major enterprise, but since he still held his job at the Peabody, he was in New York only two days a week, so Boas was its effective leader. He set about recruiting other anthropologists, ethnologists, and varied amateurs keen on collecting data. He also chose his acolytes for his own trip: a young archaeologist named Harlan Smith and the Columbia physician, psychologist, and ethnologist Livingston Farrand, who had taught a course on "primitive culture" at Columbia in 1894 and who offered to accompany Franz on an unpaid, volunteer basis. (Farrand would become full professor of anthropology at Columbia in 1903, eventually becoming president of the University of Colorado and then Cornell University.)

During this time, Marie was pregnant again. She gave birth to the new baby in April, two months before Franz and his companions left for British Columbia: they named her Gertrude Marianne, calling her Trudel. Franz never liked leaving his family, though the Boases had settled into a familiar rhythm by this point. It was to be a long trip; he didn't return until September, when Trudel was nearly six months old. But, as ever, he kept in epistolary touch with both Marie and his parents.

The accounts he sent them of this trip, which began in early June, are replete with rich descriptions of nature, through areas that still today are remote, sublime, and wild—more travelogue than study report. All along, though, he conducted the usual measuring, photographing, listening. And some recording, too: on June 6, soon after the party's arrival, an old woman "sang the song into the phonograph which serves to 'cleanse' women who had borne twins. She took bundles of fir branches and hit her shoulders and breast with them while she danced. The song imitates the growl of the grizzly bear because they believe that the children derive from the grizzly bear. An old man sang an old religious song to the sun, a prayer. The gestures were very expressive." The trip, which spanned hundreds of kilometers through untamed territory, was mostly on horseback, across mountains and along rivers. Farrand was "quite a nice traveling companion, unassuming and gay." Smith had left them for his own digging project at Port Essington soon after arriving at Spences Bridge—a place Boas had described in 1894 as "a little dump of three or four houses and a hotel right at the station," where he was "offered a dirty bed shared with a drunken workman. . . . It was worse than an Indian house." Here in 1894 he had met James Teit, a "treasure" from the Shetland Islands who knew "a great deal about the tribes" and helped him measure them—and now he encountered him again in 1897. Teit, who spoke the language of the inhabitants of the Thompson River, rapidly turned into guide and informant. The route continued through "magnificent" nature. The travelers camped, rain or shine. The horses were heavily laden, and progress was slow.

When they arrived at Puntzi Lake in the Chilcotin district of British Columbia, Franz "found the tribes so interesting that I decided to leave Farrand here for at least one month" to study their customs and physical characteristics, while Franz went on westward toward the coast and the Bella Coola, where he would continue investigating their customs, tales, and beliefs. He hired a guide to help him get there. On the way, "we saw all the Indians who live along the road. It was really funny how they all accompanied us and how we finally arrived with twenty horses. Here we left three of our horses because we don't have so much to carry any more. I hope to find George Hunt in Bella Coola and hope he has collected a lot." They reached Bella Coola on July 20. Hunt had indeed "worked very hard and well" on the "old Kwakiutl manuscripts." Anticipating Marie's birthday on August 3 (given the time needed for letters to arrive), Franz wrote to her that day: "I shall have to bring a birthday gift to you in person. What do you think about a grizzly bear skin? Write whether you want one. Or rather something from the Indians which you can then put in (or on) your [illegible]. Grizzly skins are really a bit too expensive." On August 3: "I wanted to congratulate you on your birthday, but here I am again with my

Indians. But all the time I think about you and when I shall be with you again. That will be at the best in eight weeks minus two days. That's long enough for me. . . . Kids, how I would like to play with you!"

On August 5 he reported having "finished the texts with George Hunt, two hundred and forty-four pages, and a number of songs on seventy-two more pages. That was really hard work." These would be published in 1905 as part of the Jesup publications. On August 9 he wrote to Marie that, while awaiting the steamer in Namu, he had run into George Dorsey—the anthropologist who had written *Omaha Sociology*, published in 1885, an important reference for Malinowski, Benedict, Mead, Sapir, and Boas himself. Dorsey now worked at the Field Museum; he eventually succeeded Holmes as its head. Here he was with a few others from the Field, all on a "collecting tour." The brief conversation was "very friendly." But feelings roiled: in his letter, Franz was revealingly candid about his own reaction, which seems to encapsulate the contradictions inhering in his character: "I am angry at myself, but this trip of Dorsey's annoys me very much. More than I can tell you. I am mad at myself because there is an element of envy in me which I despise but which I cannot suppress altogether. It does not help that one behaves decently when inside oneself one is as shabby as the next fellow. What makes me so furious is the fact that these Chicago people simply adopt my plans and then try to beat me to it." The defeat at the Field Museum—that "unsurpassed insult" he had experienced—still rankled. "I don't really think that his trip will interfere with my work, but this treacherous way of acting makes me awfully angry." On the one hand, "I do not want to think too much about this matter so that I won't get too angry, and I also will not act toward these people as if I were angry. I really believe that I am unselfish enough with respect to my scientific work that I wish everyone the most progress. Otherwise I would not have taken Farrand and Smith with me." On the other hand, he "was mean enough," as he wrote self-critically, not to put Dorsey and "that old ass, [Jimmy] Deans" in touch with George Hunt, and he even had written to Hunt to tell him "that he should not do anything for them. I have to do this to protect myself. I will write Putnam about it so that Jesup will see how urgent and important the publication of my results is." He knew what was at stake. Dorsey was clearly competing with Boas, who, granted, was possessive about his fieldwork, but who also felt that Dorsey wanted to make use of his sources (Hunt) and assistants (Smith). He would bring up the matter again, although he also wanted to let it go. He continued his work, collecting linguistic material and texts, and also learned how to make castings.

In September, shortly before returning to New York, he wrote to his parents that he hoped "to find the new wing of the Museum almost ready to receive everything." (The new wing, inaugurated in 1899, is known today as the Northwest Coast Hall.) "Everything," including Haida and Tsimshian castings, meant 125 boxes, dispersed between Victoria, Namu, and Alert Bay. As ever, the material objects were as crucial to his project as the immaterial ones.

Franz would return to the Northwest Coast for the Jesup expedition in 1900, working there with George Hunt, attesting to how difficult the Kwakiutl language was compared with Chinook and Tsimshian. (For the latter, in 1903 he secured the collaboration of Henry Tate, who would become his local, long-term informer until Tate's death in 1914.) Out of this enterprise, over thirty publications would emerge until 1930, many of them authored or co-authored by Boas, especially those on the Kwakwa̱ka'wakw and Bella Coola. During the Jesup years, he was of course also overseeing the Siberian exploration, and he was in charge of finding suitable participants. While on a trip to Berlin in 1898, Franz had met Wilhelm Radloff, a German-born Russian professor who specialized in the Turkik peoples and languages, who suggested to him that the ideal men for the expedition to the Bering peninsula were Vladimir Jochelson and Vladimir Bogoras. Bogoras was fluent in the Chukchee language, while Jochelson was familiar with the Yukagir. Boas knew that the reason for these men's expertise on Siberia was their ten years as political exiles there, but politically aware as he had to be, he limited himself to mentioning their "important studies in Siberia under the auspices of the Imperial Geographical Society." In early 1900, before the parties departed on what would be a long, eventful journey—first to Vladivostok, via San Francisco, and thence to Nagasaki—Boas met in New York with the two men and their wives, Sofia Bogoras and Dina Jochelson-Brodsky, both medical students in Switzerland who would take part and assist in the expedition.[15] Another team comprised ethnologist Berthold Laufer and archeologist Gerard Fowke, who traveled to the Amur River and to Sakhalin Island. We won't cover here this aspect of the Jesup expeditions. Suffice to say that, by all accounts, research conditions differed widely in Siberia from those in the Northwest, including the fact that Bogoras would be arrested a number of times over the years: in Siberia, the "principal problems were politics, climate, terrain, logistics, and the enormous distances that had to be covered by horse, and raft, or on foot. The Siberian research was a dangerous adventure. It called forth a basic toughness, even heroism, that is much less frequently required today. On the American side, the work was played out against a background of intense competition, enhanced by personal bitterness" between the New York and the Chicago museums and indeed between Putnam/Boas and Holmes, who was succeeded by competitive Dorsey, the man Boas had unhappily encountered on his 1897 trip but who, eventually, would heap praise on the AMNH.[16]

All along, while managing the expedition east and west, Boas was also teaching at Columbia as well as running what was now the university's Department of Anthropology—the first in the United States—of which he had become chair. He continued to envision curating and research as indispensably conjoined and complementary—as the organizing nexus of the anthropological discipline and mission. In November 1902, he suggested to Columbia president Nicholas Murray Butler that an undergraduate program in the field be inaugurated, "in connection with the teaching of history and the social sciences," in order to open "the eyes of students to what is valuable in foreign cultures . . . and to bring out those elements in our own civilization which are common to all mankind."[17] At the AMNH, he was overseeing colleagues' publications as well as continually obtaining data and materials for the museum's collections, working to reorganize it along the lines of the Berlin Ethnological Museum, whose director was his good friend Karl von den Steinen and where he had initially learned so much. In fact, during his summer in Europe in 1898, he had toured museums in northern Europe, not only to set up exchanges with them but also to observe their methodologies of display.[18] And of course, he continued his work on the Kwakwaka'wakw and the Bella Coola.

The work involved in managing the Jesup enterprise alone was tremendous, but its outputs were impressive. At first, Jesup was enthusiastic about the results, announcing in 1902 that its aim had "in the main been accomplished," and that no further fieldwork was necessary.[19] Only the publications mattered now, since few of the planned volumes, which Boas was in charge of editing, had yet appeared. To Boas's mind, however, the fieldwork was far from accomplished. Many materials—the usual anthropometric data, photographic portraits, skeletons and crania—had emerged out of the Jesup expeditions. But there was so much more to discover. He himself had no wish to travel to the north anymore, not for a long while—and in fact, it would be twenty-two years before he did so.[20] But other, younger colleagues could—in fact should—be back on the field, and indeed they were, collecting data from California and on the Plains for another project he led on "vanishing tribes."[21] He wrote to Jesup in 1903 that, for six years, he had given his all to this expedition to make "this work a success," and that his "whole scientific reputation is at stake in carrying the work to a successful end." He pleaded with him to continue the fieldwork.

But there was no convincing the aging, increasingly tired Jesup who, in 1902, made zoologist Hermon C. Bumpus director of the AMNH. Previously, Bumpus had taken the place of paleontogist and Columbia zoologist Henry Fairfield Osborn as Jesup's assistant. As Zumwalt tells it, this shift in governance was partly connected to the Inuit.[22] For, even though, as we know, Franz never returned to Baffin Island, he maintained his interest in the Inuit—he would in fact continue working on them for over two decades. At the AMNH, he centralized the research and display of Inuit materials, with the assistance, inter alia, of Quebecois whaling captain George Comer, who had first reached out to Boas at the Department of Anthropology in 1897, a Reverend Peck, and James Mutch, the Scottish whaling manager. (In 1900, Boas had ordered vast quantities of plaster of Paris to have Comer make molds of hundreds of Inuit faces.)[23] Boas needed this input, since he had managed to study just a few tribes during his maiden and sole voyage there, so he kept in contact with other Arctic explorers and anthropologists—and there eventually emerged out of this collaboration his 1901 book *The Eskimo of Baffin Land and Hudson Bay.*[24]

It so happens that, in 1897, Franz had asked a captain and explorer named Robert Peary to bring "a middle-aged Eskimo to stay here over winter. This would enable us to obtain leisurely certain information which will be of the greatest scientific importance." In the event, Peary brought six related individuals from Smith Sound. Boas asked Kroeber to work with them and to collect their tales. They were housed at the AMNH under the responsibility of William Wallace, chief curator and building superintendent, where some twenty thousand people had come to see them, paying a fee, but they fell ill before being moved to Jesup's property in the Bronx. Four of them died of pneumonia within a year at Bellevue Hospital. A seven-year-old boy named Minik survived. His father, Qisuk, was one of the dead. The museum staff staged his fake burial so that his body could be studied: his skeleton went on show in the museum. Wallace raised Minik, who didn't find out the truth about his father's fate until 1902—through the newspapers. (In 1909 Minik returned to Greenland, where he died in 1918 of the Spanish flu.) Wallace was then discovered to have been taking kickbacks and resigned from his position. The story became public—and deeply embarrassing. This was when Jesup named Osborn vice president, and Bumpus director.[25]

Boas, who, according to Cole, first met Bumpus at Clark, where he had been a doctoral fellow, did not get along with him at all. The atmosphere worsened, gradually but decisively, once Putnam left for Berkeley in 1903, founding the Museum for Anthropology there.[26] Putnam had been made chairman of its advisory committee in 1901, but two years later, he did not inform Boas that he would be taking up the post of director. From 1904, he would spend three months each year at Berkeley as professor of anthropology, on leave from the Peabody, and letting go entirely of what had become a part-time position at the AMNH. In effect, in 1902 Jesup had asked him to resign because his absences had a deleterious effect, though Putnam had then stayed on as "advisory curator."[27] This turnaround in 1903 surprised and hurt Franz, who felt betrayed by it, all the more since he was participating in building a program of anthropology in California—one that involved his protégé Kroeber, who was now working with Putnam. Kroeber would spend the rest of his life there, in charge of developing the Department and Museum of Anthropology at Berkeley, and publishing widely.[28] Franz also felt blindsided in 1902 concerning the creation of an archaeology department at Columbia, directed by Marshall Saville, the curator at the AMNH. The project was endowed with $100,000, gifted by Franco-American philanthropist Joseph Loubat. Franz learned of this in the newspaper, as did Jesup and Bumpus. Putnam, though aware of it, did not mention it while he was negotiating his revised status at the AMNH.[29] Sadly, Boas's relationship with Putnam never recovered from what Franz experienced as slights, if not betrayals.[30] But at least the California program was Boasian.

Other crises occurred over that year 1902. While at Lake George in July, Franz underwent surgery for appendicitis at the Albany hospital. His recovery period was not tranquil. After Powell died that September, the secretary of the Smithsonian appointed W. H. Holmes as his successor rather than William John McGee—much to Boas's displeasure. Until then, McGee had been Holmes's collaborator at the BAE, but when Powell died, he was dismissed.[31] Boas considered McGee a friend, one who had long supported him—and the BAE contributed funding to his and his students' research—despite his being an evolutionist, like Holmes. And also despite Franz's displeasure with the charter of the American Anthropological Association (AAA) established under McGee's presidency in June 1902: Boas's objection to its including amateurs was not heeded.[32] The AAA now took over the publication of *American Anthropologist*, the journal that Boas had centrally contributed to launching in March 1899, to great academic success. (The journal still exists—indeed, many articles cited here were published in its pages.) But Boas never let go of this history, which had begun with the Chicago debacle when McGee took Boas's side against Holmes, rehearsing it still in 1909 in a letter to his uncle.[33]

Meanwhile, the double workload was becoming extremely heavy. At the start of his AMNH years, in 1898, Boas had considered accepting an offer of a professorship at the University of Vienna if his current position at Columbia were not to become permanent, and if it was not able to support him in developing the university's Department of Anthropology. He knew that he must both continue the fieldwork investigating the rapidly disappearing tribes and gain a professorship, since he believed that the museum's curating and collecting mission, together with teaching, comprised deeply complementary training for his students as well as for his own research.[34] By 1904, however, running the Department of Anthropology, which had grown to comprise 140 undergraduate and 18 graduate students, required much more of his time, as he wrote to Columbia president Butler, requesting that he be given more hours. He negotiated a revised employment and payment structure with Bumpus to that effect, but it was clear that the moment was approaching to step down from his curatorial position. Bumpus's interventionist management style increasingly irked Franz: the two traded criticisms of each other's exhibition display styles. Jesup echoed Bumpus's protest that Boas's American Indian cases were badly labeled and incomprehensible, while Bumpus's Peruvian cases were much more to his liking. Bumpus then demanded alterations to Boas's Blackfoot exhibits. Jesup respected Boas, of course, but he was not in a position to defend him against the new director he had chosen, and he did genuinely prefer the latter's approach to exhibiting. Their relationship, although still cordial, was increasingly strained by Franz's remuneration requests as well as by various bureaucratic complexities.[35] There were also the delays and hugely raised costs of the expedition publications—which Boas would contractually have to complete by 1911.

Franz resigned from the AMNH in May 1905, though he stayed on for a while to wrap up the ongoing projects.[36] In Boas's place, Jesup appointed assistant curator Clark Wissler, an anthropologist who had obtained a doctorate in psychology and was Boas's university assistant. Franz respected him and felt he was needed at the university. It was another protracted, psychologically tense negotiation, in which Wissler had the last word, eventually managing to keep both positions. By the time Boas left—albeit he never entirely severed his ties with the AMNH and he continued to oversee the Jesup publications—the museum had grown tremendously, now featuring eighteen halls and six galleries. Boas had had major ambitions for it, and had planned to expand knowledge and acquisitions from the Far East as well as from Mesoamerica. His decision to leave was in part due to his inability to fulfill these ambitions. In Herbert S. Lewis's words, Franz "was more than a curator; he was an anthropological empire builder. (But his plans at the AMNH were brought low by a curator.)"[37] As Camille Joseph and Isabelle Kalinowski noted, Boas continued after 1905 to promote the notion that museums should perpetually increase their holdings for the sake of scholarship. He corresponded at length about this with the collector George Heye, to whom he sent many of the objects he had George Hunt acquire for him. In 1916, he asked Heye to donate these objects to the AMNH rather than create his own private museum.[38]

Over the years he spent at the AMNH, Franz's family had grown. Henry, or Heine, was born on February 2, 1899—named after Boas's good friend Henry Herbert Donaldson. Marie Franziska, the last of the Boas's five living children, was born on January 8, 1902. (Hete was never forgotten. Franz visited the cemetery whenever he went to Chicago, and there was an aborted attempt to move her grave to New York.) When he was just a few days old, Heine was at risk of dying from bronchitis: he was saved just in time by a nurse and doctor. This frightening event happened on February 16, 1899, the very day Franz received word that he would be named full professor of anthropology at Columbia University. But following closely on these major events came most intense grief: on February 21, his beloved father Meier died. He had suffered from a heart condition for years, so it wasn't entirely unexpected, but it was nevertheless a severe blow. As Cole puts it, "The coveted professorship now seemed meaningless; his father would never learn of it."[39]

But of course the professorship, which came through in May

1899, to take effect from July 1, wasn't meaningless at all.[40] We know now how much Boas would go on to do with it, and that his students were to become important figures in the history of anthropology. (Jacobi, still helping behind the scenes, had made an offer to Low to provide for his nephew's salary for two years.) The death of Franz's father, though deeply painful, especially given how close they were and how supportive Meier had always been, did not shift the course of Franz's life. On the contrary—on he went, fighting for what he believed in, always uncompromising though not unforgiving, giving to many, and expecting a lot from those he encountered. Other painful deaths soon followed, including that of Ssigna, his guide on Baffin Island. But Boas knew well by now how the Inuits as well as the First Nations peoples dealt with death, descendance, inheritance, tradition, transcendence, and remembrance. There was wisdom in their myths and tales—different from the Western philosophical canon that he had been trained in, to be sure, and culturally distant from the intellectual practices of a secular Jew like him—but perhaps, one speculates, therefore all the more fascinating and attractive to him.

Jesup died in January 1908. Osborn succeeded Jesup; he remained president of the trustees until 1930, accruing even more power once Bumpus was fired for "falsely accusing Osborn of financial mismanagement."[41] He believed that "much anthropology is merely opinion, or the gossip of the natives. It is many years away from being a science. Mr. Jesup and the Museum spent far too much money on anthropology."[42] It is noteworthy that Osborn was the man who, in 1922, founded the American Eugenics Society. The principles of eugenics were precisely what Boas spent his life trying to upend from within, as it were, formulating over and over again the important practical consequences of the arguments he had started building already in Baffin Island. We can refer here to an article he published in 1916, wherein he politely challenged the very grounds of eugenics, writing that "the battlecry of the eugenists, 'Nature not nurture,' has been raised to the rank of a dogma, and the environmental conditions that make and unmake man, physically and mentally, have been relegated to the background." He went on:

> Most modern biologists are so entirely dominated by the notion that function depends upon form, that they seek for an anatomical basis for all differences of function. To give an instance: they are inclined to assume that higher civilization is due to a higher type; that better health depends upon a better hereditary stock; and so on. The anthropologist, on the other hand, is convinced that many different anatomical forms can be adapted to the same social functions; and he ascribes, therefore, greater weight to the functions, and believes that in many cases differences of form may be adaptations to different functions. He believes that different types of man may reach the same civilization, that better health may be produced by better bringing up of any of the existing types of man. The anatomical differences to which the biologist reduces social phenomena are hereditary; the environmental causes which the anthropologist sees reflected in human form are individually acquired, and not transmitted by heredity.[43]

He had been trying to subvert the misuse of evolutionism for years. Ruth Bunzel, who started in 1922 as Boas's secretary and editorial assistant but, encouraged by him, became an important anthropologist, wrote in her 1962 introduction to his *Anthropology and Modern Life*, which first appeared in 1928, that it was the "ethnocentric, nineteenth-century version of cultural evolution" that he opposed. In fact, "he believed, as must all who look at the long record of man's life on this planet, in cultural evolution. It was the method and the ethnographic bias that he sought to correct."[44] He had identified the roots of this bias, its rationale, and of course its dangers. It never disappeared, as we know. But he persisted. It is worth quoting a letter from one of Boas's students, also a Jewish immigrant—a furious nocturnal outburst to his mentor one Friday night in 1924:

> Dear Professor Boas,
> . . . I cannot sleep. It's that Areopagus of morons ravaging my soul. Such a gathering! I sensed the spirit of the assemblage even before we began to speak: those bearded faces, set mouths, sallow complexions. . . . It was as if the cemeteries of the American Philosophical Society had emptied their weird contents into that hall. Why, I believe there were not as many as six persons there who as much as followed your closely-knit argument. They just sat there trying not to look asinine but failing miserably. . . . Nor did my effort to get at the kernel of their humanity via sense of humor prove any more successful. They laughed, to be sure, but as laughs that Australian bird. . . .
>
> And those spontaneous irrepressible comments of the Chairman . . . "the entire problem of Africa depends on it . . . the Negro is regarded as an equal only where there are few of him. . . . We all believe in it [the racial differences]. . . . I, as a white man . . . " I suppose you and I must have appeared to him as two colored men disguised as Jews dishing out our black magic before that . . . gathering of sapientes. . . .
>
> I'll remember that scene as long as I live.
> As ever yours,
> Alexander Goldenweiser[45]

In September 1908, Boas had spoken in Vienna at the Sixteenth International Congress of Americanists about the "Results of the Jesup Expedition." We have a report of the speech, according to which Boas, after paying tribute to the late president, "set forth the methods employed in the research. One result has been to establish evidence of the shifting of the Northwest Coast tribes. They do not seem to have been stable units, but rather in a continual state of flux. There is no longer any doubt of a connection between the peoples of Siberia and

North America. A race probably entered the American continent from Siberia before the glacial period, and later there was a remigration to Siberia. Marked ethnological differences have been noted among the races of western America. Professor Boas announced that the publications based on the Jesup Expedition will soon be completed."[46] As it happens, the final volume would never appear, partly because of continuing difficulties with the AMNH, and partly because of delays in the Siberian expedition, which became unsurpassable obstacles when the war broke out. But at least the expedition had yielded rich fruit, showing that neither peoples nor societies were ever static. There were no biological essences, no races to fall back on, only cultures with shifting borders and shifting values. The evolutionists were simply—and dangerously—wrong.

In his book *Primitive Art*, which appeared in 1922—the very year Osborn established the eugenics society—Franz developed further the notion that the constitutional features of the human psyche were common to all, that "the mental processes of man are the same everywhere." In this rich text, he drew with freedom and feeling on his decades-long, deeply invested experience on the ground with what were always the "subjects" of his studies—some became collaborators, but never did he see anyone as an "object": "Anyone who has lived with primitive tribes, who has shared their joys and sorrows, their privations and their luxuries, who sees in them not solely subjects of study to be examined like a cell under the microscope, but feeling and thinking human beings, will agree that there is no such thing as a 'primitive mind,' a 'magical' or 'pre-logical' way of thinking, but that each individual in 'primitive' society is a man, a woman, a child of the same kind, of the same way of thinking, feeling and acting as a man, woman or child in our own society." Belief systems that privileged "magical" thinking could take root in any culture: "Investigators," he wrote, tended "to forget that the logics of science—that unattainable ideal of the discovery of pure relations of cause and effect, uncontaminated by emotional bias as well as of unproved opinion,—are not the logics of life. The feelings underlying taboo are everpresent among us," for instance.[47] And emotions govern our lives wherever we are from.

Eleven years earlier, in *The Mind of Primitive Man*, he had appealed to the insights on imitation developed by sociologist and social psychologist Gabriel Tarde to make a similar point: "Unconscious and conscious imitation are factors influencing civilized society, not less than primitive society, as has been shown by G. Tarde, who has proved that primitive man, and civilized man as well, imitates not such actions only as are useful, and for the imitation of which logical causes may be given, but also others for the adoption or preservation of which no logical reason can be assigned."[48] Again: there was no difference between the minds of the "primitive" and of the "civilized." All humans were acculturated into an environment, a world, a language, emotional habits, sets of beliefs and ideas, that in turn shaped their experiences and views. This was what constituted the single perspective, which it was easy to mistake for the whole picture, as if anyone could ever achieve a neutral, god's-eye view. And this, in effect, was how apperception worked too: it applied at the individual as well as at the group level.

The centrality of art to these investigations was obvious to Boas. In early 1914, he wrote to George McAneny, president of the Board of Alderman of New York City, who happened to be married to Franz's cousin, Jacobi's daughter Marjorie. Franz had dreamed up a plan to connect art and science: there was, he wrote, "an obvious relation between science teaching in the New York schools and the natural history collections in the museums of the City, and between history teaching and the collections of art. The work of the Board of Education might be considerably enriched by systematic cooperation with museums." He foresaw the creation of a "Board of Science and Art," twinned with a "Board of Educational Development," to bring museums to all publics: "It is, therefore, worth considering whether several small museums could not serve the interests of the citizens better than constant enlargement of a few central buildings, where the schools, and particularly the branch libraries of the city, might not be utilized for this purpose, without creating the necessity of erecting many new expensive buildings or new museum wings."[49] There should be collaboration between research institutes, museums, and the like. Nothing came of this ambitious proposal. But it is clear from it that he viewed art as an intrinsic part of human culture, one that everyone should have the chance of experiencing firsthand—as indeed he had, growing up with it. He did not think of "primitive art" in any other terms.

Franz knew that by studying so-called "primitive" peoples, he was simply studying humanity, and thereby revising the concept of culture as it had been shaped by the Enlightenment. As Stocking notes, between 1894 and 1911—so, between his talk before the AAAS in Brooklyn and the publication of *The Mind of Primitive Man*—Boas did modify his way of using the term *culture* in relation to the term *civilization*. Stocking gives these examples (with his italics): "Was the *culture* attained by the ancient civilized people of such character as to allow us to claim for them a genius superior to that of any other race?" (1894); "Was the *civilization* attained by these ancient people of such character . . ." (1911). And another pair: "The general status of their *culture* was nearly equally high . . ." (1894); "The general status of their *civilization* was nearly equally high" (1911). For Stocking, this shift shows that "Boas began his career with a notion of culture that was still within the framework of traditional humanist and contemporary evolutionist usage. It was still a singular phenomenon, present to a higher or lower degree in all peoples," whereas by 1911, this singular "culture" became "civilization," and "culture" became "cultures." As Stocking states, "What is involved here is precisely the emergence of the modern anthropological concept."[50] And this new concept did not go unnoticed.

In August 1906, when Boas was just forty-eight years old, a Festschrift was produced for him. A Festschrift is an honor usually conferred on a scholar at an older age. Yet Boas was just middle-aged, and his important opus *The Mind of Primitive Man* was still five years ahead. But it was clearly not too early for the *Anthropological Papers Written in Honor of Franz Boas*, "presented to him on the twenty-fifth anniversary of his doctorate." It is possible that Jacobi had mooted the idea, according to Cole, who also notes that it came just as Boas had left the AMNH, so it also celebrated, in a way, the closing of that chapter. Boas wrote as much to the Festschrift's secretary and editor Laufer, the departmental colleague whom Franz had earlier hired for the Siberian part of the Jesup Expedition and had sent to China on behalf of the East Asiatic Committee section of the anthropology wing of the AMNH, which Jesup had established with the great philanthropist Jacob H. Schiff. Zumwalt reports Laufer writing to Boas that the Festschrift "was to serve 'as a protest against tyrants,' in reference to the treatment that Boas received from Bumpus and others at the AMNH."[51] (In 1907, Laufer departed for the Field Museum.) Cole tells us that the event "did not go smoothly," that the book's publication was delayed, and that the formal dinner following its delivery a full eight months later was cancelled because it coincided with Ernst having a near-fatal brush with pneumonia that very night.[52]

Still, it marks a passage. Introducing its many, varied authors, Herbert S. Lewis observed how widely respected Boas was, and how profoundly his contributions were already recognized—certainly enough for Jacob Schiff to have been the anthropology wing's main donor. At the same time, the number and variety of contributors and subscribers to this Festschrift are a reminder of how Boas's achievements were the product of collective efforts. They were also firmly situated within their periods and places, as Lewis points out: a German education, at a time when its academic traction was powerful and its intellectual traditions influential, and the late "Gilded Age" in America, when the wealthy were investing in culture, art, and science, as indeed did Jesup and Low. Boas, Lewis writes, "was the right man at the right place at the right time," and the Festschrift "marks the transition to a new anthropology in the United States."[53]

This new anthropology, as is now clear, used an idiographic approach and historical specificity in order to arrive at generalization, via the analysis—statistical or morphological—of vast amounts of data, area by area. As Cole observes, the generalization to a psychic unity of humankind was the basis for imagining that human evolution had progressed in "stages," but as Boas had put it in a brilliant talk, "The History of Anthropology," he gave in September 1904 at the International Congress of Arts and Sciences in St. Louis, in a session chaired by Putnam: "In no case is it more difficult to lay aside the *Kulturbrille*— to use von den Steinen's apt term—than in viewing our own culture. For this reason the literature of anthropology abounds in attempts to define a number of stages of culture leading from simple forms to the present civilization, from savagery through barbarism to civilization, or from an assumed pre-savagery through the same stages to enlightenment."[54] With the *Kulturbrille* off, one could engage in "new attempts at classification," both biological and cultural.

In fact, Boas was not so much critical of evolution as he was of "the methodology employed" to demonstrate it: he was averse to any determinism, and in particular to the comparative method and to any overinterpretation of "observed homologies and supposed similarities," because the widespread nature of a given phenomenon "proved nothing if its origins were incomparably different," in Cole's summary. There was no "grand scheme of cultural development," and to posit one distorted one's understanding both of cultures, which were plural and manifold, and of mind, whose functions permitted this variety. Boas's great nemesis in the matter of evolution was anthropologist and physician Daniel Garrison Brinton, whom he had taken to task at the 1896 AAAS meeting in Buffalo for appealing to Bastian's universal *Elementargedanken* to posit a psychic unity without defining what these universals might be.[55] Anthropologist Bradd Shore suggests that, in order to preserve such a psychic unity "while freeing himself of the racial assumptions of the evolutionist position," Boas distinguished "between cultural traditions and mental endowment as the basis for differences in mental life." This move, he posits, had a "serious cost, one that has continued to trouble modern anthropology": a separation between culture and mind, as if the mind were, so to speak, a "container" of culture, rather than culture being an "*attribute* of mind." This is how "anthropology achieved an independence from psychology. The study of culture could be dissociated from the study of mind."[56] This is also in part why debates continue to rage around "nature or nurture" well into our own century, a dichotomy that elides the fact that we are naturally cultural, and that we can in fact understand acculturation by studying the physiology of the embodied mind.

Boas is still associated today with the "four-field" ambit of this new anthropology, separate from the psychological study of the processes of cognition and emotion, that gathered physical, sociocultural, linguistic, and archaeological dimensions into what had been a disparate set of research programs. Anthropology at Columbia now brought together linguistics, ethnology, archaeology, and physical anthropology or anthropometry: Boas's graduate students were training in all those aspects of the field, often gathering at their professor's gabled house just across the Hudson, within a (then) forested area in Grantwood, New Jersey. Franz had bought land there in 1907, built a sixteen-room house, and the family had left Manhattan's Upper West Side to settle there. Stocking dates the advent of this new, fourfold definition to the 1904 talk in St. Louis. This division was an outcome of the history of the discipline such as Stocking traces it here, bringing to the fore the complex relation of anthropology to science: just as it was becoming a science, he wrote, it "ceased at the same time to lose its character of being a single science, but became a method applicable to all the mental sciences, and indispensable to all of them. We are still in the midst of this development." This development required an interdisciplinary approach: "The *general* problem of the evolution of mankind is being taken up now by the investigator of primitive tribes, now by the student of the history of civilization. We may still recognize in it the ultimate aim of anthropology in the wider sense of the term, but we must understand that it will be reached by cooperation between all the mental sciences and the efforts of the anthropologist."[57] (It is possible that today's psychology would have been embraced by Boas. At the time, however, a biological understanding of Bastianesque "elementary ideas" was not reachable.)

Toward the end of the talk, Boas spoke of distinct "biological, linguistic, and ethnological-archaeological methods in anthropology." As anthropologist Dan Hicks has argued, Brinton had in fact suggested a similar division, but history has given its birth to Boas, whose idiographic approach Brinton did not share.[58] Indeed, at the St. Louis talk, Franz called Brinton (who had died in 1899) an "extremist" for "assigning sameness of cultural traits wholly to the psychic unity of mankind," and for excluding the possibility of cultures being transmitted—in contrast to the notion of cultural transmission upheld by Ratzel, "whose recent loss we lament" (Ratzel had indeed died just a few weeks before, in early August 1904).[59]

Finances at the Department of Anthropology started becoming tight in 1908, as King reports, in part because faculty spent more time researching than teaching and, given that Columbia was already in debt, its president Butler wanted to tighten the reins. Franz had to find new sources of funding for students' research and fieldwork that, as ever, he knew was essential for the discipline to thrive. It must be noted that anthropology was an expensive discipline, and funding would always be a constant struggle, for Boas included. By remaining a philologist at the BAE, at this juncture he was able to call on its funds to support the research needed to compile what would become the two-volume *Handbook of American Indian Languages* he edited—the first volume was published in 1917, the second in 1922.[60] In 1917, he launched the *International Journal of American Linguistics*. In the meantime, Edward Sapir, who would contribute so much to the field of linguistics, had obtained his PhD with him in 1908—after an MA on Herder—and gone to Berkeley for a brief period to work with Kroeber on the state's Indigenous languages, including Yana, which was rapidly disappearing. Its last speaker was Ishi. (Sapir would return to California in 1915 to work with Ishi just before the latter died of tuberculosis.) Franz's activity as a linguist became evermore central. It was one of the "immaterial" corpuses of knowledge that Camille Joseph and Isabelle Kalinowski refer to when they note how his attention to material objects, central as it had been to his curatorial work at the museum, shifted to immaterial objects, such as the languages used to bring to life material objects and tell stories.[61] Language, which partakes of biology but is itself immaterial, was, as Regna Darnell puts it, "the piece of the classificatory triad [of race/biology and environment/culture] that renders mind rather than body the centerpiece."[62]

To satisfy the demands of university governance, Boas added new classes to the departmental offerings and designed classes for undergraduates. The undergraduate classes would grow to be very large in size, as Boas wrote to Butler in one of his many requests for extra funding: he needed assistance from graduate students to prepare lectures and materials. (There were seven-

teen lectures a week by 1910.)[63] One of these new classes, starting in the academic year 1907–8, was called "The Negro Problem." Franz had written to Booker T. Washington, the great
African American leader, activist, and educator, that "scientific
work on the Negro race" would "be of great practical value in
modifying the views of our people in regard to the Negro problem."[64] Scientific knowledge was, in other words, a political good.
In November 1906, he wrote to Andrew Carnegie requesting
funds for his proposed program, stating that "the whole attitude of our people in regard to the Negro might be materially
modified if we had a better knowledge of what the Negro has
really done and accomplished in his own native country."[65]

A few months before, on May 31, 1906, Franz had given
the commencement address at the all-Black Atlanta University
at the invitation of W.E.B. DuBois, who recalled the event:

> Few today are interested in Negro history because they feel
> the matter already settled: the Negro has no history.
> This dictum seems neither reasonable nor probable. I
> remember my own rather sudden awakening from the pa-
> ralysis of this judgment taught me in high school and in two
> of the world's great universities. Franz Boas came to Atlanta
> University where I was teaching history in 1906 and said to
> a graduating class: You need not be ashamed of your African
> past; and then he recounted the history of the black king-
> doms south of the Sahara for a thousand years. I was too as-
> tonished to speak. All of this I had never heard, and I came
> then and afterwards to realize how the silence and neglect
> of science can let truth utterly disappear or even be uncon-
> sciously distorted.[66]

Boas and DuBois would stay connected from then on. Boas got
involved with the nascent NAACP and helped procure funding
for Howard University's Center for the Study of Negro Life and
History. And he continually helped promote Black scholars, both
male and female, many of them his students, most notably Zora

Neale Hurston, who would become a well-known novelist as well as an anthropologist. His Jewish student Melville J. Herskovits, for his part, became a noted Africanist and musicologist. In the summer of 1911, both Boas and DuBois were speakers at the First Universal Races Congress, which brought together, quite radically, Europeans, Africans, and Asians at the Imperial Institute in London. (Among those present were Gandhi, H. G. Wells, and Boas's Columbia colleague John Dewey.) The congress was sponsored by the Society for Ethical Culture, created by neo-Kantian philosopher Felix Adler, whose father had been the rabbi at Temple Emmanu-El in New York, and who had studied for his doctorate at Heidelberg. Adler had created the society to gather a humanistic, anti-religious, inclusive "Judaism of the Future," one that would discard "the narrow spirit of exclusion, and loudly proclaim that Judaism *was not given to the Jews alone, but that its destiny is to embrace in one great moral state the whole family of men*," and that would proclaim freedom of thought as "the sacred right of every individual man." Its members were people like Franz—Jewish products of *Bildung* who espoused the values of 1848. Boas, pertinently, gave a lecture entitled "On the Instability of Human Types."[67]

He had firsthand experience of this necessity for freedom of thought. Remember his "Credo": "The psychological origin of the implicit belief in the authority of tradition, which was so foreign to my mind and which had shocked me at an earlier time, became a problem that engaged my thoughts for many years. In fact, my whole outlook upon social life is determined by the question: how can we recognize the shackles that tradition has laid upon us? For when we recognize them, we are also able to break them." His own ethical education had consisted in the expansion of empathy to encompass worlds far from his own, to transcend the dangerously cliquish nature of empathy. The in-group had to be expanded to "include all of humanity," rather than to identify and attack the out-group, as is usually the case. Human types, precisely, are plastic: this much Boas had demonstrated, data in hand. We are adaptable. We assimilate. For Franz, "the identification of an individual with a class because of his bodily appearance, language, or manners has always seemed to me a survival of barbaric, or rather of primitive, habits of mind." It is part of our nature, but "it must be the object of education to make the individual as free as may be of automatic adhesion to the group in which he is born or into which he is brought by social pressure," and to overcome our herd instinct. We can do it. Franz had done it—though he admitted, too, that his education conditioned him to espouse these views.[68]

Those were the views that informed Franz's 1906 talk, at a time of race riots and terrible tension. And they were indeed powerful words. One can understand DuBois's astonishment upon hearing Boas affirm: "Nothing, perhaps, is more encouraging than a glimpse of the artistic industry of native Africa. I regret that we have no place in this country where the beauty and distinctiveness of African work can be shown; but a walk through the African museums of Paris, London and Berlin is a revelation." (In fact, over the years he tried to find funds for exactly such a museum in America.) Boas's words encompassed all of humanity: he slalomed across world history to show the highs and lows of all civilizations. So, "it seems likely that at a time when the European was still satisfied with rude stone tools, the African had invented or adopted the art of smelting iron," and "when the early kingdom of Babylonia flourished the same disparaging remarks that are now made regarding the Negro might have been made regarding the ancestors of the ancient Romans," who were then "a barbarous horde that had never made any contribution to the advance of that civilization that was confined to parts of Asia." More: "It is not the first time in human history that two peoples have been brought into close contact by the force of circumstances, who are dependent upon each other economically but where social customs, ideals and—let me add—bodily form, are so distinct that the line of cleavage remains always open. Every conquest that has led to colonization had produced, at least temporarily, conditions of this kind."[69]

But then, the "best" example, one that Boas thought "illustrates the conditions that characterize your own position," was that of the European Jews: "a people slightly distinct in type, but differing considerably in customs and beliefs from the people among whom they lived. The separation of the Jew and the Gentile was enforced for hundreds of years and very slowly only were the various occupations opened to him. . . . Even now the feeling of inequality persists," however much the "old barriers have fallen," and however much "in the creative work of our times, in industry, commerce, science, and art, the Jew holds a respected place." In fact, still now, "the consciousness of the old, sharper divisions" found "expression as antipathy to the Jewish type," an antipathy that was "strong enough to sustain an anti-Jewish political party" in France. In other words, Franz could identify as a Jew with the experience of African Americans—and indeed he was encouraging a geographical and historical empathy, a felt sweep of the globe's many instances of oppression. The feelings of others could not be modified, he said, but "your race has to work out its own salvation by raising the standards of your life higher and higher, thus attacking the feeling of contempt of your race at its very roots."[70] He did not elaborate here on his suggestion that the abhorrence of a people could be mitigated by its joining privilege, or of what were the implications of tying the issue of racism with that of class. Nor did he elaborate on how contradictory it was, then, to affirm this, given that Jews could still be the object of contempt even when successful—sometimes precisely on account of their perceived success. His use of the term *salvation*, at any rate, expressed a poignant hope, especially given how history would play out.

In contemporary America, the "disparaging" attitudes concerned not just the Black population but also the manifold immigrants from all over Europe—including Catholics from Ireland and Italy—who were arriving in great numbers in those days, accompanied by the usual anxieties of those who believed immigrants brought with them both physical and moral disease. This was a period, as Herbert S. Lewis puts it in an article that explores Boas's deep political commitments, when "in addition to evolutionism, racial determinism and Social Darwinism were also in the ascendance, and these touched the emotions and socioeconomic interests of American and European elites even more. This was the era of the passage of Jim Crow laws, racial segregation, and anti-black and antiforeigner agitation." And he observes: "Despite their entrenched status in American and European intellectual and political life, however, Boas, a new immigrant, virtually alone, started to combat all of these from the very beginning of his career, drawing upon his view of humanity and on his science. Were these not political acts?"[71] Undoubtedly, at least in this writer's view, they were.

A major project was just about to begin that responded to such fears over the potentially negative impacts of eastern, southern, and central European immigration to the United States on the local population. The project was close to Boas's concerns, and indeed to his political commitments—and would also help him boost departmental income. Set up in 1907 by the United States Immigration Commission, it was known as the Dillingham Commission, chaired by Republican senator William P. Dillingham to effect "a compromise between proponents and opponents of immigration."[72] When Boas was contacted by the commission to contribute a report, he proposed to investigate the bodily changes of recent immigrants. As King puts it, "If immigration was in fact having an effect on American society, its clearest results were likely to be seen in the bodies of the newest Americans: the immigrants' children."[73] Such a study would show whether the new environment caused change or whether traits would be preserved, and if so, whether this would constitute an obstacle to the ideal of assimilation.

Boas was of course perfectly placed to engage in this study. We know that his involvement with physical anthropology started early: it was one aspect of the issue of heredity, with which he struggled for a long time. We saw how, in his obituary of Virchow, Franz also took on board the latter's interest in biological processes and his focus on variations within individual cells, which amounted to a particularist's—indeed, a historical—approach to biology.[74] While at Clark, encouraged by Hall, he had studied the impact of environment on children's growth. Now he was keen to establish how historical processes interacted with physical anthropology, and so to define what a "race" was.[75] In 1889, Francis Galton, a cousin of Darwin who in 1883 had coined the term *eugenics* and was a strong proponent of its principles, had published his famous work *Natural Inheritance*. Here, using the statistical methods and correlational calculus that he had just developed, he stated his "law of ancestral heredity," according to which an individual inherits half their heritage from each parent, a quarter from all grandparents, and so on. Out of this arose the science of biometrics, taken up and then replaced in 1896 by the method of Karl Pearson, with whom Boas corresponded.[76] And as Tanner noted, Boas "was in the forefront of the biometrical advance; all his life he taught and encouraged anthropologists in the use of statistical methods."[77] When Gregor Mendel's groundbreaking work on genes was rediscovered in 1900 (after it had been replicated for the first time), the notion of "dominant" and "recessive" traits entered the picture, changing greatly the understanding of heredity.

This is the context in which Franz, for decades, had been pursuing his biometric research and compiling his massive anthropometric data, ultimately with a view, as Stocking puts it, to understand "issues of racial process which would enable him to cast light on specific problems of the historical relationships of peoples," and on what exactly produced variations and differences between individuals and groups. The idea that humans were a domesticated species became more precise. Any variability of traits within a species—pigmentation, size, hair type, skeletal type, and so on—was only to be found in domesticated animals, not in wild ones, and this was the case with humans, whose variable characteristics had developed in geographically distinct locations, independently from each other. During the preparations for the World's Columbian Exposition in Chicago, Boas had established "the first standards for height and weight for American children," based on ninety thousand children aged five to eighteen, across six cities.[78] The upshot of his extremely detailed statistical studies, which after 1900 combined Mendelian genetics and Galtonian laws, "was a thoroughgoing critique of the hierarchical formalism of post-polygenist racial thought," in Stocking's words.[79] In 1895, he had published, in German only, his *Anthropologie der Nordamerikaner Indianer*, based on the data he had drawn for the World's Columbian Exposition, in which he presented "summary statistics, means, standard deviations, and frequency distributions of height and cephalic index for about 60 tribes," with a particular focus on the cephalic index and growth rates of "half-breeds."[80] He established, for instance, that "the half-breed children are shorter than the Indian children of the same age," and generally "half-bloods appeared to revert to one or the other ancestral form, not to a middle type," as Galton's theory would have predicted.[81] There was no average curve, only continuous variation and statistical variability. This was an important finding.

Many other reports followed, all equally rich in data, and based on very large population pools. Starting in 1903, he began to test the Mendelian hypothesis of a dominant trait, focusing for this on the inheritance of the form of the head. To this end, his friend the anthropologist Maurice Fishberg collected for him the data of forty-nine Jewish families: it was a small sample, but it confirmed, so far, the Mendelian version of heredity. In a lecture simply titled "Anthropology" that he delivered at Columbia in December 1907, Franz said it loud and clear: "All the nations of modern times, and those of Europe no less than those of other continents, are equally mixed; and the racial purity on which European nations like to pride themselves does not exist." Anthropological evidence "does not sustain the claim of superiority of any race over the others." Even if one did find "differences in form and size of the brains of different races," it was clear that "the variability within each race is so great that the small average differences between distinct racial types are almost insignificant as compared to the total range of racial variability." One had to "guard against the inference that divergence from the European type is synonymous with inferiority."[82]

In the spring of 1908, Boas embarked on the research for the Dillingham Commission, which lasted until 1910. That December 1908, he gave a talk at the AAAS in Baltimore titled "Race Problems in America," in which he clearly addressed the issues the project was to tackle. He dismissed any notion of "a pure type in any part of Europe" and broached two questions regarding the "physical characteristics of the immigrant population": the respective influence of "environment" and "intermixture," precisely what he intended to clarify for the commission.[83] This was a project "vast in scope, unexpected in outcome, and staggering in professional and public reception," in Tanner's words.[84] Picking up on the work he had begun at Clark on the cephalic index, but vastly expanding its remit and changing its starting hypothesis, Boas assembled a thirteen-strong team of students, colleagues, and assistants to measure heads of family members and take their histories, compare the sizes of those whose parents had arrived before 1880, between 1880 and 1890, and after 1890, and collate and analyze the enormous amount of data generated. The team measured a total of about eighteen thousand immigrants in New York or their children.

A majority were east European Jews—and clearly here Boas stood apart from his own Jewishness, adopting, in the words of anthropologist Leonard Glick, "the perspective of an insider contemplating the potential problems posed by the arrival of outsiders."[85] Others were southern Europeans—Sicilians, Neapolitans—and central Europeans, Bohemians, Poles, Hungarians. There were also a few Scots. As he wrote at the outset, in March 1908, to J. W. Jenks (an economist and Cornell professor) of the Dillingham Commission, the central question was "whether the American influence exerts itself more markedly than the foreign influence or vice versa," that is, "how strong is the power of assimilation of the present American type when intermarrying with types of southern and eastern Europe?"[86] The study's initial upshot was clear: "Those children, whose parents immigrated earliest, are best developed in height, as well as in weight," wrote Boas in September 1908 to Jenks. And "mental development proceeds in the same way; those whose parents have immigrated earliest, pass through school more rapidly." He was surprised to find also that among the east European Jews— "the race is very short headed"—there was "a decided tendency to an increase in length of head among the later immigrants."

The overall change in cephalic index that emerged by the end of the study was surprising. As Tanner points out, the change was not in fact very strong, but it did indicate the impact of surroundings, living conditions, climate, nutrition, and the like on body form. *Changes in the Bodily Form of Descendants of Immigrants* was published in 1912, and *American Anthropologist* printed a summary of the book by Boas under the same title, in which he also responded to critiques.[87] (He published the raw data later, in 1928, as *Contributions to the Study of Inheritance*, for the sake of transparency and to enable further study—and, according to Tanner, this was "the largest collection of family measurements ever published.")[88] The work's three main findings, to use anthropologist John S. Allen's summary of the ten points Boas outlined, were that immigrants born in America differed in type from their parents; that the longer the time elapsed between the arrival of the mother in America and the birth of a child, the stronger the impact of the American environment; and that the children of mixed parentage regressed to one or the other parental type, not to any mean—as Boas had already seen in his earlier studies. It bears mentioning that Maurice Fishberg, whom we just met, cited these findings about plasticity and made use of the data in his own massive 1911 opus, *The Jews: A Study of Race and Environment*, published at the time by Scribner's.

To Boas, these clear anatomical changes in response to changed surroundings indicated cranial and anatomical plasticity. It was an important finding for its time—when the cephalic index was the focus of so much research. Franz was perplexed as to its causes: there was no available answer to account for them.[89] The science of genetics was in its infancy, and epigenetics did not yet exist. As Susan Hegeman has pointed out, "Boas's anti-racist crusade was pre-genetic, and thus relied on the same scientific principles and kinds of evidence as his theoretical opponents, the scientific racists. In other words, Boas's critique of scientific racism was internal to that paradigm, an exercise in negative critique." It was internal to that paradigm indeed, but therefore the better poised to overturn it. Assimilation could happen because, as Hegeman writes, there was in Boas's view "no necessary relationship between the 'race,' the language, and the cultural forms and expressions of a people," which arbitrarily "converged through the historical contingencies of migration, contact, and conquest." She points out that "Boas's position as assimilated German Jew is relevant" here because he "was advocating not so much assimilation as the anti-racist point that assimilation was possible within the context of racial diversity," *pace* racist beliefs. Hence, because Boas had determined that racial typologies were "unstable" and that race and culture were "arbitrarily related to one another, he imagined cultures transcending racial classifications, and racial groups crossing cultural boundaries."[90] This was a self-portrait of sorts, too.

There were many open questions regarding biology, of course, and Boas used them as epistemic contours of sorts for the reams of data, statistical analyses, grammars, dictionaries, collections of myths and stories, and art that he gathered so methodically with his students and colleagues. It was during the period of the Dillingham Commission, in 1911, that Franz published his first popular book, *The Mind of Primitive Man* which, as we have seen repeatedly in previous pages here, reused much of the material from previous talks, synthesizing his findings and ideas "into something that might be called a worldview," as King puts it. He was able to delineate how the notion of racial hierarchy was false, or that, since "the alleged specific differences between civilized and primitive man, so far as they are inferred from complex psychic responses, can be reduced to the same fundamental psychic forms, we have the right to decline as unprofitable a discussion of the hereditary mental traits of various branches of the white race."[91] Moreover: "We have no right to explain difference in mental attitude of different groups of people, particularly of closely related ones, as due to hereditary causes, until we have been able to prove that physiological and the correlated psychological traits are hereditary, regardless of social and natural environment."[92] There were no differences between the so-called civilized and primitive: "It would be vain to try to understand the development of modern science without an intelligent understanding of modern philosophy; it would be vain to try to understand the history of mediaeval science without a knowledge of mediaeval theology; and it would be vain to try to understand primitive science without an intelligent knowledge of primitive mythology. 'Mythology,' 'theology,' and 'philosophy' are different terms for the same influences which shape the current of human thought, and which determine the character of the attempts of man to explain the phenomena of nature."[93]

He had been working his way to such a synthesis throughout the past two decades.

And the matter of mind, as we have seen from the very outset, concerned him profoundly. Just two years before, in 1909, he had returned to Clark to give a talk at a conference organized by G. Stanley Hall for the twentieth anniversary of the university. This was his "Psychological Problems in Anthropology," which he began by announcing that anthropology was akin to psychology insofar as "we are also trying to determine the psychological laws which control the mind of man everywhere, and that may differ in various racial and social groups"—a sentence that, along with many others, made its way verbatim into the 1911 book (and is cited in the introductory pages here). Adding that a detailed anthropological analysis of cultural contexts was necessary to effect such a determination, he then asked: "Are all the races of mankind mentally equally endowed, or do material differences exist?" He reiterated the important point that reactions to sense experience were "mostly determined by the habitual reactions of the society to which the individual in question belongs." The similarity of phenomena worldwide—such as marriage, law, art, and religion as well as fire production, cooking, shelters, tools, social groups, and incest prohibition—pointed to something like *Elementargedanke*, but "the occurrence of these ideas by itself does not explain clearly the psychological processes that produce them and that cause their stability," because of the extreme variability of their manifestations in the shape of plural cultures. Totemism, for instance—"a form of society in which certain social groups consider themselves as related in a supernatural way to a certain species of animals or to a certain class of objects"—was not a "single psychological problem, but embraces the most diverse psychological elements": one people may believe they are the descendants of an animal, others that it is their protector, others still have a magical relation to it, and so on.

In other words, seemingly similar anthropological phenomena were psychologically distinct, and it was impossible to deduce "psychological laws covering all of them." This also meant that the "common features," or psychic unity of humankind, could be found not in "similarities of ethnic phenomena, but in the similarity of psychological processes so far as these can be observed or inferred." Such processes included, for instance, the "symbolic significance of decorative art" for primitive tribes, or "the connection between social organization and religious belief" manifested in totemism, where "certain social classes claim privileges by the grace of God." The bases of customs, taboos, and artistic practices were automatic actions: "Certain ideas exist in his [man's] mind for which he cannot give any explanation except that they are there. The desire to understand one's own actions, and to get a clear insight into the secrets of the world, manifests itself at a very early time, and it is therefore not surprising that man in all stages of culture begins to speculate on the motives of his own actions."[94] It is fair to say that Boas's contemporary Sigmund Freud was also interested in comprehending how humans understand themselves and the "automatic" motives of their actions. And as it happens, the two men did cross paths—only once, here at the Clark anniversary conference in 1909.

We may recall that Hall had invited Freud to Clark on that occasion. This would be Freud's only visit to the United States. He gave five talks there—the fifth slot was originally Boas's, but he ceded it to Freud. Jung was present too, as were William James and Wundt's student Edward Titchener. There exists a famous photograph of these and other illustrious attendees taken by photographic studio partners Schervee and Bushong on September 10, 1909. (It depicts an all-male group, even though, to name just one, Titchener's first graduate student was a woman, Margaret Floy Washburn, and she was the first to receive a PhD in psychology in the United States, in 1894.) Freud, Jung, Sándor Ferenczi, and Titchener were among those who received honorary doctorates on that occasion—along with Boas himself. We have no trace of conversations between them, though it is highly probable that Freud and Jung attended Boas's talk. Anthropologist Kevin P. Groark notes that both Freud and Jung got immersed in ethnology after the conference "in an attempt to develop their own genetic psychological theories of psychic inheritance": it is around then that Freud started writing the essays for the journal *Imago* that would make up *Totem and Taboo*, published in 1913.[95]

Conversely, at his Lowell Institute talks the year after the Clark conference, and thus in *The Mind of Primitive Man*, Boas explicitly integrated Freud's insight that "in the study of the behavior of members of foreign races educated in European society, we should . . . bear in mind the influence of habits of thought, feeling and action acquired in early childhood, and of which no recollection is retained. If S. Freud is right in assuming that these forgotten incidents remain a living force throughout life,—the more potent, the more thoroughly they are forgotten,—we should have to conclude that many of the small traits of individuals which we ordinarily believe to be inherited are acquired by the influence of the individuals among whom [in the talk version, Boas wrote "the environment in which] the child spends the first few years of its life. All observations on the force of habit and the intensity of resistance to changes of habit are in favor of this theory."[96]

But Boas found Freud's subsequent efforts at ethnology risible. He would write these lines in the 1938 revised edition of *The Mind of Primitive Man:* "Freud's comparison of primitive culture and the psychoanalytic interpretations of European behaviors seem to lack a scientific background. They appear to me as fancies in which neither the aspect of primitive life nor that of civilized life is sustained by tangible evidence. The attempt to conceive every mental state or performance as determined by discoverable causes confuses the concepts of causality and predictability. Of course, every event has a cause, but the causes do not hang together so that they represent a single thread. Innumerable accidental causes intervene which cannot be predicted and which also cannot be reconstructed as determining the course of the past."[97] This is the passage to which Boas referred the science journalist Waldemar Kaempffert, who, in 1940, wrote to Boas asking him for further guidance on Freud's ideas about primitive people. As far as he, Kaempffert, could tell, and as he had "quoted Malinowski to the effect that the Oedipus complex did not hold among the matrilineal Trobriand Islanders in Melanesia," Freud seemed "to have been quite wrong." In his response, besides referring Kaempffert to the citation above, Boas wrote: "I think it is so obvious that Freud's ethnological theories are untenable that I have never gone very deeply into the subject. His whole procedure seems to me so illogical that I have always thought that the fashion may not last very long."[98] It made no sense to apply all too speculative psychoanalysis to anthropological data, especially as evolutionism was inherent in psychoanalysis. In his article "The Methods of Ethnology," published in 1920, Boas reiterated the stance he had taken in 1911: "While I believe some of the ideas underlying Freud's psychoanalytic studies may be fruitfully applied to ethnological problems, it does not seem to me that the one-sided exploitation method will advance our understanding of the development of human society."[99] An obverse transfer, however, would have been desirable: that the psychoanalysts use anthropological data and "get out of their armchairs and experience individual societies in depth," as anthropologist Robert Kenny puts it, so that "they would be chastened in their quest for evolutionist general laws." As it turned out, when the psychoanalysts paid attention to ethnology, they stuck instead to their armchairs and to evolutionism, believing that "psychoanalysis had revealed truths about the history of mental development that no other method had or could."[100]

And yet, not surprisingly, many of Boas's students did turn to psychoanalysis—taking on board its central psychodynamic aspects and ignoring the ethnology, which almost all agreed was indeed wrong. They were, in fact, developing Boas's mission to understand the relation of mind and culture, and superseding their mentor. In 1928, Edward Sapir—he had published his *Language: An Introduction to the Study of Speech* in 1921— reformulated Boas's skepticism with the punchy line "Psychoanalysis is less exciting as social philosopher and prophet than as clinician," accepting, then, its clinical value. Two years before, he and psychiatrist Harry Stack Sullivan had become close friends when Sapir gave a noted talk in Chicago, "Speech as a Personality Trait" (published in 1927), and they developed together interpersonal psychoanalysis, which acknowledged structurally how culture shaped the relational self at a deepest level.[101] In the mid-1930s, psychoanalyst Karen Horney, who was also a friend of Sullivan, would call on Margaret Mead to discuss how culture shaped the notion of femaleness—again, how culture and individual psyche intersected.[102]

Boas's very conception of the object or even premise of anthropological research was connected to the notion of the collective self. In that 1920 article "The Methods of Ethnology," he wrote: "The activities of the individual are determined to a great extent by his social environment, but in turn his own activities influence the society in which he lives and may bring about modifications in its form. Obviously, this problem is one of the most important ones to be taken up in a study of cultural changes." Herbert Lewis identified here echoes from the German Jews Moritz Lazarus and Heymann Steinthal, whose mid-nineteenth-century *Völkerpsychologie* had a decisive impact on Boas—and which was in some ways "thoroughly 'Boasian' before Boas's time."[103] Yet Boas had stopped short of exploring how the individual and the social were interconnected, intent as he was on preserving as separate the respective spaces of race, culture, and language. The latter had its "inner form," another category from Steinthal, and it was as such an expression of thought— necessarily collective—that was to be studied, reconstructed, and understood from within. This was why Boas generated grammars of the languages he studied with his colleagues and students as well as with members of the First Nations. This was the case, for instance, with the important Dakota grammar, published in 1941, compiled with Ella Cara Deloria, a Yankton Dakota Sioux on her father's side, whose life Franz had sustained since 1915 and whose career he had helped promote. (Later, she would work with him on a project, "Racial and Social Differences in Mental Ability," funded by Columbia.)[104] Languages, like other ethnological phenomena, at once inscribed and were inscribed in a history: they borrowed, converged, diverged.[105]

This too was a far cry from Freud's notion of verbal trans-lations of unconscious urges and conflicts. Kroeber dived deep into this realm, however: in 1917, when he was president of the American Anthropological Association, he went briefly into anal-ysis, and then practiced for five years as a lay psychoanalyst. For Boas, this was "an unfortunate aberration to be borne patiently."[106] Kroeber even wondered for a while whether he should aban-don anthropology altogether. The one area simply did not bleed into the other. But he ended up abandoning his practice in 1923, remaining with anthropology. In his 1920 review of Freud's *Totem and Taboo*, he acknowledged both sides: "However much cultural anthropology may come to lean more on the historical instead of the psychological method, it can never ultimately free itself, nor should it wish to, from the psychology that underlies it. To this psychology the psychoanalytic movement initiated by Freud has made an indubitably significant contribution, which every ethnologist must sooner or later take into consideration." But he ended with a defense of empirical, scientific work: "Eth-nology, like every other branch of science, is work and not a game in which lucky guesses score; . . . our business is first to understand as thoroughly as possible the nature of these existing phenomena [such as totemism]; in the hope that such understanding may gradually lead to a partial reconstruction of origins—without undue guessing."[107] On this front, he and his mentor were in total agreement.

For, arguably, much of Boas's life was a defense of empiricism against "undue guessing" and speculation, of laboriously obtained, carefully categorized data over grand a priori theory: he knew well how such a priori theory could reflect biases and distort truth, as well as undermine justice. But, contrary to what is often said of Boas even today, he did have a clear theoretical stance of his own, one that was on a continuum with his moral and political ideals. He translated these ideals into the energetic political activism he engaged in over his last two decades. He knew exactly what he stood for, and by maturity, not only had he consolidated his own views, he had redrawn the map of anthropology, extending the import of his thinking—in particular about culture and race—beyond the walls of academe and into the public realm, where it urgently mattered.

5

A Legacy

WHEN WORLD WAR I broke out, Franz foresaw the worst early on, writing to his then twenty-three-year-old son Ernst a week later, on August 6, 1914—while on the road toward Cranbrook in British Columbia: "My dear boy, . . . I cannot visualize how reasonable people and nations which are 'leaders of civilization' can conjure up such a terrible war. If Germany loses, such hatred will be created that it will stir up her nationalism for centuries to come; if she is victorious, such arrogance, that it will lead to the same consequence. If people would only realize what a source of hatred and misfortune the highly praised patriotism represents!" Not only was he worried about his mother and about his siblings: all patriotism was anathema to him. To younger Henry, or Heini, he wrote on August 15 from St. Eugene: "This false love for the fatherland other people call patriotism. They are forgetting that every country with its special features has to work together with other countries in order really to fulfil its duties and to be of use." In 1912, he had published "An Anthropologist's View of War," in which he gave what we would call an evolutionary psychologist's account of warfare, stemming from "the early days of mankind" of perpetual strife between small, unified, self-interested hordes, and where harming the other was self-defense. Then, as numbers increased within each horde, along with "economic complexity," so hostility diminished, though "the old feeling of specific differences between social groups" remained in racist and antisemitic attitudes: "It is not any rational cause that forms opposing groups, but solely the emotional value of an idea that holds together the members of each group and exalts their feeling of solidarity and greatness to such an extent that compromises with other groups become impossible. In this mental attitude we may readily recognize the survival of the feeling of specific differences between the hordes, transferred in part from the feeling of physical differences to that of mental differences."[1] In 1912, he had still believed in the possibility of world peace, and dared hope for it. But two years later, that belief and that hope were quickly shattered.

Soon he effectively found himself on the wrong side of history: he was the German immigrant again. He had family and friends in Germany, after all, and he had never stopped being German, of course. He was a founding member of the Germanistic Society of America, of which Uncle Jacobi was the president, and which fostered intellectual and academic collaborations between Germany and the United States.[2] He had always insisted on speaking German at home while the children were growing up: we know this from the testimonials of Ernst, who recalled that the siblings were expected to speak German between themselves as well; of Helene, with whose own children their grandfather insisted on speaking German; and of the youngest, Franziska (who became a well-known and influential dancer), who also recalled, speaking to Zumwalt, that, when they were small, Franz "would play German folksongs" at the piano, and also that Marie's cooking was Austrian.[3] The Boas family's daily life was deeply steeped in New York's German society, its Kleindeutschland and restaurants, where it was possible to be at once American, German, and Jewish without feeling much pressure to define oneself as any one thing. Franz had certainly pushed his Jewishness to the outer edges of his identity—and, arguably, to the outer edges of his thinking about identity.

But now that Germany was the enemy, Franz's position became tricky. After the sinking by the German navy of the *Lusitania* in May 1915, Americans viewed Germans as all the more threatening, potentially dangerous enemies. The German high culture that Boas had grown up in, and that had shaped him, was no longer welcome: as King tells it, Beethoven and Wagner were wiped out of concert repertoires, and monuments of Goethe and Schiller were defaced. The Germanistic Society was no more. Things got worse in 1917, when the Black Tom munitions dump in Jersey City was blown up by secret agents working for Germany. The enemy combatant, so to speak, was now on American territory. President Wilson proclaimed that "America must be kept American." As a result, German could no longer be spoken or taught in many states, those German citizens who had not become American had to register with the government and could no longer take a train, and so on. There was a concomitant rise in violent anti-German acts. This is when many people chose to Americanize their originally German names.[4]

Boas, typically and courageously—and perhaps rashly—spoke out. In a long scholarly letter published in the Sunday edition of the *New York Times* on January 3, 1915, he emphasized the need to "realize the deep emotions that sway the actions of the nations" and recounted the recent history of the aspirations to national unity among European countries, carefully showing how language and country did not map onto each other one to one, and indeed that a shared language, unlike "race," which did not exist, deepened the emotional bond within a people. He suggested that Americans were "judging by cold reasoning actions that were dictated by strong emotional causes" and weren't in a position to understand these causes. Moreover: "There is no country in which the foreign policy does not lie in the hands of a few, who can obtain, at least temporarily, popular approval of their policies by the appropriate manipulation of information." Indeed, "the basis of all our national aspirations is not an intellectual, but an emotional one, and we should be clear in regard to the emotional values underlying the thoughts of the members of each nation." And so: "We shall not learn the lesson of this war if we condemn Austria and Germany and praise ourselves on account of our higher humanity."[5] America would have reacted in the same way, he wrote, had it been in the same position.

At the end of the year, on December 6, he published another, much shorter letter, which the *New York Times* entitled "Warns of German Wrath: Professor Boas Complains of Acts Injurious to Teutonic Empires": "These are sad times for those who have the progress of mankind at heart. Not enough that the nations of Europe are destroying one another, in our own country the seeds of discord are sowed by violent partisanship, by mutual vituperation, and unwillingness to understand the basis of discordant points of view." On January 6, 1916, as anti-German sentiment was increasing, the *Times* published another letter by Boas under the title "Why German-Americans Blame America: They Think Their New Country, Having Sacrificed Its Own Ideals, Is Setting Up as the Arbiter of the World." America's ideal of "self-restraint" had already been betrayed by its "aggressive imperialism" of the 1898 Spanish-American War, and now, he argued, it was imposing its "ideals on other nations" without any right to do so. "In my youth I had been taught in school and at home not only to love the soul of my own country but also to seek to understand and to respect the individualities of other nations. For this reason, one-sided nationalism, that is so often found nowadays, is to me unendurable. The question whether this tolerant spirit is found in other nations does not concern us here. The point that concerns me is that I wish to see it realized in the country whose citizen I am." He held his adopted country to a high moral standard: he deplored its adopting patriotism and militarism, and its taking sides in so intolerant, brutal a manner.

Nor did he hold back when, in 1917, the United States was on the brink of entering the war. His letter, published two months before, on February 9 and entitled "Professor Boas Dissents: Blames the President for the Break with Germany," ended in no uncertain terms: "If we want to be true to our peaceful ideas we must retrace our steps." Boas was of course not the only citizen or public figure to express disagreement with the pro-war stance of President Wilson. Fifty representatives and six senators did so as well, and the total tally of the men who avoided or deserted the draft would amount to around 3 million.[6] But in the eyes of Butler, Franz's position was "intolerable." He was dangerously radical. John D. Prince, at the time a professor of Semitic languages at Columbia as well as a politician and diplomat, immediately wrote to the *Times* that he had "read with great regret the un-American letter written by my colleague." He had "always been politically opposed to President Wilson's policies," but now was no time for partisanship. Columbia, "almost to a man, stands for a united America." Boas would literally pay for his strong convictions: his salary was cut by the trustees, and he lost access to research funds—so colleagues and friends had to organize a fund to support him. He continued expressing his opposition nevertheless, deploring the increasing curtailment on freedom of speech.[7] In 1917, Congress passed an immigration law lowering the number of immigrants allowed, imposing a literacy test, increasing a tax payable on arrival, and excluding those from the "Asiatic Barred Zone." Later, Dillingham would introduce quotas.

After the United States had joined the war, on April 2, 1917,

Boas's own son Ernst, then twenty-six and facing the draft, decided to join the army as a medical officer instead, as a "cardio-
vascular specialist in the training camp hospitals," as he informed
his family in July. This was a source of great worry for Franz and
Marie. On July 24, 1917, Boas responded that he had no right
to criticize Ernst and that he understood his decision, but was
sorry that "thru your voluntary entry into the army [you] have
given your silent approval to the war. It is not a question (it goes
without saying?) that your army service will bring us worrisome
times, in this period of universal torture and cares. My dear boy,
no matter what you do, my best wishes go to you."[8] But it was
difficult to accept all the same. It was around then that Franz
learned of the death of Wilhelm Weike, his Baffin Island companion, with whom his family had remained close. He wrote to
Ernst, "The news of Wilhelm's death has moved me painfully. It
is very painful when one's whole youth begins to die off on all
sides. One becomes so aware of aging."[9] That Christmas, Ernst
returned home and married his fiancée Helen. In August 1918,
Henry (Heini) was drafted and sent to France, where, Zumwalt
tells us, since his French was quite good, he was employed to procure food for the commissary.[10] In October, Ernst was made chief
of the medical service. But the armistice was around the corner.

From the time of the United States' entry into war, Boas
made no more public pronouncements, resorting instead to private action and to defending many people whose views had also
gotten them into trouble. These included one of his colleagues,
linguist Leo J. Frachtenberg, who had made pronouncements
deemed critical of the government and had been dismissed, at
a time when, in the words of Melville Herskovits, "calls to ferret
out those who did not give assent to the war effort were heard
from every side," and universities were no exception.[11] Columbia was particularly keen on imposing "loyalty" on its faculty.[12]
In response, Franz "mobilized the Association of Professors, the
Evening Post, 3 senators, Keppel in the War Department," as he

recounted to Ernst. "I hope this idiotic nonsense will be stopped at once." Another colleague was psychologist James McKeen Cattell, whom Butler wanted to dismiss as "an implacable enemy" because he had tried to enlist congressmen to agitate against Wilson's conscription. And then there were the German and Austrian anthropologists who had been interned, whom Boas tried to help as well. He ardently believed in the international collaboration that science, at its best, is built on, transcending borders. After the war, he helped set up the "Emergency Society for German and Austrian Science" aimed at cultivating transatlantic collaborations and providing research funding to scientists in Germany and Austria whose work and livelihoods had been affected by the conflict and whose ability to purchase American books was jeopardized by the onerous exchange rates. (Paul Rivet, the like-minded socialist and politically engaged ethnologist who worked on South America and had founded the Musée de l'homme in Paris, was his intermediary in France.) He even helped raise funds for the Berlin Philharmonic Orchestra when Walter Damrosch became unable to do so in the face of inflation.[13]

His capacity to organize resistance in this regard, and as an activist generally, was quite remarkable. And it clearly drew on his remarkable skill in initiating, implementing, and running large-scale operations, which he developed over the years: he was an extraordinarily able administrator. Notably, in 1910, after lengthy, complex international negotiations that began in 1906, he set up the Escuela internacional of Mexico—modeled on schools of classical studies that had taken root in Italy and Greece from the 1880s—which he directed between 1911 and 1912. He traveled to Mexico for the purpose, publishing with the International Congress of Americanists the resulting *Archaeological Investigations in the Valley of Mexico by the International School, 1911–12*. The school, however, had to close in 1914 at the outbreak of the Mexican Revolution. Boas then turned to Puerto Rico, in collaboration with the New York Academy of Science—

traveling there in 1915 on a field trip to study Taino anthropometry while colleagues, including a young anthropologist named
John Alden Mason, collected folktales, songs, poetry, and more.[14]

Boas knew how to put his organizational skills to the purpose of ideas without ever losing sight of the bigger picture.
And there was, of course, a continuity between his pacifist stance
and his lifelong battle against biological racialism, itself based
on the data-driven, multidisciplinary research he spearheaded,
so minutely, across borders north and south, west and east. He
was fully aware of what he was up against. In 1916 appeared
*The Passing of the Great Race: The Racial Basis of European His-
tory*, a book by eugenicist Madison Grant. It was to become a
favorite tome of Hitler, who in 1925 wrote to Grant that its
German translation was his "bible": "A state which in this age
of racial poisoning dedicates itself to the care of its best racial
elements must someday become lord of the earth," he wrote.[15]
The book was reprinted throughout the 1920s—at a time when
the Ku Klux Klan was in its heyday. Grant, like Gobineau, argued for the superiority of a "Teutonic" or "Nordic race," which
would be "replaced" by "lower races" if immigration wasn't
stopped. He was also a friend of Roosevelt as well as a respected
environmentalist and trustee of the American Museum of Natural History. Osborn, for that matter, published a letter in the
New York Times in 1924 entitled "Lo, The Poor Nordic!" in
which he set out his "Position on the Immigration Question"
in explicitly racial, eugenically driven terms.[16] And a few years
later, in 1932, the museum would host the Third International
Congress of Eugenics.[17]

Boas's review of Grant's book for the *New Republic* appeared
in January 1917.[18] He called it

> a dithyrambic praise of the blond, blue-eyed white and of his
> achievements; a Cassandric prophecy of all the ills that will
> befall us on account of the increase of dark-eyed types.

> Fortunately, the supposed scientific data on which the author's conclusions are based are dogmatic assumptions which cannot endure criticism,

because "the whole concept of heredity as held by him is faulty," and "to speak of hereditary characteristics of a human race as a whole has no meaning." Boas was courteous to a fault, and methodical as ever in his critique, arguing "that nobody has so far succeeded in proving racial superiority, and certainly nothing like the superiority of one European type over another one; that the whole formulation of the problem as a struggle between different races is misleading." He presented an explanation of this that a defender of eugenics would not have paid much attention to, precisely because Grant wasn't interested, as Boas himself wrote, in "scientifically well founded data on which to base a theory, but its object is to show that democratic institutions and the arrival of immigrants of non-northwest-European type are a danger to the welfare of the American people." Boas cited Grant: "The altruistic ideals which have controlled our social development during the past century, and the maudlin sentimentalism that has made America 'an asylum for the oppressed,' are sweeping the nation toward a racial abyss." With sentences such as that one, Grant had in his favor, as King notes, "the deep self-confidence of Western society founded upon the observable reality of Anglo-Saxon dominance around the globe," a far more attractive and persuasive narrative than Boas's "arcane head measurements and scientific theory that flew in the face of accepted wisdom."[19] Measured expertise and wise skepticism are always harder to hear than populist dogma.

In February 1919, Franz wrote a piece for the *Nation* in which he expressed his strong disapproval of the Versailles Treaty and especially of the mandate system that was to be applied to the German empire: "Mandatories have an ugly habit of forgetting their mandates and considering their temporary charges as permanent property," that is, "annexation," with all the attendant ills of colonialism. It was time to implement what the British Labour Party stood for—the end of colonial exploitation of natives: "The essential motive for interference in the affairs of foreign countries is the need in our life for the products of these countries. When these cannot be obtained except by native labor, the native is forced to produce what we want and is exploited for our purposes."[20]

It was in the summer of that year that Franz started a correspondence with Rivet—they would exchange exactly 129 letters between then and 1941. Rivet wrote first, inviting him to contribute an article to the *Journal de la Société des Américanistes*. Franz responded that he strongly felt the need for international scientific cooperation that transcended the patriotism he abhorred so much, and also that he wanted to write the article in German in order to show his opposition to what such patriotism had spelled for the ostracized scientists in Germany. Rivet responded in terms that were very close to Boas's: "I think that humanity must increasingly work towards abolishing all nationalisms, I think that the only remedy for the current misery of humanity can only be a sincere reconciliation of all peoples, and for my part, I will try in all ways to hasten the advent of this real peace, which will not be written in a text but within hearts, and I would be ashamed to be a human if I didn't feel within me this profound conviction, this unshakeable faith."[21] To Boas, these words were a ray of sunshine. And from then on, they assisted each other as best they could. They met in person for the first time only five years later, in August 1924, in The Hague, at the important Americanists' Congress that took place there as well as in Gothenburg.

But Boas knew well how difficult it was for such words to have an impact on the polity in those dark days of patriotic America, where, instead, it was the likes of Madison Grant who were heard, loud and clear—and heeded by many. His racist voice and rousing nativist propaganda played a lobbying part in the passing of the Johnson-Reed Act in 1924, which "limited the number of immigrants allowed entry into the United States through a national origins quota," and whose main purpose "was to preserve the ideal of U.S. homogeneity."[22] The government then introduced visas, available for a fee and only for those eligible to enter the country—and that meant white. Another influential voice on the matter was that of Carl Brigham, whose book *A Study of American Intelligence*, published five years after Grant's, in 1923, was taken seriously even by the *New York Times:* he advocated "selective" immigration on the basis of a racialized and racist view of intelligence.[23] The scoring of intelligence was a recent phenomenon. In 1916, Lewis Terman, who introduced the IQ scoring scale, had transformed the intelligence test devised earlier in the century by French psychologist Alfred Binet into the Stamford-Binet Intelligence Scales, concluding that "feeble-mindedness" was hereditary. Whereupon psychologist Robert Yerkes, who also believed in a racialized intelligence hierarchy, ran this test within the army, aided by Terman and Henry Goddard. They adapted it for the civilian population in 1919 as the National Intelligence Test. These tests were the basis for Brigham's claims—including the inferior intelligence of Italian immigrants—which the *Times* echoed wholesale, without any mention of the critique Boas had made.

Boas's tendency never to compromise on his humanist ideals had led him into another spot of institutional trouble a few years earlier. Against the advice of his friend and colleague the great pragmatist philosopher and educator John Dewey, he published a piece in the December 20 issue of the *Nation* with the title "Scientists as Spies," recounting that four American anthropologists had, in 1917, "prostituted science by using it as a cover for their activities as spies" in "Central America." They had thereby violated "the most fundamental principles of professional ethics," jeopardizing the mission of science, that of "seeking the truth," as well as international cooperation. Boas was personally invested in this story, which took place in Mexico—though at the time he named neither men nor country: two of these men had used a contact that Boas had himself provided and who was arrested in Mexico as a result. One of these two was archaeologist Sylvanus G. Morley, a specialist of the Maya, who had studied the subject at Harvard and had indeed been a highly dedicated spy. The other was Samuel Lothrop, who would also serve in the Special Intelligence Service of the FBI that J. Edgar Hoover created during World War II.[24]

The immediate reaction on the part of the Anthropological Society of Washington, which had never been Boasian, determined in an official statement that Boas's article "unjustly criticizes the President of the United States and attacks the fundamental principles of American democracy," and ultimately, that its publication "deserves our emphatic disapproval."[25] On December 30, the AAA, during the annual meeting of its governing council at the Peabody in Cambridge, voted 20–10 to censure him. (Wissler, the presiding officer, was one of the two who abstained.) Bizarrely, the AAA would not formally withdraw the censure until 2005, eighty-six years after it had stripped him of office and pressured him to resign from the National Research Council (NRC), though at the time, it never removed Boas from its council, despite the censure.[26] The more harmful reaction came from the secretary of the Smithsonian, Charles D. Walcott, who had long disapproved of Franz. Now he felt justified in cancelling Boas's position as honorary philologist at the BAE and discontinuing his association with the Smithsonian—and this meant that it would no longer publish him or his students. Walcott even went further, writing about the *Nation* letter to President Wilson. Alerted by Wilson, the attorney general informed Walcott "that the Bureau of Investigation of the Department of Justice has been instructed to make a thorough inquiry into the past and present activities" of Boas, "to ascertain whether or not he has been identified with any of the pernicious radical activities in this country." Franz's FBI file would open officially in 1936, but clearly it began in 1919.[27] At the university, Butler fired Alexander Goldenweiser and reduced the department to three rooms on the seventh floor (walk-up) of Columbia's journalism building. Boas was now the only faculty. Butler could not fire so esteemed a figure. But he put a stop to the undergraduate classes, fearful of what they might inculcate in the young.

But Franz's graduate lectures were highly popular. It was in those years, in which for a while he went over to all-female Barnard in reaction to how constrained his position had become at Columbia, that three of his most outstanding students first encountered the subject with him—women who would become major anthropologists. They were Ruth Benedict and Margaret Mead, who had studied with Benedict just as Benedict received her PhD—Mead had been her first student—as well as with Boas and Ruth Bunzel. And indeed, King recounts that Boas would write to a colleague, "I have had a curious experience in graduate work during the last few years: all my best students are women."[28] There was also, notably, ethnologist Elsie Crews Parsons—feminist and socialist, and a Wall Street heiress who helped support Boas when Butler cut his funds by paying his secretary's salary as well as financing fieldwork trips for his female graduate students.[29] His early students had mostly been men: this had changed, though he had always helped promote women.[30] In 1911, for instance, he wrote a highly supportive foreword to *Half a Man: The Status of the Negro in New York*, a book by civil rights activist, co-founder of the NAACP, and suffragist Mary White Ovington, which she wrote as a fellow of the Greenwich House Committee on Social Investigations, set up in 1902, and on whose board sat Franz, along with Edwin Seligman, Livingston Farrand, and others.[31]

Boas managed not to pay too much attention to these institutional events, and he would not be left out in the institutional cold for long. By 1931, he would be elected president of the AAAS, and in late December of that year, after Franz had suffered an attack of heart angina during a party, the AAA "resolved" to "express to Dr. Franz Boas its sincere sympathy in his present illness and its hope for his prompt recovery."[32] But the crisis was significant. The Washington anthropologists had arguably been awaiting an opportunity to sideline Franz: they could not countenance his and his cohort's attacks on their version of evolutionism. During the war, the NRC's Committee on Anthropology was headed not by Boas but by people from the National Museum: Franz's rival Holmes—of whom alleged spy Morley was a protégé—and Aleš Hrdlička, who had been nominated for this position by the secretary of the Smithsonian, Charles D. Wolcott, one of the wartime "scientist-patriots" and himself no friend of Franz's. Adam Kuper reports that Holmes was incensed by Boas's letter: he wrote to an associate that it was "treacherous," lamenting "Prussian control of Anthropology in this country," which he called "the Hun regime," whose demise he called for.[33] The NRC also included Madison Grant and geneticist Charles B. Davenport—the effective leader of the eugenics movement. Anthropology, they thought, surely was not the hard science it needed to be for the war effort if, in Stocking's words, "it vocally proclaimed its independence from biology, relegated the study of man as a physical organism to a distinctly secondary position, denied in large part the significance of biological race, and raised to central theoretical importance a concept [culture] which had not yet shed the aura of dilettantish humanism."[34] From 1918, Grant and Davenport set up the Galton Society for the study of "racial anthropology." Osborn, of course, was a member. Another was government scientist John C. Merriam, chairman of the NRC.

The council eventually invited Boas back into the fold. But tensions grew between the advocates of physical anthropology and the Boasian cultural anthropologists. The *Nation* letter was

just "the trigger that released a flood of pent-up personal resent-
ment and institutional antagonism."[35] Over the next few years
of complex institutional shifts and adjustments (recounted in
detail by Stocking), Boas and the Boasians would rejoin the official ranks. But anthropology would expand beyond the remit
Franz had seen for it—with work beginning on Africa and the
Asian Pacific, notably via Kroeber and Clark Wissler, as well as
a rapprochement with psychology, institutionally enacted with
the creation of the Social Science Research Council in 1925. Franz
had weathered the storm, in any case. Stocking quotes Kroeber's description of Franz as "a true patriarch" and "a powerful
father figure," nicknamed "Papa Franz" by his students, whose
forceful personality, writes Stocking, was "instrumental in creating the professional anthropological identity which had already been emerging and was to survive and grow."[36]

For a while, the war had appeared "to have shaken Boas'
faith in the efficacy of reason," in the words of Harvey Levenstein: Franz no longer believed in the power of words to effect
change, especially seeing how deeply racism was entrenched,
and how intellectuals were disappointing, prone as they were to
betray their ideals.[37] In the September 5, 1918, issue of the *Dial*,
he published "The Mental Attitude of the Educated Classes,"
in which he performed an anthropological analysis of his own
class, that of the intellectuals, who tacitly believed "not only that
they have special knowledge but also that they are free to form
perfectly rational opinions," while in fact they were just another
instance of the fact that "there is no type of society in existence
in which such freedom exists." If "it never enters into their minds
that any other way of thinking and acting would be possible," then
"they consider themselves as perfectly free in regard to all their
actions." Such ideas, which "restrict the freedom of thought of
the individual," could lead to "serious mental struggles when
traditional social ethics come into conflict with instinctive reactions. Thus among a tribe of Siberia we find a belief that every

person will live in the future life in the same condition in which he finds himself at the time of death. As a consequence an old man who begins to be decrepit wishes to die, in order to avoid life as a cripple in the endless future, and it becomes the duty of his son to kill him. The son believes in the righteousness of this command but at the same time feels the filial love for his father." Similarly, it was "not surprising that the thought of what we call the educated classes is controlled essentially by those ideals which have been transmitted to us by past generations." Those ideals included "the ethical tendencies, the aesthetic inclinations, the intellectuality, and the expression of volition, of past times. Their control may find expression in a dominant tone which determines our whole mode of thought and which, for the very reason that it has come to be ingrained into our whole mentality, never rises into our consciousness."

Much of what we take as the rules we live by is in fact "irrational" and has an unconscious origin. It is only when these rules become conscious—when they require rational explanation, for instance—that they are justified. As Franz's student and now established anthropologist Robert H. Lowie wrote in 1937, "A matter-of-fact usage is sanctioned *ex post facto* by virtue of some supernatural decree." This was also, in Boas's words, why "it will require new efforts to free a future generation of the shackles that we are forging"—the shackles again, those *Kulturbrille*, fruit, as ever, of apperceptive processes. "When we once recognize this process, we must see that it is our task not only to free ourselves of traditional prejudice, but also to search in the heritage of the past for what is useful and right, and to endeavor to free the mind of future generations so that they may not cling to our mistakes, but may be ready to correct them." As Lowie put it, for Boas, "a cultural phenomenon is intelligible only from its past."[38]

The anthropologically distancing study of history was, in other words, ethically, politically, psychologically, and epistemically necessary. Boas used it in his own life. And it is probable that his own lucidity helped him rally after the postwar discouragement. In October 1918, he wrote in another letter to the *Nation* that since "the free expression of opinion that used to be the foundation of our liberty no longer exists," he would "vote for the Socialist party" in the next elections.[39] He was Sophie's son, after all. Activism, not quietism, was his calling—along with the continually productive research that bolstered his case against the epistemic and political dogmatists of this world. Just as this activism became all the more intense as Nazism emerged and Hitler came to power, he never lost touch with the very stuff of his work and passion.[40] He further developed theories about folklore and art—and, of course, about acculturation and culture. In 1927, a year before *Anthropology and Modern Life* came out, he published *Primitive Art*, which was based on lectures he had given in Oslo. It was an account "of the dynamic conditions under which art styles grow up," to use one citation extracted by Kroeber in his review of the book for *American Anthropologist*, where he praised it as "the soundest, most penetrating, and probably most comprehensive work existing on primitive art—and by implication perhaps on civilized."[41] Until 1924, he remained editor (having been so since 1908) of the *Journal of American Folklore*, along with Elsie Clews Parsons. From 1910 and for a good fifteen years thereafter, he was also editor of the *Columbia University Contributions to Anthropology*. Many of his students' publications appeared in those collections, and in those years. Boas nurtured all the more his students and his convictions—writing, mentoring, and organizing as feverishly as ever, and assisting all who needed his help.

There were major personal setbacks. In 1915, during surgery for a tumor located on a salivary gland, a nerve was severed, and from thereon the left side of his face drooped, partially paralyzed, while the sight from his left eye became blurry. His speech was affected as well, and he had difficulty pronouncing some sounds. He had ulcers, too, which caused distress.[42] And there were significant deaths. His mother Sophie died on February 6, 1916, aged eighty-seven, but because postal correspondence was barely functional during the war, he didn't learn of it for many months.[43] And on July 10, 1919, his Uncle Jacobi—to whom he owed so much—died. Franz wrote to Ernst—now grown up, he was "Boas's trusted counsel," as Zumwalt puts it: "I must say that the news has upset me very much, even though it was to be expected. I do not wish to live and see my strength ebb away."[44] Jacobi was eighty-nine, and had been in perfectly good health until that very day, when he felt fatigued, reported the *New York Times*, which gave him a lengthy obituary. He was at Bolton Landing on Lake George, where he normally summered, staying at his old friend Carl Schurz's house. It seems to have been as good a death as had been his life. The obituary reported that "it was his pride to give advice to the poor even more freely than to those who held out large fees."[45]

Franz had certainly lived up to his uncle's intellectual, professional, and moral expectations. He was as active as ever. And his students were rapidly going places. In 1920, Lowie published his influential anti-evolutionist *Primitive Society*, where he developed the culture concept. In his *Biographical Memoir of Franz Boas*, published in 1947, Lowie testified to Boas's reformulation of von den Steinen's dictum about the *Kulturbrille*, according to which "we must look at primitive man without the spectacles of our civilization; Boas amended it to read that we must look at *ourselves* without spectacles. He was ever aware of the preconceptions with which, as Virchow once put it, we are all 'crammed full from infancy on.' He once told me how hard he had had to struggle to overcome early rationalistic influences; and the burden of all his ethnological teaching, paralleling his linguistic position, was that every philosophy and form of behavior must be apprehended from the insider's point of view."[46] Lowie became full professor in Kroeber's department at Berkeley in 1925. Margaret Mead's *Coming of Age in Samoa: A Psychological*

Study of Primitive Youth for Western Civilisation would appear in 1928, when she was just twenty-three, with Franz's foreword. It swiftly became a major bestseller—regardless of the later controversies surrounding her use of field data.[47]

In 1922, Boas traveled north again. Here he is writing to Ernst from Victoria, having gone there for the first time in twenty-two years, with "Mama" this time, where he met up with George Hunt. The place had "really changed very much," and "seeing the people again whom I know here makes me realize how old we are." Ernst's wife Helen had just had a baby, and in this letter Franz inquired after their health. On August 30, 1922, he wrote from Spenses Bridge to Toni, who, now a concert pianist, had managed to move to the United States just before the Johnson-Reed Act went into effect:

> I worked very hard in Victoria, and Mama had a good time. We went together to the movies and to the real theater and made several little trips. At the end I even had to give a lecture. George Hunt from Fort Rupert and another Indian were here. I have a room in the library in which I do my work.
>
> The visit here is very sad. An old companion of my travels is dying of cancer of the bladder. I spend much time with him trying to give him courage. Tomorrow we leave. Five more days of mountain climbing, and then we go home again. Both of us are very glad to get back again.

In 1923, having travelled again, he wrote to Marie from Bella Bella on November 17 that Hunt was in hospital and "very depressed," as one of his daughters had just died, his older son had cancer of the spinal cord, and his oldest sister had "suffered a stroke." The dispatches from these later trips are at times melancholy, at times serene enough—at any rate, they are of course no longer the exploratory ones of the beginnings, though one can still find the curiosity, purpose, and enthusiasm that always animated him.

Margaret Mead reports that he never lost the sense of "urgency" in recording disappearing cultures: "In 1930, at the age of 72, he made a return trip to the Kwakiutl to try out a new method—the use of film—on problems of style."[48] It would be his last trip to Fort Rupert, indeed to that part of the world he'd come to know so well, and to a nation that was being reduced to "a poor fishing people." "Civilization has infringed badly on the lives of the Indians," he wrote to Toni in October.[49] He kept his promise to help advocate for them against the Canadian ban on the potlach, and he drew official attention to the dysentery epidemic that was raging there.[50] For the film, he used a sixteen-millimeter camera, and for sound, wax cylinders. George Hunt and his family, as well as other related families, worked with him, filming, for instance, Mary Hunt Johnson performing a woman's winter dance, which Boas entitled the Cannibal Dance, one of a series of clips that would total fifty-one minutes of film, intended as a study on rhythm and gesture—but would never be finished.[51] Boas, in turn, encouraged Hunt to use a camera. He knew this would be the last time he'd ever see Hunt, as he wrote to his children; he was seventy-six now, and "quite frail."[52] His last publication on the Kwakwaka'wakw would come out in 1935—two years after George Hunt had died. His daughter Helene Yampolsky Boas would edit the Kwak'wala-English dictionary, publishing it in 1948, ensuring that it was organized according to the "writing system developed by Franz Boas and George Hunt" and based on her father's original work, "itself based extensively upon Kwak'wala materials recorded by George Hunt from numerous Kwakwaka'wakw speakers and knowledge keepers from the 1890s to the 1930s."[53]

Tragedy struck over and over in the 1920s: Franz's daughter Gertrude died of polio in 1924, aged just twenty. Heine, a youth of twenty-six, died in a railroad accident the year after. And on December 16, 1929, a hit-and-run driver killed Marie as she was crossing a street on a rainy day very near the family home in Grantwood. She died in hospital a few days later, aged sixty-eight. She and Franz had been together forty-two years.

Franz had left for Chicago two days before to participate in the inauguration of the new Social Science Research Building at the university, built by architects Coolidge & Hodgdon. Over the entrance was a medallion representing a profile of Boas. Marie was dead by the time he returned. It was their son Ernst who signed the death certificate, and Helene who told their father.

He was bereft—beyond words. Only silence surrounds these colossal losses. He fell into depressive darkness. Work was his escape, his balm, and his salvation. "You know that unfortunately I have not the light spirit of others, and when I do not work, or else am intensely occupied with something else I can think of nothing but Trudel and Heini," he had written to Ernst on July 17, 1927. "They are there when I get up in the morning and when I stop work at night they are there.[54] Franz was well surrounded by people who cared. His friends, colleagues, and students were present, in particular Gladys Amanda Reichard, who had been his doctoral student and was now an established anthropologist with a position at Barnard. She wrote to Elsie Clews Parsons, who had suggested to him that he accompany her to Mexico for a field trip, not least to distract him from his grief: "He had such wonderful force of will before for Mama Franz's sake. Now I think he has it in spite of himself rather than because of himself." Yet she sensed that his altruism was such that "I think he will pull together for the sake of other people." Still, as she wrote to Kroeber the following February, "His spirit seems to be broken. Can you imagine Boas without spirit?"

To try to escape his grief, Boas did travel, to Germany to attend the International Congress of Americanists. When he returned, he left for that last trip to British Columbia. He was traveling with a Russian exchange student at Barnard named Julia Averkieva, who conducted research there. The sublime nature there continued to console him. And, as ever, he became absorbed in this world. But grief inevitably followed him. He had been there with Marie on the trip he had taken in 1922. On October 21, he wrote to Ruth Benedict, "I had to think of the lovely trip Mama Franz and I had eight years ago when we stopped off at Glacier, Lake Louise, Banff and really enjoyed the beautiful nature. It will never be like that again." Nonetheless, this trip was exciting, "the first serious fieldwork I have done for a long, long time." From Fort Rupert, on December 14, 1930, he wrote to all his children: "A year ago today I went to Chicago not knowing what fate had in store for me. I said good-bye—good-bye forever—to your mother under the viaduct over 125th street! You lost a dear Mother; and I cannot find myself since then." Later: "I will find myself eventually and do what must be done, but the real enjoyment of life is gone." Ernst had written to Franz on the occasion of that one-year anniversary: "Now that we have only you our love has grown doubly. You know how necessary you are to us, so you must take care of yourself so that you will be with us for a long, long time." Toni had sent him a telegram too, to which Franz responded, "I knew that you would think of me on that day and I was very pleased. I am so glad that I shall be back in a month from today, and yet I am dreading my return into the house which is so empty now."

When, on January 2, 1931, he received news of his election to the presidency of the AAAS by telegram to Alert Bay, he wrote to Ernst that he was tempted not to accept it. But of course he knew he had to, if only for the sake of anthropology. He received congratulations from all corners—including from President Butler, whom King calls Boas's "administrative nemesis," and who wrote, "It is not only an honor to you but to the University which you have served these many years."[55] His presidential address to the AAAS, which he delivered in June 1931 in Pasadena, was entitled "Race and Progress": in it he confronted the issue of the "intermingling of racial types" and the roots of "racial antagonism" in closed societies, in which "antagonisms

against others" were inevitable. "Although the degree of antagonism against outsiders has decreased, closed societies continue to
exist in our own civilization," wrote Boas. It was within this context that arose racial discrimination, including antisemitism:

> While in all other human societies there is no external char-
> acteristic that helps to assign an individual to his group, here
> his very appearance singles him out. If the belief should pre-
> vail, as it once did, that all red-haired individuals have an
> undesirable character, they would at once be segregated and
> no red-haired individual could escape from his class no mat-
> ter what his personal characteristics might be. The Negro,
> the East Asiatic or Malay who may at once be recognized by
> his bodily build is automatically placed in his class and not
> one of them can escape being excluded from a foreign closed
> group. The same happens when a group is characterized by
> dress imposed by circumstances, by choice, or because a dom-
> inant group prescribe for them a distinguishing symbol—like
> the garb of the medieval Jews or the stripes of the convict—
> so that each individual no matter what his own character may
> be, is at once assigned to his group and treated accordingly.[56]

Today's identity politics probably would not have been to Boas's
liking.

The department had been growing back over the 1920s,
even though Franz's office hadn't moved from its cramped quarters in Journalism Hall. His students and colleagues filled the
large Grantwood house with life, hope, passion, and energy, and
he decided to turn the impromptu gatherings that had always
happened when Marie was alive into a regular weekly seminar
each Tuesday evening. The work continued, all important: academic production, basic research, teaching, and mentoring. And
the activism as well, which was becoming increasingly urgent.

The cognitive and emotional biases that Boas himself had
analyzed and understood were also operative, inevitably, in the

case of the racially prejudiced institutions and policies he stood against. The calmly, methodically reasoned and rational, evidence-based argumentation he put forward again and again ultimately had no traction against the socially embedded mechanisms of these biases, at once imitative and emotive, as he knew them to be. His arguments were subtle, but their use by the otherwise convinced could be coarse—for instance, when he testified as expert witness at a court case in 1925 determining the "white-ness" of Armenians, he asserted that they were of European origin, but his words were used to affirm that it "was utterly impossible to classify them as not belonging to the white race."[57] His scientific caution and integrity did not always serve him well. But then, when faced with dogma, such attributes are rarely of use. And dogma was increasing. In the United States, the Ku Klux Klan, initially founded just after the Civil War, was resurgent. It had reemerged as a small group in Georgia in 1915, but now was taking the country by storm, peaking at 4 million proudly racist members, who staged brutal actions to enforce Jim Crow segregation. They were also antisemitic, anti-Catholic, and generally opposed to immigration—"America for Americans" was the slogan of the anti-immigration movement, galvanized by the war. After the 1917 Bolshevik victory in Russia, the movement demonized organized labor as well. In 1927 in Berlin, the Kaiser Wilhelm Institute of Anthropology, Human Heredity, and Eugenics was founded to promote the racist pseudoscience and the notion of racial heredity that Boas and his circle, including Herskovits, fought against. (Herskovits wrote a piece in the *Nation* in 1925 deploring the development of this pseudoscience in the United States as well as in England, Sweden, and Germany.)[58] The institute's building was partly financed by the Rockefeller Foundation, and when the Depression hit in 1929, the foundation bankrolled it entirely.

The public voice of Boas grew ever more meaningful, and he wrote for a large number of newspapers and magazines. In

August 1924, the satirist H. L. Mencken, about to launch a new magazine, *American Mercury* (published by Alfred A. Knopf), wrote to Boas to ask him for a piece: "I am preparing to set up a new monthly review in New York, and turn to you in the hope that I may interest you in it. Its scope will be rather wider than that of the existing reviews—it will attempt to cover the sciences as well as politics and the fine arts—, and, whatever its failings otherwise, it will at least avoid the defect of dulness [*sic*]. Its general position will be a common-sense one, and it will try to avoid both the utopianism of the so-called Liberals and the ignorant intransigence of the newspapers. Perhaps I may describe it by saying that almost any part of your 'Mind of Primitive Man' would fit into it admirably. Are you engaged upon any work that would fit into such a publication?" Franz certainly was—as ever. The piece that emerged out of this commission was "Question of Racial Purity" in the October issue. Herskovits tells us that, in 1926, Boas published in the *Frankfurter Zeitung* a piece with the same title in German, "Die Frage der Rassenreinheit." In 1931, the year in which he was made president of the AAAS, he received an honorary doctorate in medicine from his alma mater, the University of Kiel, fifty years after having obtained his PhD there: his talk was entitled "Rasse und Kultur," race and culture. Now was not a time to let go of the topic. He failed at first to find a publisher for it; it made "no sense printing it in a so-called liberal journal," given that those he wanted to reach "would not read it," and periodicals of another stripe "would not take it." In the end, Gustav Fischer published it in 1932 as a pamphlet.[59]

Of course Boas was not the only German Jewish intellectual engaged in fighting "the aberrations of our time"—the words he used in a letter he wrote in January 1925 to the great cultural theorist and art historian Aby Warburg. He was writing in response to a request from Aby, sent a month earlier, to help the latter with the acquisition of the latest American literature in ethnology, and in which he encouraged Boas to continue supporting German scholars, deploring the mounting racial prejudice in Germany. In 1920, Boas had founded the Emergency Society for German and Austrian Science and Art (ESGASA) to counteract the spread of prejudice that was accompanying the "gradual paralysis of intellectual life." Boas wrote that "racial prejudices seem at the present time to be epidemic all over the world." The two men came from different backgrounds—Aby was a son of Hamburg bankers—but from similar cultures, that is, the *Bildung*-informed world of secular German Jews. Aby's extraordinary library, the Kulturwissenschaftliche Bibliotek Warburg (KBW), based in his native Hamburg, would, after it was shipped to London from Nazi Germany in 1933, become the Warburg Institute. (Part of the University of London since 1945, it is still flourishing today—and it is the alma mater of the present author.) Franz and Aby started corresponding early, in 1895, after they had met in New York that fall, when Aby was there for the wedding of one of his brothers, Paul. (He married into the Kuhn, Loeb & Co. banking family. Another brother, Felix, had also married into that family. American money helped sustain the KBW and its substantial acquisitions—as well as the efforts of the ESGASA.) Aby soon fled the world of the New York financial elites, though, and took off on a major ethnological trip to Colorado, Arizona, and New Mexico. In May 1896, he attended the Hopi snake dance in Orayvi, later writing about it. He would henceforth develop anthropological methods in his own works. When he moved to Berlin in June 1896, he met Boas's friend von den Steinen. It is clear that Franz mattered to—and influenced—Aby, more than the converse: as Aby wrote to him in late 1896, Franz had "graciously afforded scientific advice concerning my Indian plans." Their correspondence stopped then, only resuming in 1924, after Franz had made a trip to Hamburg. Aby was the one to kick it off, with a long letter in which, among other things, he wrote: "We stumbled into this terrible World War in no small part because we were lulled into a foolish sense of security by the belief that racial characteristics somatically guarantee something mental, from which we now might well awaken."[60]

The two sporadically kept in touch until Warburg's death in 1929, when Fritz Saxl wholly took charge of the institute. In the summer of 1935, Franz wrote to Saxl, inquiring about materials the institute might provide on the topic of gesture.[61] Aby had long researched the expression of emotion over the centuries, inter alia through gesture and through the representation of emotional gesture in arifacts. He too was interested in the human mind and in how it represented itself—in the continuity one could find within historical and geographical spaces, and the unity one could find in variation. Franz told Saxl about his study of immigrant gestures, which he was conducting in collaboration with an Argentinian student of his, David Efron, and with an artist called Stuyvesant Van Veen, who had also produced illustrations for Boas's Kwakwaka'wakw studies: together they examined "gestures as used by immigrants and their gradual disappearance in the second generation," showing, for example, that the gestures of Jews and Italians blended over time. Assimilation happened fast. Efron would go on to publish this study's results in 1941 as *Gesture and Environment*. Earlier, in 1926, Boas had conducted an unpublished study in which freshmen students were asked to identify one another's ethnicity; one of the outcomes was that 40 percent of the Italians in a New York college were identified as Jews and vice versa.[62] Gestural styles were culturally, not racially, determined—contrary to what Nazis, of course, liked to believe.

Resistance against the forces of obscurantism was hard. But Boas did not and would not give up. There was too much to combat. The emotionally integrated rationality he believed in against the odds, that old *Herzensbildung*, was still alive within him, and it continued to inform all his writings, along with his repeated attempts to show the importance of skepticism contra dogmatism, and observation contra generalizing judgment. On October 9, 1930, he wrote to the banker Max Warburg—one of the late Aby's brothers—in response to "the question you asked me on the evening of the reception in the Warburg Library. In my opinion the only sound way to combat race prejudice is to make the pseudoscientific basis of the theory untenable. I do not believe that propaganda and publicity methods will help much because their first results will always be counter-propaganda."[63] In 1930, he was still firm in his belief that one could take off the *Kulturbrille* and combat irrationalism with reason, not emotional manipulation. This changed as the war approached. As Julia Liss observes, "The invention of the word *racism* to mean an ideology of race differences linked to inferiority and superiority, in contrast to *racialism* and *race prejudice*, is indicative of the logic of the war years."[64] On September 11, 1936, he wrote to Elsie Clews Parsons: "Unfortunately, you cannot attack emotion by reason and all we can hope for is to gain influence over those who have not yet fallen victims to the passionate beliefs of the time." It was "an almost hopeless fight." And yet, "this is no reason to give up the fight and to supply at least ammunition to those who know best how to use it."[65]

And so Boas continued on his road. In 1937, two years after the Nuremberg Race Laws were enacted in Germany, Boas sat down to be interviewed, along with his students, by journalist Joseph Mitchell for the *New York World-Telegram*. (Mitchell had begun writing for the *New Yorker* in 1933.) The process would have a transformative impact on Mitchell, turning the workaday journalist he had been into the writer he became. (Mitchell would begin writing for the *New Yorker* in 1928.) The interview was initiated by Jack Sargent Harris, a doctoral student with Ruth Benedict, Ralph Linton, and Alexander Lesser who was also working as an assistant to Boas on the research into immigrant gestures. In the introduction of a recent printing of this interview, anthropologist Robert Brightman cites a description of the interviews from the biography of Mitchell by Thomas Kunkel:

> As the two men settled into conversation, the reporter began to realize that Boas was paying more attention to him than to his questions, essentially an anthropologist observing a curious specimen—the New York newspaperman. Boas was becoming increasingly engaged—"not in me," Mitchell explained, "but in my ignorance." As Boas tried to explain his research principles, he suddenly told Mitchell, "Read this," and handed him a copy of *Anthropology and Modern Life*, which Mitchell would in fact read, and he "began telling me how to look at the world. He said, 'Don't take anything for granted, don't take yourself for granted, or your father.'" Mitchell was exhilarated by it all. He would remember coming away from the experience "feeling born again."[66]

The ability to look and listen was precisely what was being crushed in those darkening years. And Boas knew how much this ability had to be cultivated: the very principles at work in scientific inquiry were those that enabled a decent, open society to exist. The misuse of science to the ends of injustice and oppression was insufferable. Pragmatic as ever, Boas did not just put those principles to use in the formation of ideas, whether scientific or political: he continued to employ the tactical and organizational skills instrumental in setting up organizations that promoted such principles. His actions coherently followed his words. Although he was physically weakened and exhausted—his heart was fragile, as may have been the case with his father—nothing stopped him, and his academic work continued apace. He published relentlessly, as he would until the very end. Over the late 1930s, he revised *The Mind of Primitive Man* for its third edition, published his collected scientific papers, the third volume of the *Handbook of American Indian Languages*, and the *Kwakiutl Tales*. The collective volume he edited, *General Anthropology*, was published in 1938, including chapters by Lowie and

Bunzel, among others. In 1940, he published his collected essays, *Race, Language and Culture*.

The nativist passions he had been arguing against for his whole life were set to become official policy when Hitler was elected chancellor in 1933. Franz had taken what would be his last trip to Germany in 1932. On March 27, 1933, he published an open letter to President von Hindenburg protesting Hitler's appointment, declaring his solidarity with the German victims of antisemitism. He said of himself that he was "of Jewish descent but in my thoughts, in my heart and in my head, I am German." Paul Rivet helped Boas publish his letter in the French papers, as did philosopher and sociologist Lucien Lévy-Bruhl, whom Boas had met in Paris in 1929 at a meeting of the Société française de philosophie, and with whom he had been conducting a constructive debate over their disagreements about the notion of the "primitive": Lévy-Bruhl identified such a thing as a primitive mind, mostly "pre-logical."

As a direct result of the open letter, Boas's Kiel doctorate was rescinded. The very man who had nominated him for it— the director of the Anthropological Institute at Kiel, an embryologist and anthropologist named Otto Aichel—was incensed: "The Jews in Germany have presumed a part of Germany to which they are not entitled at all. . . . The government considers its duty to clean up all bad things, even the bad elements among your fellows." He accused Boas of "feeding the exorbitant propaganda against Germany" with this letter.[67] On the square before the university, the Nazis burned his *Rasse und Kultur*, the text based on the speech he gave there in 1931 when he received his honorary doctorate, among his other books, and they also burned the works of Einstein, Freud, Rosa Luxembourg, Lenin, Trotsky, and many others. According to Marxist social anthropologist Bernhard J. Stern, "This act only served to give a wider audience to Boas' views," as Boas himself knew—he asked his publishers to "use this opportunity for advertising the book again in an adequate way. I should imagine that it would have a big sale.[68] When told that his books were removed from the library, he said, reported the *New York Times*, "If they do not want to read, that is their own lookout. If people want to be crazy, what can you do about it?"[69] "Removed," as indeed there persisted some uncertainty as to whether the books had been burned. *Science* reported them removed. (In 1937, Boas affirmed that his books had been "confiscated," only "burned" in newspaper reports.) On May 10, 1933, the *Columbia Daily Spectator* reported: "The Professor said he found it most amusing that only a year and a half ago, the University of Kiel thought him sufficiently deserving of an honorary doctor's degree. That same school will be the site of the text burning. 'They can have their degree back, if they want it,' the eminent anthropologist remarked with an abrupt wave of his hand."[70]

On March 4, 1934, along with his friend Maurice Fishberg and the Yale anthropogeographer Ellsworth Huntington, he gave a talk entitled "Aryan and Semite, with Particular References to Nazi Racial Dogmas" to the Judaeans and the Jewish Academy of Arts and Sciences. In June 1934 he published a pamphlet in German, *Arien und nicht Arien*, in what one might later, in Soviet times, call "samizdat" form—"distributed by the anti-Nazi underground," as Herskovits reported, "printed on tissue-thin paper, the better to be concealed as it was passed surreptitiously from hand to hand." It was soon translated into English as *Aryans and Non-Aryans*, as well as into Spanish, and rapidly reprinted several times. Herskovits writes, "Of everything he wrote," this was the publication that "achieved perhaps the widest circulation."[71] Here Franz synthesized yet again the arguments against biological racism: "The attempt that is being made by those who are in power in Germany to justify on scientific grounds their attitude toward the Jews is built on a pseudo-science. No one has ever proved that a human being, through his descent from a certain group of people, must of necessity have certain mental characteristics. A nation is not to be defined by its descent but by its language and customs. Otherwise Germans, Frenchmen, and Italians would not be nationalities. Language and customs are determined far more by their environment in which the child grows up than by its descent, because the physical attributes, so far as they have any influence at all, occur with extraordinary variety within each group."[72] Those who were already convinced otherwise were unlikely to pay much attention to these arguments, but the ideas were worth repeating, and Franz did so, with what Glick calls his "accustomed faith in the power of rationalism to triumph over clannish hatreds and prejudices."[73]

He would use the same words in the summer of 1937 at the session "Race and Racism" of the International Population Congress in Paris—he was invited there by Rivet, its vice president. Boas had published two articles in *Races et racisme*, a journal Rivet launched in 1937 with the Groupement d'étude et d'information races et racisme, and that would be published bimonthly until 1939. For a long time these would remain Boas's only French publications. His 1910–11 study *Changes in the Bodily Forms of Descendants of Immigrants* had not been well received by the French physical anthropologists at the time, and now "at stake was not anthropologists' debate about the accuracy or relevance of measured individual differences. The challenge thrown down by Nazi race scientists demanded a more positive reception of Boas's study." His voice was urgently needed: Rivet knew that, hence his invitation, in response to Boas's expressed wish to take part.[74] Boas's turn to speak came after the convinced eugenicist Osborn stepped up to the podium, followed by talks by members of the German delegation, including eugenicist Ernst Rüden's "The Eugenics of Mental Disease," which advocated "the sterilization of all persons known to be affected by a hereditary disease." These speakers were invited precisely to set up a confrontation between eugenics and the evidence Boas, as well as Rivet and his group, marshalled against its tenets—for instance, that gestures were modified in the descendants of immigrants in America. His concluding words were that "racial descent" had no part to play in "habits of life and cultural activities." In fact, the very notion of a "race" being of any import was "at best a poetic and dangerous fiction."[75] Ruth Benedict described the event in a letter to Jules Henry (who had been a doctoral student with her and Franz): "When the first Nazi got up, Papa Franz rose to his feet at the end of five minutes and interrupted from the floor that this was propaganda and had no place in a scientific meeting; he moved that the oration be ruled out. And the congress sustained him. So the Nazis were foiled, and of course Papa Franz filled with a great soothing sense of accomplishment. The old war horse!"[76]

We humans adapt to our environments, but we are the product of these adaptations, embedded within the world, in constant, dynamic interaction with it. We create our own categories: they don't exist in nature. The notion that these adaptations constitute genetic constants and separate kinds is entirely wrong—and, of course, dangerous. It has resulted in the suffering and death of millions. It still results in misery and wars across the world. Boas, as King observes, realized that "the ideology that would have sealed his own fate as a Jew, an immigrant, and a dissident intellectual—Nazism—rested on a set of pseudoscientific foundations that had a decidedly American stamp." This pseudoscience, used to justify first slavery, then segregation in America, had been very successfully exported to Germany.

In 1938, Boas convened the University Federation for Democracy and Intellectual Freedom to gather scientists against Nazi fascism. The group produced the "Manifesto on Freedom in Science." Signed by Einstein and Oppenheimer, inter alia, the manifesto was widely publicized, including in *Time* magazine and *Science*. The *Harvard Crimson* reported on December 13, 1938: "Thirty-nine Harvard science professors, assistant professors and instructors, were among the 1,284 American scientists who signed a manifesto made public yesterday which declared that the defence of democracy is the sole means of preserving intellectual freedom and insuring scientific progress." Its "spokesman . . . , Franz Boas, professor of Anthropology, emeritus, at Columbia, said the manifesto was based on a resolution of the [AAAS] which stated that science was wholly independent of national boundaries, and 'races and creeds can flourish only when there is peace and intellectual freedom. . . . The thousands of teachers and scientists who have been exiled since Hitler came into power bear testimony to the incompatibility of Fascism and science,' Boas continued. The manifesto extended Boas' statement: 'Any attack upon freedom of thought in one sphere, even as non-political a sphere as theoretical physics, is an attack on democracy itself.'"[77] Out of this, Boas created the Lincoln's Birthday Committee for Democracy and Intellectual Freedom, announced at the Waldorf Astoria Hotel on February 12, 1939—Lincoln's birthday. Its principles were "to protect and extend intellectual freedom, to strengthen our precious heritage of American democracy, to combat propaganda for racial and religious discrimination and intolerance, to help make our schools fortresses of democracy."[78] It then expanded to become the American Committee for Democracy and Intellectual Freedom (ACDIF). Boas was its president, and the great classical scholar Moses Finkelstein was its executive secretary.

Education and communication were, then as now, crucial. Boas launched a public radio series, *On Democracy and Freedom of Thought*, advocating free education as the way to attain "freedom of the mind" and condemn "regimentation of thought by authoritarian commands or by intolerant majorities."[79] On July 17, 1939, the *New York Times* announced the campaign run by the ACDIF: "Schools Rebuked on Racial Errors: Prof. Boas Charges Many Use Textbooks That Support Nazi Doctrines—Leaders Seek Remedies—Educators, Scientists, Clergy and Book

Houses Back Information Drive." Boas reported that 66 percent of 166 school textbooks "misuse the concept of 'race' in
one way or another," teaching "what amounts to Nazi doctrines
about superior and inferior races." What instead needed to be
taught, he stated, was that "race involves the inheritance of similar physical variations by large groups of mankind, but its psychological and cultural connotations, if they exist, have not been
ascertained by science. Anthropology provides no scientific basis
for discrimination against any people on the ground of racial inferiority, religious affiliation, or linguistic heritage."[80] The ACDIF
published its pamphlet, which was widely endorsed by academ-
ics, scholars, and writers. A few days before the newspaper article appeared, Finkelstein had written to the important geneticist J.B.S. Haldane about Boas's heading a group of experts to
create a pamphlet

> directed against unscientific race teaching in American school
> textbooks. . . . We feel that it is an issue that is worthy of at-
> tention at the International Genetics Congress next month.
>   Mr. Arthur Steinberg [geneticist] of Columbia Univer-
> sity is going to attend the Congress, and he would like to talk
> to you about the pamphlet and the broad campaign which
> we have in mind.[81]

Science had to be taught and understood as an urgent priority.
The science of genetics, in particular, had to be communicated
without being twisted to serve the interests of eugenics.

And people urgently had to be rescued. Boas was involved in
the Emergency Committee in Aid of Displaced Foreign Scholars to find employment for refugee German scholars in American institutions, formed in 1933 mostly with financial support
from the Rockefeller Foundation and, among others, the Jewish Joint Distribution Committee. He helped students obtain
scholarships at American universities by having a good hundred scientists and scholars appeal to university presidents to

welcome "refugees from Fascist countries and from sections of democratic countries under Fascist control."[82] Then there were the scholars—Jewish or not. Lowie played a central role in bringing Claude Lévi-Strauss to the United States when the latter requested to join the New School for Social Research, having escaped to the south of France after the armistice. As he wrote to Lowie, he had acknowledged in his *Tristes tropiques* that Lowie's *Primitive Society* was the text that had turned him into an anthropologist. The Swiss anthropologist Alfred Métraux, now at Yale, had been "very favorably impressed" with the young Lévi-Strauss when they had met earlier in Brazil. The latter finally arrived in New York after a ten-week journey via Martinique and Puerto Rico—where he was placed under arrest in an "austere hotel" while awaiting papers from the New School and the arrival of an FBI official who could read French.[83] He started at the Free French University of the New School on November 11, 1941. He was soon joined there by the Russian linguist Roman Jakobson, who had escaped to the United States after years of wandering, and through whom Lévi-Strauss had met Boas in New York. Boas and Jakobson had befriended each other, and Franz was highly interested in his novel linguistics.

For a while, Franz worried about his old friend and accomplice Rivet—as did Lévi-Strauss. He had actively tried to locate him and to help provide financial help, notably through Nelson Rockefeller. Like Boas, Rivet had been fearlessly, publicly active against fascism. He had been the president since its founding in 1934 of the Comité de vigilance des intellectuels antifascistes. Having set up his Musée de l'homme in 1938, he had left France in June 1939, with his wife, for a field trip in South America. He then returned alone in October 1939 to take care of the museum, a month after the war had begun. The Nazis invaded France on June 14, 1940. On that very day, he published an open letter against Pétain: "France is not with you." He then opened his museum to show his dissent. It became the base for the Résistance network he established. (His colleagues in France would be assassinated in February 1942.) He was nearly arrested, but managed to escape to Bogotà, where he was as active as Boas, taking part in the founding of the Institute for Colombian Ethnology and of an ethnographic museum.[84]

The battle to help those in urgent need was in full swing. But in his own life, too, Boas had to confront opposition and difficulty. He had been emeritus professor since June 1936: President Butler, who had never been a supporter of his, had asked him in November 1935 to retire by then, not letting him do so on his own terms. It was a difficult moment, and another one of those instances of bureaucratic unpleasantness Franz had so often confronted from a young age. He had postponed retirement a few times before because, despite its prestige and importance, the department remained financially insecure, and without him at the helm, positions were at risk of being abolished. In 1931, he had tried hiring both Sapir and Kroeber when two positions had opened, but they had refused—he was disappointed, but he understood. And so he had carried on. He also needed his salary—it stood then at $12,000 a year—in order to support his sisters and their families, who had left Germany. (Annie was in Rio, Toni in New York.) Now, much to his dismay, his income was halved with his retirement. In March 1936, Karl Llewellyn, a professor of law, defended Boas in a letter to the trustees, protesting his being retired on half salary—given that Dewey, for one, had retired at full salary in 1930. He ended his letter, cited by Zumwalt, with words worth reporting here: "The man who made American Anthropology, who (with subsidies from the University cut off) still kept research going, who fought for German scholars during the suicide period of inflation, who—when his own kind had gone Hitlerite—took it on the jaw, and settled down to helping refugees—and disinterested science. And re-

mained, despite twenty years of these stresses, a scholar whom
no man can meet, without a secret sense of shame: because Boas
is the scholar a man might *hope* to be."[85]

But all Butler and the trustees gave him was the emeritus
title and the right to keep his office, to which he went twice a
week. Ruth Benedict, his heir apparent, was acting as interim
chair at the time of his retirement, and the Boasians all counted
on her taking over the chair permanently. Instead, in 1938 Butler placed Ralph Linton, much disliked by the department, in
the position. He had left Columbia for Harvard for his studies,
had never been fond of Boas, and was even less so of Benedict.
Her student Sidney Mintz reported that whenever Linton referred to her, "it was always with a good deal of animus. He
would occasionally boast publicly that he had killed her, and he
produced for me, in a small leather pouch, the Tanala material
he said he had used to kill Ruth Benedict." Apparently he feared
that she had "bewitched" him.[86] The appointment vastly soured
the atmosphere, creating factionalism within the department.
Once in position, Linton may well have assisted the FBI in opening its file on Boas and what it viewed as his possibly "Communist" circle in 1937.

Of course, the university department was not— indeed, is
not ever—the world, where Boas remained appreciated, respected, loved, and celebrated. On the occasion of his eighty-
first birthday, on July 9, 1939, he received about two hundred
birthday greetings—including a letter from President Roosevelt
and one from Einstein. For his eighty-third in 1941, there was
a telegram from Charlie Chaplin congratulating him for his
"many and great scientific achievements," and Orson Welles
sent a telegraphed message: "Terribly sorry to miss any occasion
honoring Doctor Boas."[87] None of this mattered to Butler, who
demanded that Boas leave the office by the winter of 1941–42,
also removing his title of professor emeritus. An arrangement
was found for Boas to use one room, to which he moved, and

where reportedly the space was so crammed that he could not find his files when he needed them—he tried to distribute his massive materials among libraries, and contemplated creating microfiches. Meanwhile, as he continued to struggle to find adequate funding sources, his colleagues and friends gathered forces to sustain him. He still had much to do.

Granted, he was tired and in ill health. In December 1939, he confessed to Ruth Benedict: "I feel that I am aging very rapidly. It began in the summer of 1938. My heart is very irregular and fast and I am physically weak. Walking, even a short distance, makes me short of breath."[88] And there were significant losses. Edward Sapir had died on February 4, 1939, Alexander Goldenweiser on July 6, 1940—young and suddenly—Elsie Clews Parsons on December 19, 1941, during surgery for appendicitis. Boas wrote in her obituary how much anthropology owed to her, and that "the memory of her devotion to her ideals will live on among us and lead us to emulate her example, intolerant towards ourselves, tolerant towards others, disdainful of all selfish pettiness and truthful in thought and action."[89]

But Franz was indefatigable, his energy intact. He remained as busy as ever, with increasing urgency while the war raged, and as he felt himself aging quickly. He never stopped his research—he was working on the Kwakwaka'wakw grammar and dictionary at this stage as well. Yet he still needed money. In July 1942, he wrote to Max Warburg to ask for financial help: the Columbia Council for Research in the Social Sciences did not cover all his secretarial costs, and the American Jewish Committee had stopped supporting him, apparently because he had not expressed himself with regard to Russia. On this matter, Boas wrote to Max Warburg, "I might say that my own judgment in regard to the suppression of scientific freedom in Russia was well known. As a matter of fact in Russian scientific journals I have been attacked because I have refused to have Marxian philosophy be my guide in scientific work."[90] He had never let any ideology guide his work—trying, on the contrary, to show how science could help us understand the world. Inevitably, now, he was devoting increasing amounts of time to his political engagement. Between 1940 and 1942, while the FBI was keeping close track of his life, he would write about fifteen hundred letters, a good two-thirds of which concerned political and social issues.[91]

Paul Rivet arrived in New York in December 1942. A luncheon was organized for him on December 19 at the Park Lane Hotel, cosponsored by the Latin American Refugee Fund. Rivet and Boas hadn't seen each other in five years. They were delighted to meet again. Franz sat at the speakers' table. Two days later, Franz hosted another luncheon to honor his friend, at the Columbia Faculty Club. Before setting out to the club, he had apparently dictated three letters and made some appointments for the next week. He also had a meeting with a parole officer to discuss the fate of a freedom fighter who had been jailed. He then went off to the Faculty Club.

December 21, 1942, was an exceptionally cold day, and Franz, Lévi-Strauss later wrote, sported "an astonishing faded fur hat that must have dated back to his travels among the Inuit."[92]

As Rivet recounts it, after he and Boas had recalled their first meeting in Paris, Franz told him "with his firm conviction: 'One shouldn't cease to repeat that racism is a monstrous error or an impudent lie,' and with a flash of prideful mischief he added: 'The Nazis themselves recently had to recognize the accuracy of the facts that I have found with the European immigrants to America.' Without a cry, without a complaint, we saw him tip backwards, a few groans, and a great brain had ceased to think." Linton, in a letter to Kroeber, recalled that the company had finished the main course and that "Dr. Boas was sitting back with a cigarette and a glass of wine." Lévi-Strauss was translating what Franz had told Rivet when "Boas straightened up and fell over backward." Lévi-Strauss recounts that "in mid-sentence, Boas jerked violently backwards, as under the effect of an electric shock and fell over, taking his chair with him. I was sitting next to him and hurried to help him up, but he remained motionless. Rivet, who had been an army medical officer, tried in vain to revive him; he was only able to pronounce him dead." Franz had suffered a massive heart attack, just as had happened with his father.[93]

It was a death in the midst of life, surrounded by friends, buoyed by purpose. It was also a death in the midst of war. December 1942 was cold not only in New York. Across the ocean, it was one of the coldest winters of the century, permeating one of the darkest periods of history. Boas had never stopped believing in light—precisely because nothing was fixed, nothing predictable, nothing invariable. He had always struggled with those who did not see what he saw. He had always been impatient with those who did not let him do his work. But he manifested infinite patience in trying to help people see their own shackles, their *Kulturbrille*, for what they were, showing how the natural mechanisms of apperception and habituation took hold in all cultures, all places, all landscapes. "Anthropology, the science of man, is often held to be a subject that may satisfy our curiosity regarding the early history of mankind, but of no immediate bearing upon problems that confront us," he had written in the preface to *Race, Language and Culture* on November 29, 1939. "This view has always seemed to me erroneous. Growing up in our own civilization we know little how we ourselves are conditioned by it, how our bodies, our language, our modes of thinking and acting are determined by limits imposed upon us by our environment. Knowledge of the life processes and behavior of man under conditions of life fundamentally different from our own can help us to obtain a freer view of our own lives and of our life problems." He remained convinced that understanding—of oneself and of the other—was possible, and through it, change. This is his legacy, transmitted not only to his students and disciples but also to those who may never have heard his name. One can open minds and open hearts. This is the wisdom gleaned by anthropological work. There is darkness, but there is always light.

Introduction

1. Charles King, *Gods of the Upper Air: How a Circle of Renegade Anthropologists Reinvented Race, Sex, and Gender in the Twentieth Century* (New York: Doubleday, 2019).

2. Douglas Cole, *Franz Boas: The Early Years, 1858–1906* (Seattle: University of Washington Press, 1999).

3. Rosemary Lévy Zumwalt, *Franz Boas: The Emergence of the Anthropologist* (Lincoln: University of Nebraska Press, 2019), and *Franz Boas: Shaping Anthropology and Fostering Social Justice* (Lincoln: University of Nebraska Press, 2022). Henceforth cited as Zumwalt 1, and Zumwalt 2, respectively.

4. Han F. Vermeulen, *Before Boas: The Genesis of Ethnography and Ethnology in the German Enlightenment* (Lincoln: University of Nebraska Press, 2015).

5. Margaret Mead, *Growing Up in New Guinea: A Comparative Study of Primitive Education* (New York: Blue Ribbon Books, 1930), 2.

6. See April H. Bailey, Joshua Knobe, and George E. New-

man, "Value-based Essentialism: Essentialist Beliefs about Social Groups with Shared Values," *Journal of Experimental Psychology* 50, no. 10 (2021): 1994–2014.

7. Franz Boas, "Psychological Problems in Anthropology," in *A Franz Boas Reader: The Shaping of American Anthropology, 1883–1911*, ed. George W. Stocking Jr. (1974; repr., Chicago: University of Chicago Press,1982), 243–54 (243).

8. Franz Boas, "The Limitations of the Comparative Method of Anthropology," *Science*, n.s. 4, no. 103 (1896): 901–8 (905).

9. Boas, "Psychological Problems in Anthropology," 243.

10. Lewis Henry Morgan, *Ancient Society: Researches in the Lines of Human Progress from Savagery through Barbarism to Civilization* (London: MacMillan, 1877).

11. King, *Gods of the Upper Air*, 65.

12. Franz Boas, *Anthropology: A Lecture Delivered at Columbia University in the Series on Science, Philosophy and Art, December 18th, 1907* (New York: Columbia University Press, 1908), 16, and in Stocking, *A Franz Boas Reader*, 267–81 (274).

13. See Katherina Kinzel, "Wilhelm Windelband," in *The Stanford Encyclopedia of Philosophy*, ed. Edward N. Zalta (2021), https://plato.stanford.edu/archives/sum2021/entries/wilhelm-windelband/.

14. See James W. McAllister, "Common Sense and the Difference between Natural and Human Sciences," *Inquiry: An Interdisciplinary Journal of Philosophy*, August 7, 2023.

15. Anna Ciaunica, Axel Constant, Hubert Preissl, and Katerina Fotopoulou, "The First Prior: From Co-Embodiment to Co-Homeostasis in Early Life," *Consciousness and Cognition* 21 (May 2021): 113–17.

16. Clifford Geertz, *Local Knowledge: Further Essays in Interpretive Anthropology* (1983; repr., London: HarperCollins, 1993), 16.

17. Philippe Descola, *Par-delà nature et culture* (Paris: Gallimard, 2005).

18. Stephen Jay Gould, *The Hedgehog, the Fox, and the Magister's Pox: Mending the Gap between Science and the Humanities* (New York: Harmony Books, 2003), 108. For the full letter, see Charles Darwin to Henry Fawcett, September 18, 1861, in *Darwin Corre-*

spondence Project, "Letter no. 3257," https://www.darwinproject.ac .uk/letter/?docId=letters/DCP-LETT-3257.xml.

19. Florence Weber, *Brève histoire de l'anthropologie* (Paris: Flammarion, 2015).

20. Descola, *Par-delà nature et culture,* 103 (my translation).

21. Georges-Louis Leclerc, Comte de Buffon's *Histoire naturelle, générale et particulière, avec la description du Cabinet du Roi* appeared as a thirty-six-volume encyclopedia. The first three volumes were published in 1749: *De la manière d'étudier l'histoire naturelle: Théorie de la Terre, Histoire générale des animaux,* and *Histoire naturelle de l'homme.*

22. Descola, *Par-delà nature et culture,* 94–96.

23. Tim Ingold, "Anthropology contra Ethnography," *Hau: Journal of Ethnographic Theory* 7, no. 1 (2017): 21–26.

24. Ibid.

25. Wilhelm Max Wundt, *Völkerpsychologie: Eine Untersuchung der Entwicklungsgesetze von Sprache, Mythus und Sitte* (Leipzig: Verlag von Wilhelm Engelmann, 1900).

26. Adam Kuper, "Anthropology: Scope of the Discipline," in *The International Encyclopedia of Anthropology* (Hoboken, NJ: John Wiley & Sons, 2018), 6, https://onlinelibrary.wiley.com/doi/book /10.1002/9781118924396.

27. Adolf Bastian, *Ethnische Elementargedanken in der Lehre vom Menschen,* 2 vols. (Berlin: Weidmannsche Buchhandlung, 1895).

28. Franz Boas, "Advances in the Methods of Teaching: Discussion before the New York Meeting of the American Naturalists and Affiliated Societies," *Science,* n.s. 9 (1899): 93–96 (96), reprinted in Franz Boas, *Race, Language and Culture* (New York: Macmillan, 1940), 621–25 (624).

29. Boas, *Anthropology,* 6, and in Stocking, *A Franz Boas Reader,* 268.

30. Boas, *Anthropology,* 7.

1. From Physics to Geography

1. This chapter relies to a good extent on Douglas Cole, *Franz Boas: The Early Years, 1858–1906* (Seattle: University of Washing-

ton Press, 1999); and Rosemary Lévy Zumwalt, *Franz Boas: The Emergence of the Anthropologist* (Lincoln: University of Nebraska Press, 2019) (henceforth cited as Zumwalt 1), and on their use of the correspondence.

2. Franz Boas, "An Anthropologist's Credo," *Nation* 147 (1938): 201–4 (201), and in *A Franz Boas Reader: The Shaping of American Anthropology, 1883–1911*, ed. George W. Stocking Jr. (1974; repr., Chicago: University of Chicago Press,1982), 41–42 (41).

3. As retold by Carlo Ginzburg in "Lectures de Mauss," *Annales: Histoire, sciences sociales* 6 (November–December 2010): 1303–20.

4. See Cole, *Franz Boas*, 18–20. And see Herbert S. Lewis, "'Adapt Fully to Their Customs': Franz Boas as an Ethnographer among the Inuit of Baffinland (1883–84) and His Monograph *The Central Eskimo* (1888)," in *Ethnographers before Malinowski: Pioneers of Anthropological Fieldwork, 1870–1922*, ed. Frederico Delgado Rosa and Han F. Vermeulen (New York: Berghahn, 2022), 47–82 (48).

5. Cited in Zumwalt 1, 17.

6. Alexander von Humboldt, *Cosmos: A Sketch of a Physical Description of the Universe* (London: Henry G. Bohn, 1849), 1:5–6.

7. Franz Boas, "The Study of Geography," *Science* 9, no. 201 (1887): 137–41 (137).

8. Cited in Julia E. Liss, "German Culture and German Science in the Bildung of Franz Boas," in *Volksgeist as Method and Ethic: Essays on Boasian Ethnography and the German Anthropological Tradition*, ed. George Stocking (Madison: University of Wisconsin Press, 1996), 155–84 (167).

9. Ibid., 166.

10. Boas, "An Anthropologist's Credo," in Stocking, *A Franz Boas Reader*, 42.

11. Herbert S. Lewis, "The Individual and Individuality in Franz Boas's Anthropology and Philosophy," in *The Franz Boas Papers*, vol. 1: *Franz Boas as Public Intellectual—Theory, Ethnography, Activism*, ed. Regna Darnell, Michelle Hamilton, Robert L. A. Hancock, and Joshua Smith (Lincoln: University of Nebraska Press, 2015), 19–41 (21).

12. Cited in Zumwalt 1, 31.

13. Adam Kuper, *The Invention of Primitive Society: Transformations of an Illusion* (London: Routledge, 1988), 126.

14. Cited in Zumwalt 1, 58.

15. Cited in ibid., 46.

16. Letter from Franz to Reinhard, May 18, 1877, cited in Liss, "German Culture," 167–68.

17. Zumwalt 1, 51.

18. Liss, "German Culture," 170.

19. Zumwalt 1, 49, quoting a letter to Toni dated December 3, 1870.

20. For a list of the topics he was examined on, as he reported it in letters to his parents, see Zumwalt 1, 53.

21. Cited in ibid., 64.

22. Cited in Liss, "German Culture," 172.

23. Joseph S. Lappin, J. Farley Norman, and Flip Phillips, "Fechner, Information, and Shape Perception," *Attention, Perception, & Psychophysics* 73 (2011): 2353–78 (2353).

24. Gustav Fechner, *Elemente der Psychophysik*, 1 (Leipzig: Druck und Verlag von Breitkopf und Härtel, 1860), translated as *Elements of Psychophysics* by Helmut E. Adler, ed. Davis H. Howes and Edwin Garrigues Boring (New York: Holt, Rinehart & Winston, 1966), 8.

25. Cited in Lappin, Norman, and Phillips, "Fechner, Information, and Shape Perception," 2353.

26. Franz Boas, "Über eine neue Form des Gesetzes der Unterschiedsschwelle," *Pflüger's Archiv* 26 (1881): 493–500 (abstract).

27. See Michel Espagne, "Franz Boas et la pensée géographique," in *Franz Boas: Le travail du regard*, ed. Michel Espagne and Isabelle Kalinowski (Paris: Armand Colin, 2013).

28. Letter to Jacobi, January 2, 1882, cited in Zumwalt 1, 64.

29. Franz Boas, "On Alternating Sounds," *American Anthropologist*, n.s. 2 (1889): 47–53, also in Stocking, *A Franz Boas Reader*, 72–77.

30. Michael Mackert, "Franz Boas' Early Northwest Coast Alphabet," *Historiographia Linguistica* 26, no. 3 (1999): 273–94. From abstract: "He was particularly concerned with the accurate repre-

sentation of schwa, of different series of fricatives and stops, and of so-called synthetic or alternating sounds, which he encountered in the Native American languages of British Columbia. Both Boas and Hale [Horatio Hale (1817–1896), "who had been entrusted with the supervision of Boas' activities"] believed future work would not corroborate the existence of surd-sonants (voiceless-voiced sounds) as members of triple series of consonants consisting of surds, surd-sonants, and sonants. Boas did not deny the existence of surd-sonants, but, within his theory of phonetics, he considered them as sounds that were alternately apperceived as being voiced and voiceless. Boas' first version of his BAAS alphabet and his introductory remarks to the phonetics of the Native American languages described in his BAAS reports show that practical considerations (simplicity, readability, quotability, and availability of types) and Boas' psycholinguistic interpretation of surd-sonants took priority over the latter's concerns for an accurate scientific transcription system."

31. Cited in Zumwalt 1, 64.

32. See Herbert S. Lewis, "Who's Who in the Age of Boas: The Sponsors of Anthropological Papers Written in Honor of Franz Boas (1906)," in *Bérose—Encyclopédie internationale des histoires de l'anthropologie* (Paris: Bérose, 2020), n. 34.

33. Letter to Marie, May 29, 1883, cited in Zumwalt 1, 62.

34. Letter to Jacobi, January 2, 1882, cited in Zumwalt 1, 65, and in George W. Stocking, *Race, Culture, and Evolution: Essays in the History of Anthropology*, (1968; repr., Chicago: University of Chicago Press, 1982), chap. 7: "From Physics to Ethnology," p. 137.

35. Boas to Jacobi, April 12, 1882, Franz Boas Papers, American Philosophical Society, https://diglib.amphilsoc.org/islandora/object/text%3A67958.

36. Cited in Zumwalt 1, 68.

37. Cited in ibid.

38. Cited in ibid., 72.

39. Ibid., 72–73.

40. Carlotta Santini, "Can Humanity Be Mapped? Adolf Bastian, Friedrich Ratzel and the Cartography of Culture," *History of*

Anthropology Newsletter, December 6, 2018, https://histanthro.org /notes/can-humanity-be-mapped/. See also Han F. Vermeulen, *Before Boas: The Genesis of Ethnography and Ethnology in the German Enlightenment* (Lincoln: University of Nebraska Press, 2015), 379–80.

41. Zumwalt 1, 70–71.

42. Franz Boas, "Rudolf Virchow's Anthropological Work," *Science* 16 (1902): 441–45, in Stocking, *A Franz Boas Reader*, 35–41.

43. See Adam Kuper, "Anthropology: Scope of the Discipline," in *The International Encyclopedia of Anthropology*, ed. Hilary Callen (New York: John Wiley & Sons, 2018), 2.

44. George W. Stocking Jr., "Primitive Man in Evolutionary Anthropology," in *Race, Culture, and Evolution*, 114.

45. See Rainer Baehre, "Early Anthropological Discourse on the Inuit and the Influence of Virchow on Boas," *Études Inuit Studies* 32, no. 2 (2008): 13–34.

46. E. H. Ackerknecht and H. V. Vallois, *Franz Joseph Gall: Inventory of Phrenology and His Collection* (Madison: University of Wisconsin Medical School, 1956), 28–31, quoted in "Franz Josef Gall," https://grants.hhp.uh.edu/clayne/HistoryofMC/HistoryMC/Gall .htm.

47. See Friedrich Pöhl, "Assessing Franz Boas' Ethics in His Arctic and Later Anthropological Fieldwork," *Études Inuit Studies* 32, no. 2 (2008): 35–52.

48. Adolf Bastian, *Die humanistischen Studien in ihrer Behandlungsweise nach comparativ-genetischer Methode auf naturwissenschaftlicher Unterlage. Prolegomena zu einer ethnischen Psychologie* (Berlin: Ferdinand Dümmler, 1901), iii, cited in Santini, "Can Humanity Be Mapped?"

49. Adolf Bastian, *Die Denkschöpfung umgebender Welt aus kosmogonischen Vorstellungen in Cultur und Uncultur* (Berlin: Ferdinand Dümmler, 1896), cited in Santini, "Can Humanity Be Mapped?"

50. Cited in Santini, "Can Humanity Be Mapped?" quoting Karl Rosenkrantz, *Psychologie, oder, die Wissenschaft vom subjektiven Geist* (Königsberg: Gebrüder Bornträger, 1863).

51. Cited in Zumwalt 1, 73.

52. Ibid., 74.

53. See ibid., 76–77.

54. Cited in Santini, "Can Humanity Be Mapped?": see Adolf Bastian, "Die Stellung des Kaukasus innerhalb der geschichtlichen Völkerbewegungen," *Zeitschrift für Ethnologie* 4 (1872): 2.

55. See Santini, "Can Humanity Be Mapped?"

56. Cited in Santini, "Can Humanity Be Mapped?": see Ratzel, *Anthropogeographie*, vol. 2 (Stuttgart: J. Engelhorn, 1899), 615.

57. Cited in Zumwalt 1, 80.

58. Baehre, "Early Anthropological Discourse," 24.

59. Zumwalt 1, 81.

60. Ibid., 82.

61. Ibid., 91.

62. Ibid.

63. Ibid., 94.

2. From Geography to Anthropology

1. Franz Boas to Abraham Jacobi, May 2, 1883, Franz Boas Papers, American Philosophical Society, https://diglib.amphilsoc.org/islandora/object/text%3A68110.

2. See Rainer Baehre, "Early Anthropological Discourse on the Inuit and the Influence of Virchow on Boas," *Études Inuit Studies* 32, no. 2 (2008): 24.

3. Ludger Müller-Wille, ed., *Franz Boas among the Inuit of Baffin Island, 1883–1884: Journals & Letters,* trans. William Barr (1998; repr., Toronto: University of Toronto Press, 2016).

4. Cited in Kenn Harper, "The Collaboration of James Mutch and Franz Boas, 1883–1922," special issue, "Franz Boas and the Inuit," *Études Inuit Studies* 32, no. 2 (2008): 55.

5. Franz Boas, "An Anthropologist's Credo," *Nation* 147 (1938): 201–4 (201), and in *A Franz Boas Reader: The Shaping of American Anthropology, 1883–1911,* ed. George W. Stocking Jr. (1974; repr., Chicago: University of Chicago Press, 1982), 41–42 (opening paragraphs published here under the title "The Background of My Early Thinking").

6. Harper, "The Collaboration of James Mutch and Franz Boas," 108.

7. Cited in Douglas Cole and Ludger Müller-Wille, "Franz Boas' Expedition to Baffin Island, 1883–1884," *Études Inuit Studies* 8, no. 1 (1984): 54: *Petermanns Mitteilungen* (Perthes, 1885), 80:1–100.

8. Franz Boas, "A Journey in Cumberland Sound and on the West Shore of Davis Strait in 1883 and 1884," *Journal of the American Geographical Society of New York* 16 (1884): 242–72, and cited in Herbert S. Lewis, "'Adapt Fully to Their Customs': Franz Boas as an Ethnographer among the Inuit of Baffinland (1883–84) and His Monograph *The Central Eskimo* (1888)," in *Ethnographers Before Malinowski: Pioneers of Anthropological Fieldwork, 1870–1922*, ed. Frederico Delgado Rosa and Han F. Vermeulen (New York: Berghahn, 2022), 47–82 (54).

9. Franz Boas, "Polar Expedition of Charles Francis Hall," *Berliner Tageblatt*, September 4, 1883, cited in Herbert Lewis, "Boas in Baffinland," from Boas, *Arctic Expedition, 1883–1884: Translated German Newspaper Accounts of My Life with the Eskimos*, ed. Norman F. Boas and Doris W. Boas (private edition).

10. Franz Boas, "A Year among the Eskimo," *Journal of the American Geographical Society of New York* 19 (1887): 383–402, and printed in Stocking, *A Franz Boas Reader*, 44–45.

11. Franz Boas, *The Central Eskimo: Sixth Annual Report of the Bureau of Ethnology to the Secretary of the Smithsonian Institution, 1884–1885* (Washington, DC: Government Printing Office, 1888).

12. Charles King, *Gods of the Upper Air: How a Circle of Renegade Anthropologists Reinvented Race, Sex, and Gender in the Twentieth Century* (New York: Doubleday, 2019), 62.

13. Boas, "A Year among the Eskimo," in Stocking, *A Franz Boas Reader*, 44–55.

14. Rosemary Lévy Zumwalt, *Franz Boas: The Emergence of the Anthropologist* (Lincoln: University of Nebraska Press, 2019) (henceforth cited as Zumwalt 1), 117–18.

15. Franz Boas to Marie Krakowizer, February 19, 1884, cited in Müller-Wille, *Franz Boas among the Inuit of Baffin Island*, 185; and

Müller-Wille citation quoted in Friedrich Pöhl, "Assessing Franz Boas' Ethics in His Arctic and Later Anthropological Fieldwork," *Études Inuit Studies* 32, no. 2 (2008): 37–38.

16. Zumwalt 1, 118.

17. Lewis, "'Adapt Fully to Their Customs,'" 53, 52: "His professional ethnographic contributions are contained in his Habilitation thesis, *Baffin-Land: Geographische Ergebnisse* (1885, in German), more than a dozen journal articles, and the important monograph *The Central Eskimo* (1888)."

18. See Cole and Müller-Wille, "Franz Boas' Expedition to Baffin Island, 1883–1884," 52.

19. Cited in Zumwalt 1, 130.

20. As reported in Lewis, "'Adapt Fully to Their Customs,'" 65–66.

21. Müller-Wille, *Franz Boas among the Inuit of Baffin Island*, 173.

22. Ibid, 171.

23. Isaiah Lorado Wilner, "Transformation Masks: Recollecting the Indigenous Origins of Global Consciousness," in *Indigenous Visions: Rediscovering the World of Franz Boas*, ed. Ned Blackhawk and Isaiah Lorado Wilner (New Haven: Yale University Press, 2018), 7.

24. Zumwalt 1, 118–19. I rely on her account here and in the following paragraph.

25. Ibid., 121.

26. Ibid. 121–22.

27. Ibid., 143–44.

28. Cole, *Franz Boas*, 87.

29. Cole and Müller-Wille, "Franz Boas' Expedition to Baffin Island, 1883–1884," 59.

30. Cited in Cole, *Franz Boas*, 87.

31. Ibid., 96.

32. See Douglas Cole, "Franz Boas and the Bella Coola in Berlin," *Northwest Anthropological Research Notes* 16, no. 2 (Fall 1982): 119: Franz Boas, "Captain Jacobsen's Bella Coola Indians," *Berliner Tageblatt*, January 25, 1886.

33. Since he had lost his photographic plates, he included instead photographs of himself in Inuit garb, prosaically executed in a photo studio in Minden.

34. See Brooke Penaloza-Patzak, "An Emissary from Berlin: Franz Boas and the Smithsonian Institution, 1887–88," *Museum Anthropology* 41, no. 1 (2018): 30–45.

35. This account is based on Cole, *Franz Boas*, 98–100.

36. Cited in Stocking, *A Franz Boas Reader*, 87–88.

37. Ibid., 59–60.

38. Leonard Glick, "Types Distinct from Our Own: Franz Boas on Jewish Identity and Assimilation," *American Anthropologist* 84 (1982): 545–65 (548).

39. He used this expression "shackles of tradition" repeatedly, and notably as late as 1938, in the "Anthropologist's Credo" he published in the *Nation*. See also Cole, *Franz Boas*, 133.

40. Ronald P. Rohner, ed., *The Ethnography of Franz Boas: Letters and Diaries of Franz Boas Written on the Northwest Coast from 1886 to 1931*, trans. Hedy Parker (Chicago: University of Chicago Press, 1969). My account here cites from his "Letter-Diary to Parents" of 1886.

41. See Friedrich Pohl, "Assessing Franz Boas' Ethics in His Arctic and Later Anthropological Fieldwork," *Études Inuit Studies* 32, no. 2 (2008): 35–52.

42. Cited in Zumwalt 1, 167.

43. King, *Gods of the Upper Air*, 223.

44. Matthew Vollgraff, "Faustian Bargains: The Legends and Legacies of German 'Liberal Ethnology'" (review of H. Glenn Penny, *Im Schatten Humboldts: Eine tragische Geschichte der deutschen Ethnologie*, 2019), *History of Anthropology*, July 11, 2020.

45. Rohner, *The Ethnography of Franz Boas*, 76.

46. See Cole, *Franz Boas*, 123–27, for an analysis of the article.

3. Exploring Minds

1. George W. Stocking, "Dogmatism, Pragmatism, Essentialism, Relativism: The Boas/Mason Museum Debate Revisited," *History of Anthropology Newsletter* 21, no. 1 (June 1994): 3; Brooke

Penaloza-Patzak, "An Emissary from Berlin: Franz Boas and the Smithsonian Institution, 1887–88," *Museum Anthropology* 41, no. 1 (2018): 30–45 (34).

2. Penaloza-Patzak, "An Emissary from Berlin."

3. Stocking writes in "Dogmatism, Pragmatism, Essentialism, Relativism," 3–4: "On the one hand, Mason and Powell come across as pragmatic American democrats, appealing for a flexible, functional, utilitarian arrangement, holding theory lightly, accepting that there might be a variety of approaches and of audiences, and perhaps just a bit patronizing of the arrogant ethnographic novice, who, signing himself as 'Dr. Franz Boas,' wrapped himself in the authoritative mantle of Germanic scholarship. By contrast to the two merely initialed Americans (O. T. and J. W.), Boas does indeed [seem] more dogmatic, more insistent on getting practice articulated with correct theory, more inclined to justify his position by appeal to a particular authority (Adolph Bastian)—with his own authority marked in signature by what was at that time still a characteristically Germanic academic title."

4. Boas, "The Principles of Ethnological Classification," in *A Franz Boas Reader: The Shaping of American Anthropology, 1883–1911*, ed. George W. Stocking Jr. (1974; repr., Chicago: University of Chicago Press, 1982), 61–77 (62).

5. Herbert S. Lewis, "Boas, Darwin, Science, and Anthropology," *Current Anthropology* 42, no. 3 (June 2001): 387.

6. Herbert S. Lewis, "The Individual and Individuality in Franz Boas's Anthropology and Philosophy," in *The Franz Boas Papers*, vol. 1: *Franz Boas as Public Intellectual—Theory, Ethnography, Activism*, ed. Regna Darnell, Michelle Hamilton, Robert L. A. Hancock, and Joshua Smith (Lincoln: University of Nebraska Press, 2015), 23–24; and Franz Boas, Mss.B.B61.5, Franz Boas Papers, American Philosophical Society, Philadelphia.

7. Cole, *Franz Boas*, 129.

8. Lewis, "Boas, Darwin, Science, and Anthropology," 387.

9. Cole, *Franz Boas*, 129.

10. Lewis, "Boas, Darwin, Science, and Anthropology," 4, cit-

ing Mason's response from *Science* 9, 534–35; and Stocking, "Dogmatism, Pragmatism, Essentialism, Relativism," 5.

11. Stocking, "Dogmatism, Pragmatism, Essentialism, Relativism," 11.

12. Rosemary Lévy Zumwalt, *Franz Boas: The Emergence of the Anthropologist* (Lincoln: University of Nebraska Press, 2019) (henceforth cited as Zumwalt 1), 175–79.

13. For this and all quotes from Boas, see Ronald P. Rohner, ed., *The Ethnography of Franz Boas: Letters and Diaries of Franz Boas Written on the Northwest Coast from 1886 to 1931*, trans. Hedy Parker (Chicago: University of Chicago Press, 1969), 86–104.

14. Zumwalt 1, 182–83.

15. Ibid., 183.

16. Franz Boas, *Anthropology and Modern Life* (1928; repr., New York: Dover, 1986), 15.

17. Regna Darnell, "Franz Boas's Legacy of 'Useful Knowledge': The APS Archives and the Future of Americanist Anthropology," *Proceedings of the American Philosophical Society* 162, no. 1 (March 2018): 1–14 (13).

18. Boas, *Anthropology and Modern Life*, 15.

19. See Irene Candelieri, "'I Will Always Remain as a Physician . . . Hungering for Knowledge, Hungering for Understanding': Franz Boas's Psychophysics and Anthropology of Sound," ESPSS 2021 *Book of Abstracts*. See also Andreas Roepstorff, Jörg Niewöhnerc, and Stefan Beck, "Enculturing Brains through Patterned Practices," special issue, "Social Cognition: From Babies to Robots," *Neural Networks* 23, nos. 8–9 (2010): 1051–59.

20. Marian W. Smith, "Boas' 'Natural History' Approach to Field Method," in *The Anthropology of Franz Boas: Essays on the Centennial of His Birth*, ed. Walter Goldschmidt (Millwood, NY: American Anthropological Association, 1974), 46–60 (51).

21. Franz Boas, "On Alternating Sounds," *American Anthropologist*, n.s. 2 (1889): 47–53 (50). This view has been revived today with the notion that the brain is a predictive organ.

22. Charles Briggs and Richard Bauman, "'The Foundation of

All Future Researches': Franz Boas, George Hunt, Native American Texts, and the Construction of Modernity," *American Quarterly* 51, no. 3 (1999): 479–528 (479).

23. Cole, *Franz Boas,* 129.

24. Isaiah Lorado Wilner, "Transformation Masks: Recollecting the Indigenous Origins of Global Consciousness," in *Indigenous Visions: Rediscovering the World of Franz Boas,* ed. Ned Blackhawk and Isaiah Lorado Wilner (New Haven: Yale University Press, 2018), 6. He writes: "Making use of another people's masks as found objects, they code-switched Boas to their mnemonic logic, transmitting their messages to him. The embodied materialism of this meeting, in which ideas moved through masks, blankets, and even scars, accommodated Boas's German ideas about culture, for the ornate carvings of the Northwest Coast showed that this so-called 'primitive' people, in fact, possessed a richly developed civilization."

25. "Sigmund Freud and G. Stanley Hall: Exchange of Letters," *Psychoanalytic Quarterly* 29, no. 3 (1960), 307–16. The study is entitled *Adolescence: Its Psychology and Its Relations to Physiology, Anthropology, Sociology, Sex, Crime, Religion and Education.*

26. Cole, *Franz Boas,* 121–27.

27. Franz Boas, "Summary of the Work of the Committee in British Columbia," in *Report of the British Association for the Advancement of Science for 1898* (London, 1899), 667–82, reprinted in *A Franz Boas Reader: The Shaping of American Anthropology, 1883–1911,* ed. George W. Stocking Jr. (1974; repr., Chicago: University of Chicago Press, 1982); "Fieldwork for the British Association, 1888–1897," 92.

28. Ibid., 94–95.

29. Franz Boas, *The Mind of Primitive Man: A Course of Lectures Delivered before the Lowell Institute, Boston, Mass., and the National University of Mexico, 1910–1911* (1911; repr., New York: Macmillan, 1922), 163. See also the citation and analysis in William W. Speth, "The Anthropogeographic Theory of Franz Boas," *Anthropos* 73 (1978): 7–8.

30. Rohner, *The Ethnography,* 113.

31. Cole, *Franz Boas,* 141.

32. J. M. Tanner, "Boas' Contributions to Knowledge of Human Growth and Form," in Goldschmidt, *The Anthropology of Franz Boas*, 76–111.

33. Ibid., 76.

34. Ibid., 77, 78.

35. Ibid., 84.

36. Franz Boas, "Some Recent Criticisms of Physical Anthropology," *American Anthropologist*, n.s. 1 (1899): 98–106, cited in Tanner, "Boas' Contributions," 94–95.

37. Ibid., 82.

38. Cole, *Franz Boas*, 142–43.

39. Zumwalt 1, 200–202.

40. Ibid., 207.

41. Charles King, *Gods of the Upper Air: How a Circle of Renegade Anthropologists Reinvented Race, Sex, and Gender in the Twentieth Century* (New York: Doubleday, 2019), 213.

42. Ibid., 62.

43. Cole, *Franz Boas*, 152; Zumwalt 1, 217.

44. See Raymond Corbey, "Ethnographic Showcases, 1870–1930," *Cultural Anthropology* 8, no. 3 (1993): 338–69 (338).

45. King, *Gods of the Upper Air*, 62.

46. Cole, *Franz Boas*, 153.

47. Cited in Zumwalt 1, 158.

48. Cole, *Franz Boas*, 156. King, *Gods of the Upper Air*, 67, reminds us that here debuted the zipper, Juicy Fruit chewing gum, and Cream of Wheat breakfast cereal.

49. Cole, *Franz Boas*, 160.

50. Ibid., 235.

51. King, *Gods of the Upper Air*, 85.

52. Franz Boas, "Human Faculty as Determined by Race," in Stocking, *A Franz Boas Reader*, 221–42 (222).

53. Franz Boas, "The Cephalic Index," *American Anthropologist*, n.s. 1, no. 3 (July 1899): 448–61.

54. Boas, "Human Faculty as Determined by Race," 223.

55. Ibid., 242.

56. Franz Boas, *Anthropology: A Lecture Delivered at Columbia*

University in the Series on Science, Philosophy, and Art, December 18, 1907 (New York: Columbia University Press, 1908), 11, in Stocking, *A Franz Boas Reader,* 267–81 (271).

57. See Regna Darnell, "Mind, Body, and the Native Point of View: Boasian Theory at the Centennial of *The Mind of Primitive Man,*" in Darnell et al., *The Franz Boas Papers,* 3–17 (9).

58. Boas, "Human Faculty as Determined by Race," 228. See also Helen Leach, "Human Domestication Reconsidered," *Current Anthropology* 44, no. 3 (June 2003), 349–68.

59. Stocking, *A Franz Boas Reader,* 220. See also Julia E. Liss, "Diasporic Identities: The Science and Politics of Race in the Work of Franz Boas and W.E.B. Du Bois, 1894–1919," *Cultural Anthropology* 13, no. 2 (1998): 127–66.

60. George W. Stocking Jr., "Franz Boas and the Culture Concept in Historical Perspective," *American Anthropologist* 68 (1966): 867–82.

61. Rohner, *The Ethnography of Franz Boas,* 177–80, also cited in Zumwalt 1, 249.

62. See Curtis M. Hinsley Jr. and Bill Holm, "A Cannibal in the National Museum: The Early Career of Franz Boas in America," *American Anthropologist,* n.s. 78, no. 2 (June 1976): 306–16 (312).

63. See ibid. for the whole account.

64. Cole, *Franz Boas,* 201.

65. Cited in Zumwalt 1, 251.

66. See Stocking, *A Franz Boas Reader,* "Kathlamet Texts," 116, printed in *Bulletin n. 26, Bureau of American Ethnology* (Washington, DC: Government Printing Office, 1901), 5–7, 34–38.

67. Cole, *Franz Boas,* 166.

68. Ibid., 179.

69. Cited in Zumwalt 1, 244.

70. The book also contained 168 songs, 33 of which had scores. See Rainer Hatoum, "Franz Boas and George Herzog Recording of Kwakwaka'wakw Chief Dan Cranmer (1938)," Library of Congress, https://www.loc.gov/static/programs/national-recording-preservation-board/documents/Boas-Herzog_Recording-Dan-Cramer.pdf.

71. Cole, *Franz Boas*, 184.

72. Zumwalt 1, 261–62.

4. A New Field

1. Rosemary Lévy Zumwalt, *Franz Boas: The Emergence of the Anthropologist* (Lincoln: University of Nebraska Press, 2019) (henceforth cited as Zumwalt 1), 305.

2. See Charles King, *Gods of the Upper Air: How a Circle of Renegade Anthropologists Reinvented Race, Sex, and Gender in the Twentieth Century* (New York: Doubleday, 2019), 221.

3. Zumwalt 1, 304.

4. See George W. Stocking, "Franz Boas and the Founding of the American Anthropological Association," *American Anthropologist*, n.s. 62 (1960), 1–17. Stocking tells us that in 1899, the Anthropological Club merged with the American Ethnological Society, while in Washington, the Anthropological Society absorbed forty-nine members of the Women's Anthropological Society.

5. Cited in Zumwalt 1, 268.

6. Franz Boas, "The Limitations of the Comparative Method of Anthropology," *Science*, n.s. 4, no. 103 (1896): 901–8.

7. Christopher Brakken, "The Police Dance: Dissemination in Boas's Field Notes and Diaries, 1886–1894," in *The Franz Boas Papers*, vol. 1: *Franz Boas as Public Intellectual—Theory, Ethnography, Activism*, ed. Regna Darnell, Michelle Hamilton, Robert L. A. Hancock, and Joshua Smith (Lincoln: University of Nebraska Press, 2015), 43–64 (55).

8. Franz Boas, *The Mind of Primitive Man* (New York: Macmillan, 1922), 176–96.

9. See Kenn Harper, "The Collaboration of James Mutch and Franz Boas, 1883–1922," special issue, "Franz Boas and the Inuit," *Études Inuit Studies* 32, no. 2 (2008): 53–71 (58–59).

10. Zumwalt 1, 310.

11. Cited in Cole, *Franz Boas*, 188.

12. Cited in Zumwalt 1, 269.

13. Cited in Cole, *Franz Boas*, 189, and in Zumwalt 1, 270.

14. Cited in Zumwalt 1, 271. About *Globus*, see Kirsten Bel-

gum, "Popularizing the World: Karl Andree's 'Globus,'" *Colloquia Germanica* 460, no. 3 (2013): 245–65.

15. Zumwalt 1, 283–84.

16. Stanley A. Freed, Ruth S. Freed, and Laila Williamson, "Capitalist Philanthropy and Russian Revolutionaries: The Jesup North Pacific Expedition (1897–1902)," *American Anthropologist*, n.s. 90, no. 1 (March 1988): 7–24 (9). The article provides a full account of the Russian adventure.

17. See Herbert L. Lewis, "The Passion of Franz Boas," *American Anthropologist* 103, no. 2 (2001): 447–67 (455).

18. See Isabelle Kalinowski, "Franz Boas, le Musée d'histoire naturelle de New York et la galerie de Dresde," *Revue germanique internationale* 21 (2015): 113–32.

19. Freed, Freed, and Williamson, "Capitalist Philanthropy," 21.

20. Cole, *Franz Boas*, 218.

21. Ibid., 287.

22. Zumwalt 1, 305–11.

23. See Camille Joseph and Isabelle Kalinowski, "Franz Boas, une anthropologie de la variation," *La vie des idées* (Collège de France), September 4, 2020, https://laviedesidees.fr/Franz-Boas -une-anthropologie-de-la-variation. The authors refer to W. Gillies Ross, "George Comer, Franz Boas, and the American Museum of Natural History," *Études Inuit Studies* 8, no. 1 (1984): 145–64, and suggest that for Boas, an "objective" study was only possible on the basis of the largest possible number of objects, requesting from Comer about 140 of them. They write: "La saisie de traits pertinents présupposait en effet un travail de différenciation qui ne pouvait être accompli en l'absence d'un matériau suffisamment étendu pour autoriser des mises en relation, l'observation de constantes ou de variations, le repérage des facteurs cruciaux ou accessoires. L'anthropologue défendait le principe de collectes extensives, opérées 'sans discrimination,' au nom d'une prudence méthodologique interdisant à ce stade l'exercice prématuré de 'l'interprétation.'"

24. Zumwalt 1, 307; and Joseph and Kalinowski, "Franz Boas."

25. For a full account, see Zumwalt 1, 305–11.

26. Cole, *Franz Boas*, 242–51.

27. Ibid., 231–33.

28. See Ralph W. Dexter, "The Putnam-Kroeber Relations in the Development of American Anthropology," *Journal of California and Great Basin Anthropology* 11, no. 1 (1989): 91–96 (91).

29. Cole, *Franz Boas*, 232–33.

30. Ibid., 225–29.

31. *A Franz Boas Reader: The Shaping of American Anthropology, 1883–1911*, ed. George W. Stocking Jr. (1974; repr., Chicago: University of Chicago Press, 1982), 21.

32. Cole, *Franz Boas*, 236–37, and Stocking, *A Franz Boas Reader*, 285. See also Stocking, "Franz Boas and the Founding of the American Anthropological Association," 1–17.

33. Stocking, *A Franz Boas Reader*, 303–6.

34. Zumwalt 1, 301–4.

35. Stocking, *A Franz Boas Reader*, 242–51.

36. See Freed, Freed, and Williamson, "Capitalist Philanthropy," for the full account.

37. See Herbert S. Lewis, "Who's Who in the Age of Boas: The Sponsors of Anthropological Papers Written in Honor of Franz Boas (1906)," in *Bérose—Encyclopédie internationale des histoires de l'anthropologie* (Paris: Bérose, 2020), 23.

38. Joseph and Kalinowski, "Franz Boas."

39. Cole, *Franz Boas*, 180.

40. Zumwalt 1, 304.

41. Rosemary Lévy Zumwalt, *Franz Boas: Shaping Anthropology and Fostering Social Justice* (Lincoln: University of Nebraska Press, 2022) (henceforth cited as Zumwalt 2), 446, n. 85.

42. Ibid., 39.

43. Franz Boas, "Eugenics," *Scientific Monthly* 3, no. 5 (November 1916): 471–78 (472).

44. Ruth Bunzel, introduction to *Anthropology and Modern Life*, by Franz Boas (New York: Norton, 1962), 9–10.

45. Herbert S. Lewis, "Searching for Boas in the Archives," *History of Anthropology Review*, December 13, 2018, https://histanthro.org/bibliography/archives/searching-for-boas-in-the-archives/;

Mss.B.B61, Franz Boas Papers, American Philosophical Society, Philadelphia.

46. George Grant MacCurdy, "The Sixteenth International Congress of Americanists," *American Anthropologist*, n.s. 10, no. 4 (October–December 1908): 650–60 (651). See Lewis, "Searching for Boas in the Archives."

47. Franz Boas, *Primitive Art* (New York: Dover, 1922), 2.

48. Boas, *The Mind of Primitive Man*, 116.

49. See Alan H. McGowan, "Franz Boas, the Arts, Education, and Science," *Insights of Anthropology* 6, no. 1 (2022): 386–88.

50. George W. Stocking Jr., "Franz Boas and the Culture Concept in Historical Perspective," in *American Anthropologist* 68 (1966): 867–82, referring to Boas, "Human Faculty as Determined by Race," *Proceedings of the American Association for the Advancement of Science* 43 (1894): 301–27, and *The Mind of Primitive Man* (New York: Macmillan, 1911), 6–8.

51. Zumwalt 2, 31.

52. Cole, *Franz Boas*, 286–89.

53. Lewis, "Who's Who," 22.

54. George W. Stocking Jr., "Guardians of the Sacred Bundle: The American Anthropological Association and the Representation of Holistic Anthropology," in *Learned Societies and the Evolution of the Disciplines*, ed. S. B. Cohen, D. Bromwich, and G. W. Stocking (New York: American Council of Learned Societies, 1988), 17–25.

55. Cole, *Franz Boas*, 262–65.

56. Bradd Shore, *Culture in Mind: Cognition, Culture, and the Problem of Meaning* (Oxford: Oxford University Press, 1996), 22. The cognitive sciences are still grappling with this split today.

57. Franz Boas, "The History of Anthropology," in Stocking, *A Franz Boas Reader*, 23–36 (35).

58. See Dan Hicks, "Four-Field Anthropology: Charter Myths and Time Warps from St. Louis to Oxford," *Current Anthropology* 54, no. 6 (December 2013): 753–63. Hicks notes, "Unmentioned by Stocking, the proceedings of the St. Louis congress included a much clearer account of a four-field model for anthropology. This

was a paper by Alfred Cort Haddon—then lecturer in ethnology at Cambridge University—on the theme of 'Ethnology: Its Scope and Problems'" which "made reference not to his own recently published scheme but to a fly sheet circulated by Daniel Garrison Brinton (1837–89) more than a decade previously. The fly sheet to which Haddon referred was Brinton's *Proposed Classification and International Nomenclature for the Anthropological Sciences*, published in 1892, which set out the four subdivisions of anthropology: (1) somatology (physical and experimental anthropology), (2) ethnology (historic and analytic anthropology), (3) ethnography (geographic and descriptive anthropology, and (4) archaeology (prehistoric and reconstructive anthropology)." Further, it was Brinton who, in Hicks's view, held the first professorship of anthropology in the United States, as "he was appointed professor of ethnology and archaeology at the Academy of Natural Sciences, Philadelphia, and professor of American linguistics and anthropology at the University of Pennsylvania in 1884." It is a potentially important historical revision, but a full consideration of its grounds and implications, and of how Hicks analyzes this story, would take more space than is available here.

59. Boas, "The History of Anthropology," 30.

60. Cole, *Franz Boas*, 287.

61. Joseph and Kalinowski, "Franz Boas." The stories collected by Boas in 1927 from the Chehalis people have been published as *Chehalis Stories*, ed. Jolynn Amrine Goertz with the Confederated Tribes of the Chehalis Reservation (Lincoln: University of Nebraska Press, 2018).

62. Regna Darnell, "Mind, Body, and the Native Point of View," in Darnell et al., *The Franz Boas Papers*, 11.

63. Zumwalt 2, 93.

64. Charles King, *Gods of the Upper Air: How a Circle of Renegade Anthropologists Reinvented Race, Sex, and Gender in the Twentieth Century* (New York: Doubleday, 2019), 95–96.

65. Published in Stocking, *A Franz Boas Reader*, 316–18.

66. W.E.B. DuBois to Franz Boas, February 13, 1929, in *W.E.B. DuBois Papers*, series 1: *Correspondence*, University of Massachusetts

at Amherst, ms 312, https://credo.library.umass.edu/view/series
/mums312-s01. In 1929, DuBois wrote to Franz asking him to
write an article for the *Crisis* to address: "1) Is there a new American Negro race being developed? 2) What has intelligence testing
proven regarding Negro ability? 3) What recent studies or investigations throw light upon the African Negro?"

67. See Leonard Glick, "Types Distinct from Our Own: Franz
Boas on Jewish Identity and Assimilation," *American Anthropologist*
84 (1982): 555–56.

68. Franz Boas, "An Anthropologist's Credo," in Stocking, *A
Franz Boas Reader*, 42, and cited in Glick, "Types Distinct from
Our Own."

69. See Zumwalt 2, 101, and 456, n. 12.

70. Franz Boas, "The Outlook for the American Negro," in
Stocking, *A Franz Boas Reader*, 301–16.

71. Lewis, "The Passion of Franz Boas," 453.

72. Robert F. Zeidel, "A 1911 Report Set America on a Path of
Screening Out 'Undesirable' Immigrants," *Zócalo Public Square*, July
16, 2018.

73. King, *Gods of the Upper Air*, 96–97.

74. See George W. Stocking Jr., "The Critique of Racial Formalism," in his *Race, Culture, and Evolution: Essays in the History of
Anthropology* (1968; repr., Chicago: University of Chicago Press,
1982), 161–94 (165–69).

75. Ibid., 166.

76. Ibid., 167.

77. J. M. Tanner, "Boas' Contributions to Knowledge of Human
Growth and Form," in *The Anthropology of Franz Boas: Essays on the
Centennial of His Birth*, ed. Walter Goldschmidt (Millwood, NY:
American Anthropological Association, 1974), 85.

78. Ibid., 84.

79. Stocking, "The Critique of Racial Formalism," 169–70.

80. R. L. Jantz, "Franz Boas and Native American Biological
Variability," special issue, "Population Biology of Late Nineteenth-
Century Native North Americans and Siberians: Analyses of Boas's
Data," *Human Biology* 67, no. 3 (1995): 345–53 (346).

81. Franz Boas, "The Anthropology of the North American Indian," in Stocking, *A Franz Boas Reader,* 191–201 (196), and Cole, *Franz Boas,* 269.

82. Franz Boas, *Anthropology: A Lecture Delivered at Columbia University in the Series on Science, Philosophy, and Art, December 18, 1907* (New York: Columbia University Press, 1908), in Stocking, *A Franz Boas Reader,* 267–81 (273).

83. Franz Boas, "Race Problems in America," in Stocking, *A Franz Boas Reader,* 313–30 (323).

84. Tanner, "Boas' Contributions," 99.

85. Glick, "Types Distinct from Our Own," 545.

86. Franz Boas, "Changes in Immigrant Body Form," in Stocking, *A Franz Boas Reader,* 202–14 (204).

87. Franz Boas, "Changes in the Bodily Form of Descendants of Immigrants," *American Anthropologist,* n.s. 14, no. 3 (July–September 1912): 530–62.

88. Tanner, "Boas' Contributions," 99.

89. See John S. Allen, "Franz Boas's Physical Anthropology: The Critique of Racial Formalism Revisited," *Current Anthropology* 30, no. 1 (February 1989): 79–84 (81). "The results of the immigrant study made Boas quite receptive to the genotype/phenotype/pure-line theories of Wilhelm Johannsen. Boas cited Johannsen in both editions of *The Mind of Primitive Man.* In the 1911 version, which he prepared before he was fully aware of the results of the immigrant study, he used Johannsen's work on pure lines to support his own findings that local, 'primitive' races were often identifiable as very distinct types . . . and argued that they represented the 'characteristic development of a stable type.' In 1938, after more than 20 years of assimilating the results of the immigrant study, he found Johannsen's work useful in a very different way. Now he emphasized the plasticity of Johannsen's beans—that even though they were self-fertilizing, much variability could be found in the descendants of any single bean . . . : 'There are so many uncontrollable conditions that influence the development of the organism that even with identical ancestry the same form and size cannot be expected. . . . We are dealing with the fundamental difference be-

tween a constant and a variable phenomenon which must be clearly held in mind if we want to understand the meaning of the term 'race.' In 1911, Boas used Johannsen's work to support the idea of racial stability; in 1938, he used it to justify the notion of racial plasticity. It is a change in perspective that would not have occurred had he not done the immigrant study, and it clearly reflects the change in his thinking with regard to race that the study brought about—this despite the fact that he 'fully realized the smallness of the changes observed' in the immigrant study."

90. Susan Hegeman, "Franz Boas and Professional Anthropology: On Mapping the Borders of the 'Modern,'" *Victorian Studies* 41, no. 3 (1998): 455–83 (470, 471).

91. King, *Gods of the Upper Air,* 10; Boas, *The Mind of Primitive Man,* 16.

92. Boas, *The Mind of Primitive Man,* 117.

93. Ibid., 204.

94. Franz Boas, "Psychological Problems in Anthropology," in Stocking, *A Franz Boas Reader,* 243–54.

95. Kevin P. Groark, "Freud among the Boasians: Psychoanalytic Influence and Ambivalence in American Anthropology," *Current Anthropology* 60, no. 4 (August 2019): 559–88 (562). See also Robert Kenny, "Freud, Jung and Boas: The Psychoanalytic Engagement with Anthropology Revisited," *Notes and Records: The Royal Society Journal of the History of Science* 69, no. 2 (2015): 173–90.

96. Boas, *The Mind of Primitive Man,* 121.

97. Ibid., 176.

98. Groark, "Freud among the Boasians," 561.

99. Franz Boas, "The Methods of Ethnology," *American Anthropologist,* n.s. 22, no. 4 (1920): 311–21 (319–20, 321):

The theologians who interpreted the Bible on the basis of religious symbolism were no less certain of the correctness of their views, than the psycho-analysts are of their interpretations of thought and conduct based on sexual symbolism. The results of a symbolic interpretation depend primarily upon the investigator who arranges phenomena according to his leading concept. In order to prove the applicability of the symbolism of psycho-analysis, it would be necessary to show that a symbolic interpretation from other entirely different points of view would not be equally plausible, and that explanations that leave out symbolic significance or reduce it to a minimum, would not be adequate.

While, therefore, we welcome the application of every advance in the method of psychological investigation, we cannot accept as an advance in ethnological method the crude transfer of a novel, one-sided method of psychological investigation of the individual to social phenomena the origin of which can be shown to be historically determined and to be subject to influences that are not at all comparable to those that control the psychology of the individual.

100. Kenny, "Freud, Jung and Boas," 180.

101. Stanley S. Newman, review of *Psychiatrist of America: The Life of Harry Stack Sullivan*, by Helen Swick Perry, *Historiographia Linguistica* 10, nos. 1–2 (1983): 135–38; Groark, "Freud among the Boasians," 568.

102. See Karen Horney to Margaret Mead, February 8, 1935, Library of Congress, https://www.loc.gov/exhibits/mead/field-sepik .html#143a.

103. See Herbert S. Lewis, "The Individual and Individuality in Franz Boas's Anthropology and Philosophy," in Darnell et al., *The Franz Boas Papers*, 25. And see Ivan Kalmar, "The Völkerpsychologie of Lazarus and Steinthal and the Modern Concept of Culture," *Journal of the History of Ideas* 48, no. 4 (1987): 671–90 (671). Kalmar argues that "Boas never lost touch with German colleagues. It is inconceivable that he would have invented the pluralist idea of culture independently while it was so common in Germany. And to be fair to Boas, he never claimed he did invent it. It seems clear that he simply introduced to the American public an idea that was already widely and passionately held by liberal anthropologists in Germany" (684).

104. Zumwalt 2, 301.

105. See the excellent entry "Boas, Franz," in *International Encyclopedia of the Social Sciences*, ed. David L. Sills (New York: Macmillan, 1968), 9–110 (104).

106. Quoted in Groark, "Freud among the Boasians," 566.

107. Alfred L. Kroeber, "Totem and Taboo: An Ethnologic Psychoanalysis," *American Anthropologist*, n.s. 22, no. 1 (1920): 48–55 (55).

5. A Legacy

1. Franz Boas, "An Anthropologist's View of War," *Advocate of Peace (1894–1920)* 74, no. 4 (1912): 93–95. Also cited in Julia E. Liss, "Franz Boas on War and Empire: The Making of a Public Intellectual," in *The Franz Boas Papers*, vol. 1: *Franz Boas as Public Intellectual—Theory, Ethnography, Activism*, ed. Regna Darnell, Michelle Hamilton, Robert L. A. Hancock, and Joshua Smith (Lincoln: University of Nebraska Press, 2015), 293–324.

2. Rosemary Lévy Zumwalt, *Franz Boas: Shaping Anthropology and Fostering Social Justice* (Lincoln: University of Nebraska Press, 2022) (henceforth cited as Zumwalt 2), 196.

3. Ibid., xxxviii.

4. Charles King, *Gods of the Upper Air: How a Circle of Renegade Anthropologists Reinvented Race, Sex, and Gender in the Twentieth Century* (New York: Doubleday, 2019), 108–9.

5. "Kinship of Language a Vital Factor in the War: Dr. Franz Boas, Professor of Anthropology at Columbia University, Writes of European Nationalism and the Great Conflict," *New York Times*, January 3, 1915, 72.

6. See Michael Kazin, *War against War: The American Fight for Peace, 1914–1918* (New York: Simon & Schuster, 2017), reviewed by Adam Hochschild, "When Dissent Became Treason," *New York Review of Books*, September 28, 2017.

7. King, *Gods of the Upper Air*, 110.

8. Cited in Herbert L. Lewis, "The Passion of Franz Boas," *American Anthropologist* 103, no. 2 (2001): 447–67 (457).

9. Both letters cited in Zumwalt 2, 178.

10. Ibid., 179.

11. Melville J. Herskovits, *Franz Boas: The Science of Man in the Making* (New York: Charles Scribner's Sons, 1953), 116.

12. Zumwalt 2, 175, mentions the Benjamin N. Cardozo Lecture on Academic Freedom given by President Lee Bollinger in 2005, in which Bollinger referred to this dark episode in Columbia's history.

13. Herskovits, *Franz Boas*, 118.

14. For a detailed account of this episode, see Zumwalt 2, chap. 4, 122–72: "Folklore and Ruins in Mexico and Puerto Rico." See also Eleanor M. King, "An Early Archaeological Multinational: The Story of the Escuela Internacional of Mexico" (paper presented at the 71st Annual Meeting of the Society for American Archaeology, San Juan, Puerto Rico, 2006); *Daniel Schávelzon: Arqueología Urbana*, https://www.danielschavelzon.com.ar/?p=554.

15. Cited in King, *Gods of the Upper Air*, 115.

16. Henry Fairfield Osborn, "Lo, the Poor Nordic! Professor Osborn's Position on the Immigration Question," *New York Times*, April 8, 1924, 18.

17. See Devon Stillwell, "Eugenics Visualized: The Exhibit of the Third International Congress of Eugenics, 1932," *Bulletin of the History of Medicine* 86, no. 2 (2012): 206–36.

18. Franz Boas, "Inventing a Great Race," *New Republic*, January 13, 1917, 305–7.

19. King, *Gods of the Upper Air*, 111.

20. Franz Boas, "Colonies and the Peace Settlement," *Nation*, February 15, 1919, cited in Harvey A. Levenstein, "Franz Boas as Political Activist," *Anthropological Society Papers* 29 (1963): 15–24 (21).

21. Christine Laurière, "L'anthropologie et le politique, les prémisses: Les relations entre Franz Boas et Paul Rivet (1919–1942)," *L'homme: Miroirs transatlantiques* 187–88 (2008): 69–92 (70, 74–75). Rivet's letter in the original French: "Je crois que l'humanité doit tendre de plus en plus à abolir tous les nationalismes, je crois que la présente misère humaine ne trouvera son remède que dans une réconciliation sincère de tous les peuples et pour ma part, par tous les moyens, je chercherai à hâter le jour de cette vraie paix, qui ne sera pas dans un écrit, mais dans les cœurs et j'aurais honte

d'être un homme si je ne sentais pas en moi cette profonde conviction, cette foi inébranlable."

22. For the Johnson-Reed Act, see https://history.state.gov/milestones/1921–1936/immigration-act.

23. Levenstein, "Franz Boas as Political Activist," 19.

24. On Lothrop, see David Price, "Anthropologists as Spies," *Nation*, November 20, 2000.

25. Cited in Zumwalt 2, 204.

26. See George W. Stocking Jr., "The Scientific Reaction against Cultural Anthropology, 1917–1920," in *Race, Culture, and Evolution: Essays in the History of Anthropology* (1968; repr., Chicago: University of Chicago Press, 1982), 270–307. This and the previous paragraph rely on Stocking's telling.

27. Zumwalt 2, 209, 221, 196–223 generally for a fuller account of the episode.

28. King, *Gods of the Upper Air,* 119.

29. This paragraph relies on Stocking, "The Scientific Reaction." Zumwalt 2 reports that Boas gave her a portrait of himself that bore the inscription: "Elsie Clews Parsons, fellow in the struggle for freedom from prejudice," which she mentioned in a letter to Lowie in January 1938 (423).

30. See Zumwalt 2, 41, for a list of his early students and generally her chap. 2, "Franz Boas and His Early Students, 1901–1915," 40–95, and chap. 3: "Preponderance of Women Students," 224–73.

31. Mary White Ovington, *Half a Man: The Status of the Negro in New York* (New York: Longmans, Green, 1911), https://wellcome collection.org/works/rk2xfcvp.

32. Zumwalt 2, 296–97.

33. Cited in Adam Kuper, *The Invention of Primitive Society: Transformations of an Illusion* (London: Routledge, 1988), 149.

34. Stocking, "The Scientific Reaction," 289.

35. Ibid., 292.

36. Ibid., 305–6.

37. Levenstein, "Franz Boas as Political Activist."

38. Robert H. Lowie, "Franz Boas," in *The History of Ethnological Theory* (New York: Farrar & Rinehart, 1937), 128–55 (145).

39. Franz Boas, "A Sturdy Protest," *Nation*, October 19, 1918, in *A Franz Boas Reader: The Shaping of American Anthropology, 1883–1911*, ed. George W. Stocking Jr. (1974; repr., Chicago: University of Chicago Press, 1982), 335.

40. Levenstein, "Franz Boas as Political Activist," 21–22.

41. Alfred L. Kroeber, review of *Primitive Art*, by Franz Boas, *American Anthropologist* 31, no. 1 (January–March 1929): 138–40.

42. Zumwalt 2, 174, cites a letter from Franz to his friend Oskar Bolza, a mathematician in Germany he had met during the Clark days: "Last spring I had another trouble caused by ulcers in the intestine, which put me into pretty bad condition for about six months."

43. See ibid.

44. Ibid., xxxii, 423.

45. "Dr. Abraham Jacobi Dies Suddenly at 89; Dean of American Medical Profession Stricken at His Summer Home on Lake George. Honored by Universities. Foremost Authority on Pediatrics Had Been Head of Great Societies—Compatriot with Schurz. Began His Career Here 65 Years Ago. Accused of Treason and Imprisoned. Professor in Many Colleges. His Comment on Dr. Osler's Praise," *New York Times*, July 12, 1919, 9.

46. Robert H. Lowie, *Biographical Memoir of Franz Boas, 1858–1942* (National Academy of Sciences of the United States of America Biographical Memoirs, vol. 24, 9th memoir, 1947), boas-franz.pdf (nasonline.org) 317, partly cited in Zumwalt 2, 92–93.

47. Zumwalt 2, 249–50, tells us that in 1926, Franz had hired Mead's mother, sociologist Emily Fogg Mead, who had worked on Italian immigrants, to conduct anthropometric work on a community of rural Italians in Philadelphia: she also went to Italy to find out about families and backgrounds.

48. Margaret Mead, "Apprenticeship under Boas," in *The Anthropology of Franz Boas: Essays on the Centennial of His Birth*, ed. Walter Goldschmidt (Millwood, NY: American Anthropological Association, 1974), 29–45 (43).

49. Zumwalt 2, 283, 286.

50. Ibid., 287–89.

51. "A Collaborative Reframing of Kwakiutl Film and Audio Recordings with Franz Boas, 1930," Burke Museum, https://www.burkemuseum.org/collections-and-research/culture/bill-holm-center/kans-hilile-making-it-right.

52. Zumwalt 2, 289.

53. See APA Islandora Repository Text Collection American Council of Learned Societies Committee on Native American Languages, American Philosophical Society [ACLS Collection] Section W1a.21: Kwakiutl dictionary, https://diglib.amphilsoc.org/islandora/object/text:166522#page/1/mode/1up.

54. Quotations from letters in this paragraph and the next are cited in Zumwalt 2, 274–79.

55. Ibid., 278–80, for these two paragraphs, and King, *Gods of the Upper Air*, 234.

56. Franz Boas, "Race and Progress," *Science*, n.s. 74, no. 1905 (1931): 1–8 (7). And see Leonard Glick, "Types Distinct from Our Own: Franz Boas on Jewish Identity and Assimilation," *American Anthropologist* 84 (1982): 556–57.

57. Liss, "Franz Boas on War and Empire," 302.

58. Melville J. Herskovits, "Brains and the Immigrant," *Nation*, February 11, 1925.

59. Zumwalt 2, 359–60.

60. See Brooke Penaloza-Patzak and Claudia Wedepohl, "Franz Boas and Aby Warburg: The Complete Correspondence, 1895 to 1928," *W. 86th* 30, no. 1 (2023): 71–90 ("Introduction," 71–75). Correspondence translated by Brooke Penaloza-Patzak: see 76, 78. Penaloza-Patzac and Wedepohl observe (71), the "cursory" nature of Boas's responses to Warburg's generally effusive letters, writing, "Warburg's overtures across disciplinary boundaries were driven by his desire to reform art history and its methods; Boas's reserve by his disinclination to engage those he deemed amateurs, tempered by a shrewd appreciation for the United States–based Warburg brothers and their extended family as generous patrons of the sciences."

61. See Anna Speyart, "Boas, Saxl and Wind on Race, Gesture

and Art," *Mnemosyne: The Warburg Institute Blog*, https://warburg
.sas.ac.uk/blog/boas-saxl-and-wind-race-gesture-and-art. She recounts further that

> on 13 March 1936, Gertrud Bing wrote to Boas to ask if
> he would be willing to provide the Warburg Library with
> a copy of his *Kwakiutl Culture as Reflected in Mythology*
> (New York, 1935), a recent book the Library was "very
> anxious to have." In return, Bing offered to send any of
> the Warburg Institute's own publications to Boas and en-
> closed a list for him to choose from. "Please excuse this
> request," she explained. "You know, of course, that our po-
> sition is such that we are obliged to obtain some of the
> important books for our Library by this means."
>
> Indeed, Boas arranged for a copy to be sent to the In-
> stitute. The volume in question stands next to Boas's other
> books on Kwakiutl culture in the Warburg Library, where
> users of the Library can consult it today. The story behind
> this acquisition is an interwar attempt at scholarly collabo-
> ration, in which researchers sought to support each other's
> work by sharing their expertise and exchanging biblio-
> graphical materials. In doing so, the scholars stretched
> across the boundaries of their academic disciplines to defy
> racist ideologies with a deeper understanding of cultural
> difference and its development. They experienced the ef-
> fects of such ideologies directly, and their concerns con-
> tinue to be relevant to us today.

62. Glick, "Types Distinct from Our Own," 558, reporting
Herskovits, *Franz Boas.*

63. Mss.B.B61, Franz Boas Papers, American Philosophical
Society, Philadelphia.

64. Liss, "Franz Boas on War and Empire," 307.

65. Cited in Zumwalt 2, 399.

66. Cited in Robert Brightman, introduction to *Joseph Mitchell, "Man—with Variations": Interviews with Franz Boas and Colleagues,
1937,* ed. Robert Brightman (Chicago: Prickly Paradigm, 2017),

1–25 (3), from Thomas Kunkel, *Man in Profile: Joseph Mitchell of the "New Yorker"* (New York: Random House, 2015).

67. Cited in Zumwalt 2, 364–65. Aichel would die soon after, in 1935.

68. Bernhard J. Stern, "Franz Boas as Scientist and Citizen," *Science & Society* 7, no. 4 (1943): 289–320 (299), cited in Zumwalt 2, 358.

69. "Dr. Boas on the Blacklist," *New York Times*, May 6, 1933, 8, cited in Zumwalt 2, 357.

70. *Columbia Daily Spectator*, May 10, 1933, 1.

71. Herkovits, *Franz Boas*, 117. Also cited in Glick, "Types Distinct from Our Own," 559.

72. Franz Boas, *Aryans and Non-Aryans* (New York: Information and Service Associates, 1934), 11.

73. Glick, "Types Distinct from Our Own," 559.

74. Christine Laurière, "Franz Boas and Paul Rivet's Relationship: Militancy as a Scientific Commitment," *History of Anthropology Newsletter* 36, no. 1 (2009): 10–21 (16); Laurière, "L'anthropologie et le politique," 84–85. See also Zumwalt 2, 388.

75. Cited in King, *Gods of the Upper Air*, 308–9.

76. Cited in Zumwalt 2, 389.

77. "Resolution Urges Scientists to War on Fascist Forces," *Harvard Crimson*, December 13, 1938, https://www.thecrimson.com /article/1938/12/13/resolution-urges-scientists-to-war-on/.

78. Cited in Zumwalt 2, 390.

79. Ibid.

80. "Schools Rebuked on Racial Errors," *New York Times*, July 17, 1939, 21. And see Zoe Burkholder, "Franz Boas and Anti-Racist Education," *Anthropology News*, October 2006, 24–25.

81. Letter from the American Committee for Democracy and Intellectual Freedom to JBS Haldane, HALDANE/4/21/3/3, Haldane Papers, Wellcome Collection, London.

82. Zumwalt 2, 391.

83. Lévi-Strauss recounted his epic journey to New York in an early chapter of *Tristes tropiques:* see Claude Lévi-Strauss, *Tristes tropiques* (1955; repr., Paris: Plon, 2018), 25–34 (31–32).

84. Zumwalt 2, 393–98.

85. Ibid., 402–3.

86. Ibid., 410–11.

87. Ibid., 416–19.

88. Ibid., 414.

89. Ibid., 425.

90. Franz Boas to Max Warburg, Mss.B.B61, Franz Boas Papers.

91. Susan Krook, "Franz Boas (a.k.a. Boaz) and the F.B.I.," *History of Anthropology Newsletter* 16, no. 2 (1989): 9.

92. Claude Lévi-Strauss's foreword to Boas's *Indian Myths and Legends from the North Pacific Coast of America,* cited in "Claude Lévi-Strauss' Testimony on Franz Boas," *Études Inuit Studies* 8, no. 1 (1984): 7–10.

93. Krook, "Franz Boas"; Zumwalt 2, 426–27.

ACKNOWLEDGMENTS

I WOULD LIKE to thank Ileene Smith for giving me the opportunity to write this book in the Jewish Lives series. I am not trained
as an anthropologist, and when I said yes, without a moment of
hesitation, I had no more than a general sense of who Boas was—
just enough to know he was an important and interesting figure.
Life circumstances (including Covid) repeatedly interrupted my
acquaintanceship with Franz after then, but I gradually got to know
him and admire him. Writing about him has been challenging, in-
spiring, and transformative, and the field of anthropology I discovered, none too soon, has much enriched my thinking and my understanding of the world. Once finished, the manuscript benefited
from the sensitive and clarifying copyediting of Robin DuBlanc.

Over the years, I have had the opportunity to discuss Franz
Boas and anthropology with a number of people who have given
me ideas, information, opportunities, resources, and guidance. A
special thank-you to, in alphabetical order: Laura Bossi, Stefanos
Geroulanos, Edgardo C. Krebs, Adam Kuper, Valentina Mann, Rahul

Oka, Aaron Peck, Andreas Roepstorff, John Tresh, and Matthew Vollgraff for crucial conversations, and to Herbert S. Lewis for his meaningful encouragement and for catching errors in his careful reading of the text. Thanks to Bill Sherman for hosting me as an associate fellow of my alma mater, the Warburg Institute—whose founder Aby Warburg sustained a correspondence with Boas—and for inviting me to give a talk on Franz Boas that helped shape the introduction and plan for the book. Versions of this talk were also hosted by Fay Bound Alberti at York University, by Fatima Felisberti at Kingston University, and by the History of Science and Medicine Working Group in the history department of the European University Institute in Florence.

I would like to thank also those friends, acquaintances, or colleagues who egged me on and helped with questions or provocations: Sophie Basch, Kelly Burdick, Craig Burnett, Ophelia Deroy, Alessandro Duranti, Katerina Fotopoulou, Vittorio Gallese, Maya Gratier, Justine Grou-Radenez, Isabelle Heineman, Siri Hustvedt, Lauren Kassel, Mériam Korichi, Spencer Matheson, Linn Carey Mehta, Turi Munthe, Kalypso Nicolaidis, Elinor Ochs, Gloria Origgi, Giulia Oskian, Maël Renouard, Philippe Rochat, Catherine Rubin, Bill Sherman, Marcello Simonetta, Karin Templin, Manos Tsakiris, and Ananya Vajpeyi.

I dedicate this book to my rapidly growing sons, Vigo and Amos, in the hope that the values Boas fought for with all his might will suffuse the world they inherit.

INDEX

FORTHCOMING TITLES INCLUDE:

Hannah Arendt, by Masha Gessen
The Ba'al Shem Tov, by Ariel Mayse
Walter Benjamin, by Peter Gordon
Bob Dylan, by Sasha Frere-Jones
George Gershwin, by Gary Giddins
Ruth Bader Ginsburg, by Jeffrey Rosen
Jesus, by Jack Miles
Josephus, by Daniel Boyarin
Louis Kahn, by Gini Alhadeff
Mordecai Kaplan, by Jenna Weissman Joselit
Carole King, by Jane Eisner
Henry Kissinger, by Dennis Ross
Fiorello La Guardia, by Brenda Wineapple
Mahler, by Leon Botstein
Norman Mailer, by David Bromwich
Robert Oppenheimer, by David Rieff
Rebecca, by Judith Shulevitz
Philip Roth, by Steven J. Zipperstein
Edmond de Rothschild, by James McAuley
Jonas Salk, by David Margolick
Stephen Sondheim, by Daniel Okrent
Susan Sontag, by Benjamin Taylor
Gertrude Stein, by Lauren Elkin
Sabbatai Tsevi, by Pawel Maciejko
Billy Wilder, by Noah Isenberg
Ludwig Wittgenstein, by Anthony Gottlieb